D1154123

# OXFORD MODERN LANGUAGES
# AND LITERATURE MONOGRAPHS

# FRANCISCO DE QUEVEDO
# AND THE
# NEOSTOIC MOVEMENT

BY

HENRY ETTINGHAUSEN

OXFORD UNIVERSITY PRESS

1972

*Oxford University Press, Ely House, London W. 1*

GLASGOW  NEW YORK  TORONTO  MELBOURNE  WELLINGTON
CAPE TOWN  IBADAN  NAIROBI  DAR ES SALAAM  LUSAKA  ADDIS ABABA
DELHI  BOMBAY  CALCUTTA  MADRAS  KARACHI  LAHORE  DACCA
KUALA LUMPUR  SINGAPORE  HONG KONG  TOKYO

PRINTED IN GREAT BRITAIN
AT THE UNIVERSITY PRESS, OXFORD
BY VIVIAN RIDLER
PRINTER TO THE UNIVERSITY

FOR
MERCEDES AND DIEGO

# PREFACE

IN his lifetime Francisco de Quevedo Villegas (1580–1645) was known throughout Europe for his satirical *Sueños* and his picaresque novel, the *Buscón*. In Spain, where he was the best-selling writer of the seventeenth century, he was famous besides as a poet, polemicist, and moralist. If today he is generally acknowledged to be one of the most complex, even contradictory, authors of the Golden Age, his own contemporaries found it no easier to arrive at a balanced view of a man who counted among his earliest published works in prose the life of a Valencian saint and a book of lavatory jokes. While his enemies publicly denounced his writings to the Inquisition, his friends and admirers did not tire of praising his wit and his wisdom. When, as they frequently did, they compared him with the classics, more often than not it was with Seneca. One admirer declared that Quevedo is as subtle and profound as Seneca; another, that his concise, unaffected learning makes one lose the urge to read Seneca; a third, that he is (after either the orator and philosopher or the philosopher and tragedian) a third Seneca; and more than one, that he writes like Seneca turned Christian. His 'Christian Stoicism', long regarded as part of a so-called *senequismo* supposedly more or less innate in 'the Spanish character', has only recently begun to receive critical attention and to be recognized as belonging to a movement which spread across much of Europe at the turn of the seventeenth century.[1] However, the precise nature and the development of his interest in the Stoics and their teachings, his place in the Neostoic movement, and the relationship between his Stoical works and the rest of his writings are still in need of careful definition. In tackling these problems the advantages of a work-by-work approach have seemed to me to outweigh those of an analysis by topics which would, in particular, have made it impossible to observe the functions of his Stoical ideas and his views on the

---

[1] See esp. A. Rothe, *Quevedo und Seneca: Untersuchungen zu den Frühschriften Quevedos* (Geneva/Paris, 1965), and K. A. Blüher, *Seneca in Spanien: Untersuchungen zur Geschichte der Seneca-Rezeption in Spanien vom 13. bis 17. Jahrhundert* (Munich, 1969).

Stoics in context. The terms Stoical, Senecan, and Epictetan have been used freely to refer to ideas, arguments, and attitudes which, while Quevedo may sometimes have taken them from other sources, either ultimately derive from or else coincide with sentiments expressed by the Stoics in general or by Seneca or Epictetus in particular.

On publishing this revised and shortened version of a doctoral thesis submitted at the University of Oxford, I gladly take the opportunity of recording my gratitude to those who have given me inspiration, guidance, and co-operation, especially to Professor P. E. Russell for suggesting the subject of my thesis and patiently supervising its progress; to Professor Nigel Glendinning for his constant encouragement and help; to Professor E. M. Wilson, Dr. R. W. Truman, Dr. C. A. Jones, Mr. A. E. Douglas, and Mr. J. D. Fox for their constructive criticism and advice; to Professor J. O. Crosby for generously putting his bibliographical expertise and material at my disposal; to the Count of Doña Marina for allowing me access to the copy of Seneca's works annotated by Quevedo; to the late Mr. W. G. Chapman for initiating me in Spanish literature; to Dr. P. J. S. Whitmore for first awakening in me an interest in the history of ideas; and to the staffs of the libraries and archives in which I have worked.

It is also a pleasure to thank my father and Professor Ian Michael for their help in checking proofs and eliminating some stylistic obscurities.

# CONTENTS

# CONTENTS

# ABBREVIATIONS AND REFERENCES

*BP*  Quevedo, *Obras completas*, ed. F. Buendía, i, 'Obras en prosa' (Madrid, 1961).

*CS*  *La cuna y la sepultura para el conocimiento propio y desengaño de las cosas agenas*, ed. L. López Grigera (Madrid, 1969).

*EQ*  *Epistolario completo de D. Francisco de Quevedo-Villegas*, ed. L. Astrana Marín (Madrid, 1946).

*OP*  Quevedo, *Obra poética*, ed. J. M. Blecua, 4 vols. (Madrid, 1969– ).

*Q*  Quevedo, *Obras*, ed. A. Fernández-Guerra y Orbe and F. Janer, Biblioteca de Autores Españoles, vols. xxiii, xlviii, and lxix (Madrid, 1946–53).

In addition to these, the abbreviations for titles of periodicals and collections listed in *The Year's Work in Modern Language Studies* are used in the footnotes.

Unless otherwise stated, Quevedo's works in prose and his verse translation of Epictetus' *Manual* are cited from *Q*, whose accentuation is modernized, and those not included in *Q* are cited from *BP*. His verse is cited from *OP*; his correspondence generally from *EQ*.

With the exception of *Naturales Quaestiones* (for which the Budé edition has been used), unless otherwise stated the works of Seneca and Epictetus are cited from the Loeb edition.

Biblical references are to the Vulgate.

# INTRODUCTION

NEOSTOICISM has been depicted in recent years as constituting an important part, even one pole, of European thought in the sixteenth and seventeenth centuries. Thus, H. C. Haydn's concept of 'Counter-Renaissance' is defined very largely as the reaction against proud reliance on human reason associated especially with writers of a Stoical bias, and A. Adam opposes to an Augustinian 'religion de salut' a 'religion d'essence intellectuelle' which he sees first and best exemplified in the Neostoic works of Justus Lipsius.[1] Whether or not these contrasts were in reality so clear-cut, Neostoicism certainly contributed very much to the establishment of a Renaissance secular ethic which could be formulated either as an alternative to or as support for Christian moral teaching. Neostoicism is described by one critic as 'la réaction du christianisme contre le stoïcisme qui tend en quelque sorte à le supplanter' and by another as 'the reconciliation of the "more wholesome" ideas of pagan Stoic thought with the moral exhortations of Christian ethics'.[2] Both take account of the fact that Neostoicism involved interaction between Stoicism and Christianity, but neither description is entirely satisfactory. On the one hand, while some Christian moralists, especially in the seventeenth century, did react against Stoic philosophy, they are more aptly termed anti-Stoics than Neostoics. On the other, although reconciliation was the aim of most of the writers who showed an interest in Stoicism, it was not a primary object of them all. In view of the radical changes undergone by Stoic thought in classical times, particularly at Seneca's hands, and the fact that the Neostoic movement was an international phenomenon, it would be surprising if Neostoicism could be neatly pigeonholed. Rather, as has recently been argued, the movement should be thought of as one important part of a

---

[1] See H. C. Haydn, *The Counter-Renaissance* (New York, 1950), esp. pp. 79 ff., and A. Adam, *Sur le problème religieux dans la première moitié du XVII<sup>e</sup> siècle* (Oxford, 1959), *passim*.

[2] L. Zanta, *La Renaissance du stoïcisme au 16<sup>e</sup> siècle* (Paris, 1914), p. 333; J. L. Saunders, *Justus Lipsius. The Philosophy of Renaissance Stoicism* (New York, 1955), p. xiv.

thoroughly eclectic compound of classical and Christian elements which together made up Renaissance ethics, involving 'a more frequent and more general recourse to the moral maxims and principles of the stoics, a more systematic attempt to adapt them to orthodox Christian sentiment'.[3]

Stoicism had from the beginning strongly affected Christian thought. The belief that Seneca, if not actually a crypto-Christian, had stood at least in thought very close to Christianity is voiced by several of the Fathers. Tertullian's famous phrase, 'Seneca saepe noster', Lactantius' recommendation of the Roman's works to all 'qui volent scire omnia', and Jerome's inclusion of him in his list of saints all helped encourage the Middle Ages to think of Seneca as *princeps ethicorum, fons philosophiae*, and even *theologus*.[4] Seneca's attenuation of many Stoic teachings—in particular his view that the soul is incorporeal and capable of immortality, his transformation of the immanent Stoic Logos into something approaching a transcendental, personal god, his modification of Stoic 'apathy', and his insistent preaching of the need to prepare for death—naturally made his writings, both genuine and apocryphal, the favourite source of Stoic ideas throughout the Middle Ages and after. However, not even Seneca's mild, Platonicizing version of the extreme rationalism, materialism, and determinism of the early Stoa could be adopted without question. Augustine, while sharing the widespread belief in the Stoic's friendship with Paul, had gone out of his way to point out those things in Stoic philosophy which he thought irreconcilable with Christianity. Among them he reckoned the doctrine of the absoluteness of virtue and the corollary that all vices are equal, confidence in the efficacy of reason unaided by grace to attain virtue, the definition of free will as freedom to wish that things may happen as they are bound to happen, and the notion of liberty by suicide.

Thanks to the accident of his place of birth, Seneca was revered in Spain as in no other country as the type of the philosopher

[3] A. Levi, *French Moralists. The Theory of the Passions, 1585 to 1649* (Oxford, 1964), p. 54.
[4] For the influence of Stoicism on the Fathers and in the Middle Ages, see J. Stelzenberger, *Die Beziehung der frühchristlichen Sittenlehre zur Etik der Stoa* (Munich, 1933); M. Spanneut, *Le Stoïcisme des Pères de l'Église, de Clément de Rome à Clément d'Alexandrie* (Paris, 1957); and K.-D. Nothdurft, *Studien zum Einfluß Senecas auf die Philosophie und Theologie des zwölften Jahrhunderts* (Leyden/Cologne, 1963).

*par excellence*. If, as M. Bataillon argues, Neostoicism reached Spain relatively late, it is no less true that Spanish enthusiasm for Seneca had been considerable since at least the thirteenth century.[5] The inclusion of a 'Romance de la muerte de Séneca' in at least two sixteenth-century collections of verse suggests that his Stoic suicide stirred the popular imagination.[6] Certainly his name was proverbial as a synonym of wisdom.[7] Indeed, it has been argued that Senecan Stoicism took root in medieval Spain alongside Aristotelian ethics, and even that medieval Spanish literature as a whole is characterized above all by its fondness for Seneca.[8] While this may be thought something of an overstatement, it does at least hold good for the reign of John II of Castile.

It is largely due to John's patronage that many of Seneca's most important works, as well as several of the medieval collections of *sententiae* attributed to him, had already been translated by the time printing reached Spain, and that no Latin edition of any of his philosophical works appeared in Spain before the present century.[9] These mid-fifteenth-century translations represent one of the first attempts in the Renaissance to popularize Seneca and to establish his philosophical writings as a guide to right living. Seventy-five of his Epistles were translated at the direction of Fernán Pérez de Guzmán, the uncle of the Marquis of Santillana; the *converso* Pero Díaz de Toledo translated the apocryphal

---

[5] See M. Bataillon, *Erasmo y España. Estudios sobre la historia espiritual del siglo XVI*, trans. A. Alatorre, 2nd ed. (Mexico/Buenos Aires, 1966), p. 772. For the revival of Spanish interest in Seneca in the thirteenth and fourteenth centuries, see K. A. Blüher, *Seneca in Spanien. Untersuchungen zur Geschichte der Seneca-Rezeption in Spanien vom 13. bis 17. Jahrhundert* (Munich, 1969), pp. 42 ff.

[6] The *romance* is to be found in *Cancionero llamado flor de enamorados* (Barcelona, 1562) and *Rosa gentil* (Valencia, 1573), reprinted in *Floresta. Joyas poéticas españolas*, ed. A. Rodríguez-Moñino (Valencia, 1953– ), ii, fols. 112ᵛ–113ʳ, and viii, fols. 4ᵛ–5ʳ.

[7] The saying, 'Es un Séneca', is to be found in one of the earliest collections of Spanish proverbs (see Francisco de Espinosa, *Refranero (1527–1547)*, ed. E. S. O'Kane, *BRAE*, Anejo XVIII (Madrid, 1968), p. 218). Blüher (p. 80) cites the same proverb, described as 'antiguo y muy vsado', in a work by Ambrosio de Morales published in 1574.

[8] See P. Fr. M. Gutiérrez, *Fr. Luis de León y la filosofía española del siglo XVI* (Madrid, 1885), p. 26, and F. López Estrada, *Introducción a la literatura medieval española*, 2nd ed. (Madrid, 1962), p. 123.

[9] For what seems to be the one exception to this statement, the Latin edition of the spurious *Proverbia* thought to have been printed in Valencia *c.* 1496, see C. L. Penney, *Printed Books 1468–1700 in the Hispanic Society of America* (New York, 1965), s.v. 'Seneca'.

*Proverbia Senecae* and *De moribus* and wrote a commentary on the former;[10] and translations of *De vita beata* and *De providentia* (two Books) and of two spurious works make up the *Cinco libros de Séneca* of Alonso de Cartagena, Bishop of Burgos. The *Proverbios* (Zamora, 1482) and *Cinco libros* (Seville, 1491) were the first Senecan translations to be printed in any language, and the production of the Spanish presses reflects a steady demand for Seneca in Spanish up to the middle of the sixteenth century. No less remarkable than the longevity of the fifteenth-century translations is the fact that, to judge by the number of editions published, the medieval pseudo-Senecan *Proverbios* were twice as popular as either the semi-spurious *Cinco libros* or the genuine, though incomplete, *Epístolas*.[11] The survival in Spain of medieval attitudes towards the classics is also implied by the appearance in the second half of the sixteenth century of new collections of Senecan *sententiae*.[12]

The fashion for Seneca at John's court has been attributed in part to the isolation of a cultured minority for whom the Stoic's philosophy provided detachment from calamities as well as a sense of superiority.[13] To judge by Cartagena's dedication of his *Cinco libros*, the king himself showed a predilection for Seneca's works, and in the prologue to his version of *De providentia* he reveals that he undertook his translation at royal command and surmises that were Seneca alive he would undoubtedly pay homage to King John! As for Pero Díaz, he dedicated his commentary on

[10] N. G. Round, 'Pero Díaz de Toledo: a Study of a 15th-Century *Converso* Translator in his Background', unpubl. D.Phil. thesis presented in the University of Oxford, 1966, pp. 573–4, states that Pero Díaz was also commissioned to translate *De moribus* and identifies his translation with a version represented in two manuscripts in the Biblioteca Nacional, Madrid. I am indebted to Dr. Round for allowing me to consult his thesis.

[11] Each of these translations was last published in the 1550s, by which time the *Proverbios* had been printed thirteen times (a Seville, 1526, edition not mentioned by Blüher (p. 112, n. 64) is referred to by Bataillon (p. 50, n. 26)), the *Cinco libros* five times, and the *Epístolas* six times.

[12] Fr. Luis de Granada devoted the first two of the three Books of his *Collectanea moralis philosophiae* (Lisbon, 1571) to Seneca and Plutarch; a second edition appeared under the title *Loci communes philosophiae moralis* (Cologne, 1604). Two collections of exclusively Senecan *sententiae* had both appeared in 1555: *El libro de oro de Seneca, o sea sus aforismos morales* (Coimbra) and a Spanish translation of Erasmus' *Flores Lucii Annaei Senecae* by Juan Martín Cordero (Antwerp).

[13] See N. G. Round, 'Renaissance Culture and its Opponents in Fifteenth-Century Castile', *MLR*, lvii (1962), esp. 204–15.

the *Proverbios* to John's heir, Prince Henry, and recommended this work to him as 'quasi regla o doctrina de todo nuestro biuir'.[14] However, Seneca's influence in Spain in the fifteenth century was not confined to translations of his works. The Marquis of Santillana, who appears himself also to have been a translator of Seneca and a patron of Senecan translation and who owned a sizeable collection of his works in Latin, Italian, and Spanish, was deeply affected by him.[15] Not only are Seneca and Cicero the principal classical sources of his *Centiloquio*, but his *Comedieta de Ponça* presents a Senecan solution to the problem of Fortune within the bounds of Christian Providence.[16] Seneca's fullest and most direct influence is to be seen in his *Bias contra Fortuna*, written around 1450. Although Santillana's object in this dramatic poem was to console an imprisoned cousin, he allows the philosopher Bias to voice Senecan recommendations for suicide.[17] Stoical overtones are also strong in Pero Díaz's dialogue on the Marquis's death,[18] and, as the *Celestina* and its imitations show, the impact of Senecan *sententiae* made itself felt at the end of the fifteenth and in the first half of the sixteenth century in novelesque as well as moralizing literature.[19]

New intellectual currents played an important part in the continuation and development of the vogue for Seneca in the sixteenth century. Whether or not Neostoicism actually accelerated the decline of Erasmus' influence in Spain, the new movement from northern Europe answered a need similar to that which Erasmianism had satisfied previously.[20] This was the need for a brand of Christianity which, by taking account of the solutions to

[14] *Prouerbios y sentencias de Lucio Anneo Seneca . . .* (Antwerp, 1552), fol. 154ʳ.

[15] That Santillana translated Seneca is suggested by the remark in Juan de Lucena's *Libro de vita beata*: 'Tu de caualleria, de re publica, de fe cristiana escreuiste vulgar, y las obras famosas del moral Séneca nuestro vulgarizaste' (cited in A. Bonilla y San Martín, *Fernando de Córdoba ¿1425–86? y los orígenes del renacimiento filosófico en España. Episodio de la historia de la lógica* (Madrid, 1911), p. 30.) For the works of Seneca in his library, see M. Schiff, *La Bibliothèque du marquis de Santillane* (Paris, 1905), pp. 124–31.

[16] See R. Lapesa, *La obra literaria del Marqués de Santillana* (Madrid, 1957), esp. pp. 149, 210.

[17] See Lapesa, p. 219. Santillana's *Proverbios* were appended to Seneca's in the edition cited in note 14, above.

[18] See *Diálogo y razonamiento en muerte del Marqués de Santillana*, in A. Paz y Meliá, *Opúsculos literarios de los siglos XIV a XVI* (Madrid, 1892), pp. 245–360.

[19] See J. L. Heller and R. L. Grismer, 'Seneca in the Celestinesque Novel', *HR*, xii (1944), 29–48.     [20] See Bataillon, *Erasmo y España*, pp. 772–3.

ethical problems provided by the classics, should place due stress upon the feasibility of leading a moral life largely through the exercise of reason and will. In his *Enchiridion militis Christiani* Erasmus made self-knowledge the basis of a Christian philosophy embodying largely humanist wisdom.[21] Neostoicism may be said to date from the revaluation of Seneca represented by Erasmus' edition of his works, first published in 1515 and destined to remain unsurpassed for seventy years until the appearance of Muret's edition in 1585 and of Justus Lipsius' twenty years later. Whereas in 1514 Erasmus had produced his own collection of adages culled from Seneca, Plutarch, and Aristotle and was to publish in 1528 his *Flores Lucii Annaei Senecae*, his edition for the first time brought together all the Roman's philosophical works and abandoned virtually all the spurious texts. His attitude towards Seneca may be gauged by his statement that he considered the Stoic's works essential reading for all Christians.[22] Among his followers, Vives in particular shared his admiration for Seneca. His *Ad sapientiam introductio* defines wisdom as correct judgement, treats all things except virtue and vice as 'indifferent', and borrows direct from *De ira* in order to condemn anger;[23] and in a treatise on poverty he quotes a lengthy passage from *De beneficiis*.[24] Despite Inquisitorial expurgation and prohibition after the middle of the sixteenth century, Erasmus' influence in Spain can be traced well into the next.[25] Much of the spirit of his inner piety was absorbed by the same Counter-Reformation which officially branded him *auctor damnatus*. The upsurge of mysticism in Spain in the second half of the sixteenth century can be regarded as the Erasmian ideal forced into a new channel.[26]

Although it is hard to find any clear sign of interest in Stoicism in the *Ratio studiorum*, in which Aristotle is set down as the classical

---

[21] See E. F. Rice, Jr., *The Renaissance Idea of Wisdom* (Cambridge, Mass., 1958), pp. 159 ff.

[22] Cited in H. A. E. van Gelder, *The Two Reformations in the Sixteenth Century* (The Hague, 1961), p. 170.

[23] See *Introducción a la sabiduría*, BAE, lxv (*Obras escogidas de filósofos*) (Madrid, 1873), pp. 239, 240, 248.

[24] See *Del socorro de los pobres, o de las necesidades humanas*, BAE, lxv, p. 270. The passage cited is *De benef.* I. i. 9–13.

[25] See A. Castro, 'Erasmo en tiempo de Cervantes', *RFE*, xviii (1931), 329–89, and O. H. Green, 'Erasmus in Spain, 1589–1624', *HR*, xvii (1949), 331–2, and 'Additional Data on Erasmus in Spain', *MLQ*, x (1949), 47–8.

[26] See J. H. Elliott, *Imperial Spain, 1469–1716* (London, 1963), pp. 237–40.

authority on moral philosophy, the Jesuit education reflected the influence of Erasmianism in its deliberate combination of Christian dogma and classical letters.[27] By their example and through their propaganda the Jesuits helped inculcate an ideal of self-sufficiency and indifference to 'externals' strikingly similar to that taught by the Stoics. The importance attached by the Society to self-knowledge and control, most vividly illustrated in Loyola's *Spiritual Exercises*, is well known. So, too, is the likelihood that the Latin plays written and produced at Jesuit schools contributed towards interest in the Stoa.[28] Whilst, admittedly, the majority of all educated men in Catholic Europe owed their education to the Jesuits, it is probably no accident that the leading figures in the Neostoic movement and many writers of the period who took an interest in the Stoics went to Jesuit colleges.[29]

One aspect of the Counter-Reformation which has an especially close connection with Stoic attitudes is martyrdom, for many of the accounts of which Jesuits provided the subject-matter as well as the authors. The reports seemingly vie with one another in their descriptions both of the tortures inflicted upon the victims and of the superhuman impassivity and joy they displayed. The account of the death in Japan of six Franciscans, three Jesuits, and seventeen Japanese Christians addressed to Philip III in 1601 is not at all untypical in its repeated use of the words constancy and fortitude, so dear to Seneca. Chapter XIII, entitled 'Como crucificaron a los Santos Martyres y de la fortaleza con que padecieron', contains such remarks as 'Echose bien de ver su constancia, quan de gana, con quanto animo y espiritu yvan a dar su vida por Christo' and 'passaron todos veynte y seys su gloriosa carrera con increyble constancia, y marauillosa fortaleza'.[30] It is only surprising that one must wait for Quevedo before one finds Christian martyrs explicitly compared with Stoic heroes. While the Stoics did not urge their disciples actually to go out and look for suffering, their teachings concerning the right attitude to adopt in adversity could hardly fail to appeal in an age for which

[27] See M. Batllori, 'La agudeza de Gracián y la retórica jesuítica', *Actas del Primer Congreso Internacional de Hispanistas*, ed. C. A. Jones and F. Pierce (Oxford, 1964), p. 64.     [28] See Blüher, *Seneca in Spanien*, p. 246, and n. 19.
[29] This holds good for, among others, Montaigne, Lipsius, and Quevedo.
[30] Juan de Santa María, *Relacion del martirio que seys Padres descalços franciscos, tres hermanos de la Compañia de Iesus, y diecisiete Iapones christianos padecieron en Iapon* (Madrid, 1601), fols. 135ʳ, 139ʳ.

martyrdom constituted spectacular proof of spiritual superiority over heathen and heretic.

An essential factor in the rise of the Neostoic movement was the psychological need for comfort couched in persuasive tones. Adam attributes the force of Augustinian 'salvationist' religion at the beginning of the seventeenth century to the wars of religion: 'C'est parmi les massacres, dans un monde où l'on pille et où l'on tue, dans un monde qui semble plonger dans le chaos, que le nouvel augustinisme a pris naissance.'[31] That world is, of course, also the one in which Neostoicism flourished, and the same under-lying reality goes far towards explaining why the two attitudes contrasted by Adam were closely related and not in practice mutually exclusive.[32] If, as he says, the Neostoics preached optimistic faith in the rational order of things, this is precisely because in the main they felt the need to persuade themselves, as well as their readers, that the chaos around them was only apparent chaos. The fact that many of them, Montaigne, Lipsius, and Du Vair included, were, like Seneca and Cicero, by nature unstoical is not proof of insincerity. On the contrary, Senecan heroics in the face of adversity should be expected to appeal most forcefully to men most in need of them. Like the Stoicism of Greece and Rome, Neostoicism filled a spiritual void left by the collapse of social and economic as well as ideological order.

There can be little doubt that the crisis in the Spanish economy at the turn of the seventeenth century was propitious to the adoption of Neostoic views. If in France Neostoicism provided consolation at the end of the wars of religion,[33] and both Lipsius' *De constantia* and Du Vair's *De la constance* were written out of a need for personal comfort, what J. Lynch terms 'Spain's first great crisis in the modern period' between 1598 and 1620 provided a rich soil for Stoical ideas.[34] It is no coincidence that the first forty years of the seventeenth century saw the publication of an entirely new series of Spanish translations of Seneca. With only two exceptions, one of which is Quevedo's *De los remedios de*

---

[31] Adam, *Sur le problème religieux*, p. 14.

[32] St. Francis of Sales' success in combining Augustinian theology with Neostoic ethics is remarked upon by Levi, *French Moralists*, p. 126.

[33] See H. Busson, *La Pensée religieuse française de Charron à Pascal* (Paris, 1933), p. 382.

[34] *Spain under the Habsburgs*, ii, *Spain and America, 1598–1700* (Oxford, 1969), 10.

*cualquier fortuna*, these are all translations of genuine works, and they are presented by their translators as sources of political wisdom and moral counsel. Many of the translators, like those at the court of John II, were connected with the higher aristocracy and dedicated their translations to the king and his ministers. Thus, Fr. Gaspar Ruiz Montiano's version of *De beneficiis*—entitled *Espejo de bienhechores y agradecidos* (Barcelona, 1606)—is dedicated to the Duke of Infantado, whose chaplain he was; Juan Melio de Sande's *Dotrina moral de las epistolas que Luzio Aeneo Seneca escrivio a Luzilo* (Madrid, 1612) is addressed to the Duke of Alcalá, whom he served as secretary; Alonso de Revenga y Proaño, equerry to the queen, dedicated his translation of *De clementia* (Madrid, 1626) to the Duke of Medina de las Torres; and Licenciado Pedro Fernández Navarrete directed his *Siete libros de L. Æ. Seneca* (Madrid, 1627) to the Conde-Duque de Olivares and his translation of *De beneficiis* (Madrid, 1629) to Philip IV himself, to whom he acted as chaplain.[35]

The new translations were for the most part presented as containing teachings useful to Christians, an attitude which reflects the spirit of Neostoicism as well as such extreme Spanish attempts at this period to make a Christian of Seneca as may be found in the Jesuit La Higuera's fraudulent chronicle of Flavius Dexter.[36] While the translators avoid committing themselves to the view that Seneca was actually a crypto-Christian, they go out of their way to stress the proximity of his moral philosophy to Christianity and frequently omit or adapt un-Christian notions in his works. Ruiz Montiano, for instance, links Senecan *beneficium* with Christian charity and changes references to the gods into the singular 'porque la gente vulgar no lea cosa que no sea conforme a nuestra Religion Christiana', and Melio de Sande states in his prologue that he paraphrased the Epistles 'en sentido Catolico'.[37] As for the writer of the *aprobación* for Melio de Sande's translation, he declares that 'este Filosofo de tal manera habló en estas meterias [*sic*], quanto a razones morales, que si llegara su especulacion a la

---

[35] These translations are treated in detail by Blüher, *Seneca in Spanien*, pp. 319–25.

[36] See C. Aubertin, *Étude critique sur les rapports supposés entre Sénèque et saint Paul* (Paris, 1857), pp. 30–2.

[37] *Espejo de bienhechores y agradecidos* (Barcelona, 1606), fol. +7ʳ; and *Dotrina moral de las epistolas que Luzio Aeneo Seneca escrivio a Luzilo* (Madrid, 1612), fol. ¶2ᵛ.

practica, y la practica a la verdadera Fè, fuera vn Doctor excelentis-
simo en la Filosofia Christiana moral'.[38]

Inasmuch as they express their views on the Stoa, the translators
are rarely critical. Whereas in his *Collectanea moralis philosophiae*
(Lisbon, 1571), the first of whose three Books is devoted to
Seneca, Fr. Luis de Granada denounced Stoic apathy and fatalism,
the Stoic teaching concerning suicide, and the doctrine that all
vices are equal,[39] Melio de Sande praises Seneca for 'vna ex-
celente Dotrina moral, disposicion de la verdadera sabiduria. El
dessengaño de las cosas humanas. La ley de la vida, que las ajusta
y endereça. El sufrimiento en las aduersidades y contrarios
sucessos. El conocimiento de las falsas opiniones, y la justa
estimacion de cada cosa';[40] and Revenga y Proaño, denying that
the rigour of Stoic ethics exceeds the capacity of human nature,
refers anti-Stoics to *De vita beata* and to Lipsius' 'libros de
doctrina Estoica', i.e. the *Manuductio ad stoicam philosophiam*
and *Physiologia Stoicorum*, the major theoretical writings of the
Neostoic movement.[41] However, none of the Senecan translators
displays anything like the personal commitment to the Stoa of the
first Spanish translators of Epictetus' *Manual*.

It is probably thanks to Hernán Núñez de Guzmán, the only
Spanish Senecan scholar of note in the sixteenth century apart from
Martín Antonio del Río,[42] that Salamanca produced the first
two translations of Epictetus, for he had left to the rector of the
University the copy from which was published the only Greek
text of Epictetus to appear in Spain in the period (Salamanca,
1555). The first translation of the *Manual* was made by his pupil
and successor in the Chairs of Greek and Rhetoric, Francisco
Sánchez 'El Brocense', whose learning impressed even Lipsius.[43]

---

[38] *Dotrina moral*, fol. ¶ 3ᵛ.
[39] See *Collectanea*, fol. π8ʳ.                    [40] *Dotrina moral*, fol. ¶ 2ᵛ.
[41] *Los dos libros de clemencia; escritos por Lucio Anneo Seneca, Filosofo Español*
(Madrid, 1626), fol. 98ʳ.
[42] Hernán Núñez's commentary, *In omnia L. Annaei Senecae philosophi scripta
... castigationes utilissimae* (Venice, 1536), is frequently cited in Lipsius' edition of
Seneca. J. Sandys, *A History of Classical Scholarship* (Cambridge, 1921), ii. 158,
mistakenly refers to this commentary as 'an edition of Seneca'. Del Río wrote
a number of commentaries on the Tragedies (see N. Antonio, *Biblioteca Hispana
Nova* (Madrid, 1783-7), ii. 102).
[43] See A. F. G. Bell, *Francisco Sánchez El Brocense* (Oxford, 1925), p. 99.
El Brocense's translation, *Dotrina del estoico Filosofo Epicteto, que se llama
comunmente Enchiridion*, was first published at Salamanca in 1600 and then, in
1612, at Madrid, Barcelona, and Pamplona.

Although he considered the doctrine of apathy harsh and rigid
and condemned outright the Senecan concept of Fortune, Sánchez
none the less declared that, but for his references to the gods,
Epictetus recalls Ecclesiastes and the writings of the Apostles,
and he expresses his regret at having reached the 'tan buen puerto'
of Stoicism late in life.[44] It is as much on account of this personal
attachment to Stoicism as because of his specific comparisons
between Stoic and Christian thought that he deserves to be called
the first Spanish Neostoic.[45] As for the second translator of the
*Manual*, Gonzalo Correas, who was also Professor of Greek at
Salamanca and lectured on Epictetus,[46] he declares in his translation, published by the University Press in 1630, that he first
read the *Manual* before going up to Salamanca and that even at
that early age he had found its teaching 'mui konforme á la ke
leía en los santos Evanxelios'.[47] If the harshness of Stoic ethics
and Epictetus' references to the gods were corrected, he says,
following El Brocense, this philosopher would be seen to teach
the same as any good Catholic. Correas' view that the pagan
Epictetus is a remarkable example to Christians, 'konsiderando
kuanta es maior nuestra obligazion, ke la suia',[48] is one which
Quevedo was to extend to the Stoics as a whole.

The penetration of Stoical ideas and attitudes into moralizing
and consolatory literature reaches a climax at the turn of the
seventeenth century.[49] The deceptiveness of appearances and
of 'common-sense' opinions, the misery and brevity of life, the
inevitability of death and the need to prepare for it, and the
decrying of 'external' goods in general are some of the Stoical
views which become commonplaces of the moralists. In Spain,
even Sancho Panza is acquainted with Stoical clichés about death
'según nos lo dicen por esos púlpitos'.[50] In such leading Jesuit
moralists of the last third of the sixteenth century as Pedro de

---

[44] Sánchez, *Dotrina* (Madrid, 1612), fol. 16ᵛ.

[45] See Blüher, *Seneca in Spanien*, pp. 281 ff.

[46] See E. Alarcos García, ed., *Arte de la lengua española castellana*, by Gonzalo
Correas (Madrid, 1954), pp. xi, xiii.

[47] *El Enkiridion de Epikteto, i la Tabla de Kebes, filosofos estoikos* . . . (Salamanca, 1630), p. 7. On p. 7 Correas also states that he had earlier published a
Greek–Latin edition of the *Manual*, but no copy of it is known.

[48] Correas, *El Enkiridion*, p. 7.

[49] Levi, *French Moralists*, p. 55, points to the vogue for 'titles with a stoic
resonance' as a symptom of increased interest in the Stoa in the last decades
of the sixteenth century.                           [50] *Don Quixote*, II. vii.

Rivadeneira and Juan de Mariana, and in the Dominican Luis
de Granada, Seneca is the chief secular guarantor for revealed
truth.[51] More often than not, however, it is impossible to separate
Stoic from Christian elements. An example is Part II of the
Franciscan Diego de Estella's *Libro de la vanidad del mundo*
(Salamanca, 1576), in which Stoical themes are supported exclusively by biblical texts. Another is Juan de Horozco y Covar-
rubias' *Paradoxas christianas contra las falsas opiniones del mundo*
(Segovia, 1592), in which it is said of the Stoics that they 'trataron
de algunas verdades que conformauan con la verdad que se
trasluzia en ellos, y se descubrio a todo el mundo en la escuela
de Christo', and which, like the more famous *Emblemas morales*,
abounds in Stoical topics.[52] In the poems of Fr. Luis de León,
first published by Quevedo, Horatian, Neoplatonic, Stoical, and
Christian sentiments are fused together. Far from implying opposition to the Stoics, the fact that he treats Stoicism as inferior
to Christianity is typically Neostoic.[53]

Just as Spanish Senecanism in the fifteenth century drew
heavily on the work of Italian humanists,[54] so neither did Spanish
interest in the Stoics at the turn of the seventeenth century arise
in isolation. Throughout the previous century, despite restrictions
on relations with intellectual circles abroad, Spain was not cut
off from European currents of thought.[55] By a happy chance the
relaxation of intellectual censorship at the end of the century
coincided with the consolidation of the Neostoic movement.
By another, the most prestigious promoter of that movement
enjoyed close and fruitful relations with Spain. Despite his
flirtations with Protestantism, Justus Lipsius was admired by
Spaniards from an early date. Even before he left Leyden to return
to Louvain and the Church of Rome in 1591, his works were

[51] See Blüher, *Seneca in Spanien*, pp. 260–76.

[52] *Paradoxas*, fol. *5^r. Among the most obviously Stoical Paradoxes are I. vii,
'Que la fortuna es mas de temer quando es prospera que quando es aduersa',
and I. xvi, 'que el rico y el pobre, el poderoso y el que poco puede todos son
iguales en esta vida'. For the Stoical element in Spanish emblematic literature,
see Blüher, op. cit., pp. 258–9.

[53] See Gutiérrez, *Fr. Luis de León*, p. 289 n. 1, and A. F. G. Bell, *Luis de
León. A Study of the Spanish Renaissance* (Oxford, 1925), p. 219. Gutiérrez,
pp. 286–7, holds that Fr. Luis's motto, *Ab ipso ferro*, was an imitation of Epictetus' *Sustine et abstine*. For Seneca's influence on Spanish poetry in the second
half of the sixteenth century, see Blüher, op. cit., pp. 228–43.

[54] Blüher, op. cit., pp. 101 ff.                [55] See Elliott, *Imperial Spain*, p. 219.

sought after and read by Spanish scholars.[56] Particularly after his appointment as royal chronicler by Philip II four years later, the eager requests from Spaniards for his latest works and for news of his future projects redoubled. Spanish men of letters were soon among those throughout Europe who made certain of reading his commentaries on classical authors and his treatises on Roman antiquities as they came off the Plantin press. Two of his works, the *Politica* and *De constantia*, were translated into Spanish and published early in the seventeenth century. They were among the eight works by Lipsius in the library of Baltasar Gracián's patron, Vicencio Juan de Lastanosa,[57] while Latin editions of both works were among the nineteen by the Fleming owned by Olivares.[58]

The translator of the *Politica* was Philip II's ambassador to England and France, Bernardino de Mendoza, whose dedication to 'la nobleza española que no entiende la lengua Latina' praises among Lipsius' qualities as a writer 'su mucha dotrina, variedad de leccion, elegancia y breuedad de estilo'.[59] As for the translator of *De constantia*, Lipsius' first essay in re-establishing Stoic moral philosophy, although the title-page gives his name as Juan Baptista de Mesa, the historian and bibliographer Tomás Tamayo de Vargas claimed that his translation was usurped by one Fr. Hernando de Luxán and published under a false name.[60] The suggestion that Mesa or Luxán usurped Tamayo's *privilegio* would seem to be the most likely solution to the puzzle.[61] Whoever he was, the translator provided the non-Latin-reading public in Spain with their first serious introduction to Neostoicism.

Several of Lipsius' Spanish correspondents heard direct from him about the progress of his work on the Stoa.[62] However,

---

[56] See A. Ramírez, *Epistolario de Justo Lipsio y los españoles (1577–1606)* (Madrid, 1966), p. 9 n. 18.

[57] See K.-L. Selig, *The Library of Vicencio Juan de Lastanosa, Patron of Gracián* (Geneva, 1960), nos. 508, 534, 535, 553, 571, 572, 599, 697, and 753 (presumably the same edition as 535). Lastanosa also owned copies of Spanish and Latin editions of Seneca.

[58] See 'Biblioteca selecta del Conde Duque de San Lucar, Gran Canciller' (c. 1744), Real Academia de la Historia, Madrid, MS. D/119.

[59] *Los seys libros de las politicas o doctrina Ciuil de Iusto Lipsio* . . . (Madrid, 1604), fol. ¶5ᵛ. The *fe de erratas* and *licencia* are both dated 1599.

[60] See 'Iunta de Libros La maior que España ha visto en su lengua Hasta el año de MDCXXIV', Biblioteca Nacional, Madrid, MS. 9752, ii, s.v. 'Tamayo'.

[61] See G. A. Davies, 'The Influence of Justus Lipsius on Juan de Vera y Figueroa's *Embaxador* (1620)', *BHS*, xlii (1965), 173.

[62] See Ramírez, *Epistolario*, e.g., pp. 274, 277, 294, 302, 322.

since he died barely two years after the publication in 1604 of his *Manuductio ad stoicam philosophiam* and *Physiologia Stoicorum*, his correspondence gives disappointingly little indication of the reception accorded in Spain to these two works. Intended as introductions to his edition of Seneca, both systematize the corpus of Stoic doctrine from Zeno to Epictetus and define the frontiers separating Stoic from Christian teaching.[63] The fact that they were both dedicated to such powerful Spanish noblemen as the Duke of Frías and the Count of Fuentes must have ensured that they reached at least as wide a Spanish public as his earlier works. Surprisingly, however, neither Lastanosa nor Olivares seems to have owned a copy of either book; and, while Spanish references to Lipsius abound in the seventeenth century, specific mention of his work on the Stoa is comparatively rare. He appears rather to have been known in Spain for his prose style and for his scholarship generally. The translator of *De constantia* does, admittedly, state that his style is laconic because he was a Stoic, but this is something of an exception.[64] The Maestro in Antonio de Liñan y Verdugo's *Guía y avisos de forasteros que vienen a la corte* (Madrid, 1620) simply gives Lipsius as an example of one who created new prose styles while still respecting antiquity.[65] In a lecture delivered in Zaragoza, the poet and historian Lupercio Leonardo de Argensola referred to his correspondence with Lipsius and exhorted a youthful audience to emulate the Fleming's research into the Roman army by studying the Spanish armies of the *Reconquista*.[66] In a work entitled *Novedades antiguas de España*, Tamayo de Vargas refers to Lipsius as 'Principe de la erudicion i prudencia';[67] Juan de Piña mentions his name beside those of Tacitus, Persius, and Martial;[68] Francisco Cascales praises the grammarian Bartolomé Jiménez Patón by declaring that 'nos quita el desseo de los Escaligeros, Lipsios, y Bulegeros de la Tramontana';[69] and Lope de Vega's *Los melindres de Belisa*

[63] See Saunders, *Justus Lipsius* (*passim*).
[64] See *Libro de la constancia de Iusto Lipsio* (Seville, 1616), fol. A1$^r$.
[65] See *Guía y avisos*, ed. [M. de Sandoval] (Madrid, 1923), p. 217.
[66] See L. and B. Leonardo de Argensola, *Obras sueltas* (Madrid, 1889), i. 319–21.
[67] *Novedades antiguas de España* (Madrid, 1624), fol. 63$^r$.
[68] See *Varias fortunas* (Madrid, 1627), fols. ¶5$^v$–¶6$^r$.
[69] B. Jiménez Patón, *Discurso de los tufos, copetes, y calvas* (Baeza, 1639), fol. 66$^r$. Cascales' last reference is to Jules-César Boulenger (Bulengerus) (1558–1628), who, like Lipsius, wrote several works on Roman customs.

has yet another reference to him as the type of the philosopher.[70] When in his *Laurel de Apolo* (Madrid, 1630) Lope called Quevedo 'Lipsio de España en prosa', he was probably thinking of our author's style and erudition rather than his interest in the Stoics.[71] However, Lipsius' long-awaited and much-publicized work on Stoic philosophy and the translation into Spanish of two of his most important works can hardly have failed to leave their mark. There can be little doubt that, for instance, the great renewal of interest in Seneca at the beginning of the seventeenth century owed much to his influence. Certainly in the case of Quevedo the Neostoic movement, and Lipsius in particular, supplied a powerful new stimulus to the age-old appeal of Seneca in Spain.

It would almost be strange had Francisco de Quevedo not been attracted by the Stoics' consolation for misfortune and exhortations to self-reliance. His life was dogged by continual reverses of fortune: ill health, penury, imprisonment, lawsuits, and a disastrously short-lived marriage to an elderly widow punctuated a brilliant career as diplomat and writer. But two periods—apart from the final imprisonment in León from 1639 to 1643 during which he composed his last Stoical works, *La constancia y paciencia del santo Job* and *Providencia de Dios*—were decisive for his development as a Neostoic. The first, marked by what seems to have been an acute and prolonged crisis of conscience, dates from about 1609 until his departure for Italy in 1613. There is every indication that at this period Quevedo felt deeply distressed by the more frivolous of his early writings and by his conduct as a university wit. The year 1609 saw him become a member of the pious Congregación del Oratorio del Olivar and dedicate to the Duke of Osuna his translations of Anacreon and of pseudo-Phocylides' *Carmen admonitorium*, one of his earliest essays in Christianizing a classical author.[72] By this time he had already written his

---

[70] 'Lipsio con capa y espada / Fama inmortal tiene y goza' (I. xvii).

[71] A. Rothe, *Quevedo und Seneca. Untersuchungen zu den Frühschriften Quevedos* (Geneva/Paris, 1965), p. 3, implies the opposite. Other early references to Lipsius are noted by Ramírez, *Epistolario*, p. 19 n. 55.

[72] See S. Bénichou-Roubaud, 'Quevedo helenista (el *Anacreón castellano*)', *NRFH*, xiv (1960), 51–72, and D. G. Castanien, 'Quevedo's *Anacreón castellano*', *SP*, lv (1958), 568–75, and 'Quevedo's Translation of the Pseudo-Phocylides', *PQ*, xl (1961), 44–52. The only attempt at a full-scale biography is L. Astrana Marín, *La vida turbulenta de Quevedo* (Madrid, 1945), but it is entirely lacking in documentation. The best general study is still E. Mérimée, *Essai sur la vie et les œuvres de Francisco de Quevedo (1580–1645)* (Paris, 1886).

*España defendida*, a host of satirical *Cartas*, *Premáticas*, *Memoriales*, and *Genealogías*, as well as at least the first three of his *Sueños*, which reveal highly critical attitudes towards contemporary Spain, life in general, and himself in particular. The 'true "schizo-phrenic" duality in the character of our satirist' clearly bothered him no less than it has his biographers.[73] Even at this early stage in his career he is constantly depicting himself with embarrassing self-abasement as morally reprehensible. Already in one of his early *Memoriales* we find him describing himself in a series of antithetical *conceptista* puns as 'hombre de bien, nacido para mal ... que ha tenido y tiene, así en la corte como fuera della, muy grandes cargos de conciencia; dando de todos muy buenas cuentas, pero no rezándolas; ordenado de corona, pero no de vida ... corto de vista, como de ventura ... falto de pies y de juicio';[74] in the dedication of his second *Sueño* to the Count of Lemos in 1607 he declares: 'Bien sé que a los ojos de vuecelencia es más endemoniado el autor que el sugeto';[75] and in the fourth, dedicated to Osuna some three to five years later, he describes himself as 'todo en poder de la confusión, poseído de la vanidad de tal manera, que en la gran población del mundo, perdido ya, corría donde tras la hermosura me llevaban los ojos, y adonde tras la conver-sación los amigos, de una calle en otra, hecho fábula de todos; y en lugar de desear salida al laberinto, procuraba que se me alargase el engaño'.[76] That this is not merely a literary pose is sug-gested by the miserably humble letter he sent his friend Tamayo de Vargas in 1612 together with his first Stoical work,[77] and the abjectly repentant one he sent his aunt the following year with the series of poems he entitled 'Lágrimas de un penitente'.[78]

---

[73] H. Iventosch, 'Quevedo and the Defense of the Slandered: The Meaning of the *Sueño de la muerte*, the *Entremés de los refranes del viejo celoso*, the *Defensa de Epicuro*, etc.', *HR*, xxx (1962), 98 n. 11. Ch. 8 of O. H. Green, *Courtly Love in Quevedo* (Boulder, Col., 1952), gives a large selection of critical opinion on the question of Quevedo's duality.

[74] *Q*, I. 472b–473a.          [75] *Q*, I. 302.          [76] *Q*, I. 326.

[77] In this letter, citing the sentence 'Lascivos son mis escritos, pero mi vida buena', quoted at the end of *Anacreón castellano*, he comments: 'Yo, al revés, malo y lascivo, escribo cosas honestas, y lo que más siento es que han de perder por mí su crédito, y que la mala opinión que yo tengo merecida, ha de hacer sospechosos mis escritos' (*EQ*, p. 15).

[78] The second, and last, sentence of this letter reads: 'Sólo pretendo, ya que la voz de mis mocedades ha sido molesta a vuesa merced y escandalosa a todos, conozca por este papel mis diferentes propósitos, y ruegue a Dios nuestro Señor me dé su gracia' (*EQ*, p. 17).

A second major crisis followed some twenty years later and reached its height with the appearance of Quevedo's name on the 1632 Index. Far from being what Mérimée calls 'un de ces changements dont la cause secrète échappe trop souvent au biographe',[79] its causes appear if anything clearer than those of the first and seem to stem mainly from problems which beset him as a writer. To begin with, in the late 20s and early 30s the attacks of his literary enemies produced in him a veritable persecution mania. As early as 1608 he had written in the dedication of the third *Sueño*, 'yo acá esfuerzo la paciencia a maliciosas calumnias que al parto de mis obras (sea aborto) suelen anticipar mis enemigos',[80] and the prefaces to the subsequent *Sueños* show him becoming progressively more irate with his critics. The first *Sueño* had been refused publication in 1610, the censor maintaining that it was likely to lead readers into sin and that its author was either ignorant of the Scriptures or else had set out to make fun of them.[81] The *Sueños* appeared in Castile only in a thoroughly revised version some twenty years later, their title, *Juguetes de la niñez y travesuras del ingenio*, reflecting their author's desire to play down his best-selling but, for him, potentially dangerous work.[82] In his preface he explains that when he wrote these satires 'la sazón de mi vida era por entonces más propia del ímpetu que de la consideración'.[83] Two more problems, and the reasons why his name appeared on the Index, were piracy and the publication of works falsely purporting to be by him. A year after his appearance on the Index he declared in the preface to *La cuna y la sepultura* his intention to publish everything he had written, because 'siendo bastantes mis ignorancias para culparme, la malicia ha añadido a mi nombre obras impresas y de mano que nunca escribí'.[84] However, his professional troubles at this time did not end here, for the same period saw him come under the heaviest censure of his career. When in 1630 he submitted his *Cuento de cuentos* to the censor he found himself branded a heretical and scandalous

---

[79] Mérimée, *Essai*, p. 100.                                    [80] *Q*, I. 308.

[81] See Quevedo, *Vida del Buscón. Sueños y discursos*, Colección Crisol, no. 15, 6th ed. (Madrid, 1964), p. 295.

[82] The Index of 1640 mentions an edition of the *Juguetes* version of 1629, but the first known edition is Madrid, 1631. In the four previous years, the *Sueños* had appeared outside Castile in at least eleven editions.

[83] *Q*, I. 294.

[84] *Q*, II. 76. See *Novus index librorum prohibitorum et expurgatorum* (Seville, 1632), p. 399.

author.[85] In 1628 his defence of St. James of Compostela as sole patron of Spain had been countered in three different tracts and had resulted in his banishment from court.[86] His *El chitón de las tarabillas*, published pseudonymously two years later, was greeted by another caustic pamphlet, and to 1630 also is ascribed a *Memorial* denouncing the *Política de Dios*, *Buscón*, *Sueños*, and *Discurso de todos los diablos*.[87] Finally, the year 1635 saw the publication of Juan de Jáuregui's *El Retraído*, a bitter satire on *La cuna y la sepultura*, and of *El tribunal de la justa venganza*, the most vicious onslaught of all, on whose title-page Quevedo was named 'Maestro de Errores, Doctor en Desverguenças, Licenciado en Bufonerias, Bachiller en Suciedades, Cathedratico de Vizios, y Proto-Diablo entre los Hombres'.

It is surely no accident that this second crisis was accompanied by a spate of Stoical writing and that thereafter our author published only serious works. The appearance in 1630 of the *Doctrina moral del conocimiento propio y del desengaño de las cosas ajenas* marks the beginning of a new attempt on his part to prove himself respectable. His first publication after the appearance of his name on the Index was *La cuna y la sepultura*, a more explicitly Christian version of the same work. In 1635 he published his translations of Epictetus and pseudo-Phocylides together with his essay on the Stoics and defence of Epicurus and, three years later, his translation and imitation of the pseudo-Senecan *De remediis fortuitorum*. His *Virtud militante*, which appeared posthumously in 1651, was written between 1634 and 1636. Significantly enough, it is in the dedication of this work and of *La cuna y la sepultura* that he most strongly contrasts his character and his writings, maintaining that it does not detract from their value if he has not practised what they preach.[88]

The three periods at which Quevedo turned most actively to Stoicism—the third being that of his imprisonment in León

---

[85] See the *censura* by Fr. Juan Ponce de León, *BP*, pp. 363a–366a.

[86] See the list of 'Escritos contra Quevedo', *Q*, I. lxxxix–xc.

[87] See M. Menéndez Pelayo, *Historia de los heterodoxos españoles*, vii (Santander, 1948), pp. 710–24.

[88] In his dedication of *La cuna y la sepultura* to D. Juan de Chaves y Mendoza in 1633 he writes: 'Yo, señor, por desquitar la culpa que tiene quien escribe lo que no obra, lo dedico a vuesa señoría que lo obra y no lo escribe' (*BP*, p. 1191a). In the dedication of the first part of the *Virtud militante* to D. Pedro Pacheco he writes: 'le ofrezco este tratado, que podría tener algo bueno, por causa de ser yo tan malo' (*BP*, p. 1227a).

towards the end of his life—mark the high points of personal crises in his life. As in the cases of Montaigne and Lipsius, the attraction exercised on him by the ideals of Stoic imperturbability and self-reliance evidently stood in direct proportion to his own need for an effective shield against adversity and to his essentially unstoical nature. His appeals to his readers to concern themselves only with 'internals' often give the impression of being addressed as much to his own wayward self as to them. Like his jokes at his own lameness and short-sightedness, they suggest a need to ward off the barbs aimed at him by others by anticipating them himself. O. H. Green observes that Quevedo's 'confessions of moral inadequacy . . . are in themselves expressive of a certain moral integrity which characterizes the man'.[89] These confessions, but for which we should know next to nothing about his personal failings, are, however, suggestive of more. His urge to confess, both privately to his correspondents and publicly to his readers, suggests that his shortcomings horrified him. If, in Green's words, he is guilty of 'recurrent truancy' and 'one must not think of a conversion',[90] one should not underestimate his efforts to reform. By his confessions he seems to want to make it clear that he 'knew better'. If he could not live the Stoic ethic to his satisfaction, he could still try to teach it, to himself as well as to others.

Quevedo's earliest documented contact with the Neostoic movement is his brief correspondence with Justus Lipsius, begun in 1604 when he was still a student of theology in Valladolid and interrupted shortly before the Fleming's death two years later.[91] Quevedo was moved to write to Lipsius out of interest in one of his latest works, De Vesta et Vestalibus (Antwerp, 1603). In his first letter to him he tells Lipsius that, having seen some of his fellow-countrymen trying their hands at the Virgins but leaving them intact, he has been inspired by Lipsius' treatise to write about them himself.[92] His esteem for Lipsius is clear from the outset in his declaration that he will submit to him for his correction whatever he writes. As if to prove that he is in earnest he

---

[89] *Courtly Love in Quevedo*, p. 79.　　　　　　　　[90] Ibid., p. 76.

[91] For Quevedo's education and the view that the Stoics were not taught either at the Colegio Imperial in Madrid or at the University of Alcalá, see Rothe, *Quevedo und Seneca*, pp. 18–23. His relations with Lipsius are studied in *EQ*, Appendix I, pp. 509–24, and R. Lida, 'Cartas de Quevedo', *Letras hispánicas: estudios, esquemas* (Mexico/Buenos Aires, 1958), pp. 103–8.

[92] See Ramírez, *Epistolario*, p. 387.

appends to his letter a note, almost as long as the letter itself, commenting on Lipsius' interpretation of a passage from Arnobius. In his reply, although the aged scholar makes no mention of this note or of Quevedo's project, he does express his pleasure that the young man had read and approved of his treatise, informs him that it is about to appear in an enlarged, annotated edition, and promises to send him a copy—an offer which Quevedo takes up in his second letter. If, apparently, Lipsius was not keen to encourage competition with his *De Vesta*—and Quevedo, too, seems to have left the Virgins untouched—our twenty-four-year-old student could take heart at the effusively expressed wish that he be always inclined to learning and virtue and remain well disposed towards his new friend.[93] In his very first letter to him the great humanist of Louvain had admitted him to the circle of his noble and scholarly correspondents.

While Quevedo was involved with the Vestal virgins, Lipsius was busy with other things. In his reply to the Spaniard's first letter he tells him that he is wholly given over to Seneca and refers to the recently published *Manuductio* and *Physiologia*. In view of his subsequent attachment to the Stoa, and to Seneca in particular, Quevedo's response—'Seneca noster te totum habet, et non aliter totum Senecam habere possumus'—must be taken as more than mere repartee.[94] It may also be thought symbolic that the Fleming ends his second, and last surviving, letter to Quevedo by again mentioning his major works on the Stoics and declaring that he would send him copies of them were he not so far away. Either from what he had heard about our author or from what he gathered from his letters, he obviously considered that he might be interested in his writings on the philosophy of the Stoa. Whether in fact Quevedo received it as a gift from its author or obtained it by other means, he certainly read the *Manuductio* and made it his business to spread its message in Spain. He also knew Lipsius' editions of Seneca, Tacitus, and Velleius Paterculus.[95]

[93] See Ramírez, *Epistolario*, p. 391.

[94] Ramírez, op. cit., p. 400. It is curious to see how Quevedo echoes the sentiments of Alfonso de Valdés' letter of 1529 written to Erasmus soon after the publication of the latter's edition of Seneca (see Blüher, *Seneca in Spanien*, p. 185).

[95] For Quevedo's use of Lipsius' Seneca, see Appendix I. In *Providencia de Dios* (*Q*, II. 180a) he refers to Lipsius' commentary on Tacitus. He refers to the edition of Velleius Paterculus in his second letter to Lipsius (see Ramírez, op. cit., pp. 400–1, 402 n. 525).

Quevedo's second letter to Louvain reveals that he knew the translator of the *Politica*, Bernardino de Mendoza. In fact, he informs Lipsius of the translation's recent appearance in print and of the translator's death some three months before, and we find that on Mendoza's advice he had considered undertaking or had already embarked upon a second project of Lipsian inspiration.[96] This, the defence of Homer against the strictures of Julius Caesar Scaliger, received the Fleming's encouragement and was, it seems, carried out.[97] As R. Lida remarks, in view of the notorious rivalry between Lipsius and the younger Scaliger, his successor at Leyden, Quevedo's satirical digs at Scaliger father and son in several of his works should be regarded as so many blows struck in defence of his mentor.[98]

Quite apart from the common intellectual interests which their correspondence revealed to them, it must have been gratifying to Quevedo and Lipsius to find that their views on the political situation were practically identical. The grief felt by the latter at seeing his country torn asunder by war comes over clearly in his first letter. Adapting a passage from Catullus, he describes the Netherlands as the common grave of Europe and Asia and laments that theirs is an age of steel.[99] In reply Quevedo flatteringly asserts that it is only thanks to Lipsius' writings that their times can be said in any way to emulate the classical Golden Age, and he speaks of his own country in the same pessimistic vein as Lipsius of his. If Spanish gold and soldiers are being consumed in the Netherlands, at home Spaniards have fallen prey to sloth and ignorance. The despair which had sparked off Lipsius' first essay in Stoicism now inspires the author of the *Sueños* to exclaim: 'Quid de mea Hispania non querula voce referam?'[100] Starting out as he had with the greatest admiration for the acknowledged leader of the Neostoic movement, their brief exchange of letters doubtless constituted the most decisive stimulus to his own interest in the Stoa.

His correspondence with Lipsius was, however, by no means Quevedo's only contact with the Neostoic movement. Indeed, he

---

[96] See Ramírez, p. 400. For Quevedo's sonnet on Mendoza's death, later adapted for that of Luis Carrillo y Sotomayor, see *OP*, I. 463.

[97] Although it does not survive, it is referred to in his *Anacreón castellano* (written by 1609), but without making it clear whether the defence was already composed (see *Q*, III. 438b).

[98] See 'De Quevedo, Lipsio y los Escalígeros', *Letras hispánicas*, pp. 159 ff.

[99] See Ramírez, p. 391.                         [100] Ibid., p. 400.

is most probably the only Spaniard to have had connections with all four of its leading figures as well as with a large number of other Spaniards with a Stoical bent. By 1609 he knew of Guillaume du Vair's translation of Lamentations, he consulted his translation of Epictetus for his own translation of the *Manual*, and he had at least heard of the *Philosophie morale des stoïques*.[101] However, there is no evidence that he knew *La Sainte Philosophie*, which, like his own Stoical works, treats Stoic topics from a more clearly Christian standpoint. As for Gaspar Scioppius, whose *Elementa philosophiae stoicae moralis* (Mainz, 1606) is the only work of the period comparable in aim and scope with Lipsius' *Manuductio* and *Physiologia*, he was in Madrid in 1613–14 and, according to Quevedo's first biographer, corresponded with our author.[102] Quevedo is also the first Spaniard known to have read Montaigne, whom, in his satire on Richelieu, he calls the oracle of political aphorisms and whose *Essais* he describes in his *Defensa de Epicuro* as 'libro tan grande, que quien por verle dejara de leer a Séneca y a Plutarco, leerá a Plutarco y a Séneca'.[103] He also knew the first Spanish translator of the *Essais*, Baltasar de Zúñiga, another correspondent of Lipsius, and he may have inspired one Diego de Cisneros to become the second.[104]

As regards his relations with Spaniards connected with the Neostoic movement, besides Bernardino de Mendoza, Quevedo knew Tamayo de Vargas, the translator of Lipsius' *De constantia*; and in 1612 he sent him his first known Stoical work.[105] Whether or not they met, he was also an admirer of El Brocense, on whose translation of Epictetus he based his own version of the *Manual*, and whose translations of Horace and Petrarch are appended to Quevedo's edition of the poet Francisco de la Torre.[106] Lupercio

---

[101] See Quevedo, *Lágrimas de Hieremías castellanas*, ed. E. M. Wilson and J. M. Blecua, *RFE*, Anejo LV (Madrid, 1953), p. 10; and p. 26, below.

[102] See P. A. de Tarsia, 'Vida de Don Francisco de Quevedo Villegas', *Vida y obras posthumas de Don Francisco de Quevedo Villegas*, x (Madrid, 1794), 24. Tarsia's Life was first published in 1663.

[103] *Q*, III. 425. See V. Bouillier, *La Fortune de Montaigne en Italie et en Espagne* (Paris, 1922), p. 55, and J. Marichal, 'Montaigne en España', *NRFH*, vii (1953), 262–4.

[104] See Marichal, pp. 263–4. Quevedo dedicated to Zúñiga his commentary on a letter from Ferdinand of Aragon to the first viceroy of Naples (see *Q*, I. 170).

[105] See *EQ*, pp. 13–16.

[106] See *Obras del Bachiller Francisco de la Torre* (Madrid, 1631), fols. 131ʳ–144ᵛ. In his *España defendida y los tiempos de ahora*, written in 1609, Quevedo refers

Leonardo de Argensola, another of Lipsius' Spanish correspondents and, like our author, a poet influenced by Seneca, is thought by Fernández-Guerra and Astrana Marín to have been the friend to whom he sent his third *Sueño* in 1608.[107] There is no doubt that another correspondent of Lipsius, the Professor of Theology at Salamanca and Canon of Seville Cathedral, Manuel Sarmiento de Mendoza, was on good terms with him. In 1628 his *Milicia evangélica* appeared with a preface by Quevedo in which he contrasts the voyages of gold-seekers with those of missionaries in search of martyrdom; in 1631 Quevedo dedicated to him his edition of the poems of Luis de León based on a manuscript lent him by Sarmiento; and four years later he addressed to him one of the 'Fantasmas' which make up the second, Stoical, part of the *Virtud militante*.[108]

Another friend of Quevedo's was the first Spanish biographer of Seneca, Juan Pablo Mártir Rizo, whose erudite *Historia de la vida de Lucio Anneio Seneca español* (Madrid, 1625) he mentions in his *Perinola*.[109] In 1625 he had written a preface for another work by Mártir Rizo, and the latter in turn came to his defence in the heated debate over the proposal that St. Teresa should be made co-patron of Spain.[110] As for Seneca's second biographer, Juan Francisco Fernández de Heredia, he dedicated his *Seneca y Neron*, first published pseudonymously in 1642, to the son of Quevedo's patron and friend, the Duke of Medinaceli, and it is likely that the two writers knew each other.[111] Quevedo also knew intimately two of Seneca's translators, the poet Luis Carrillo y Sotomayor and the editor of his own verse, Jusepe Antonio González de Salas. In the introduction to the third Muse, *Melpómene*, the latter provides the only surviving evidence of Quevedo's interest in Seneca's tragedies when he relates that Quevedo knew by heart the *Troades*, a translation of which González de Salas appended to his *Nueva idea de la tragedia antigua* (Madrid,

---

to El Brocense as 'cuidadoso y docto español' (*BP*, p. 517b). For the indebtedness of his translation of Epictetus to El Brocense, see below, pp. 58–60.

[107] See *Q*, I. 307 n. (a), and Astrana Marín, *Vida turbulenta*, p. 141.
[108] See *Q*, II. 482a/b, 483a–484b, 149a ff.
[109] See *Q*, II. 477b.
[110] See *Q*, II. 480a/b, and I. xc, no. 241.
[111] In May 1634 Quevedo's friend, the Duke of Medinaceli, corresponded with Fernández de Heredia about the dowry of Quevedo's wife (see *EQ*, pp. 272–5). For the two biographies of Seneca, see Blüher, *Seneca in Spanien*, pp. 374–8.

1633).[112] As regards Carrillo y Sotomayor, both he and his brother Alonso were friends of Quevedo in his university days, and the posthumous *Obras de Don Luys Carrillo y Sotomayor* (Madrid, 1611), containing the short-lived poet's translation of *De brevitate vitae*, also included a *silva* and an epitaph by Quevedo, the latter a rare and early example of his ability to imitate Seneca's Latin. He may indeed have been thinking of his friend's translation as well as of his untimely death when he made him speak in this epitaph of life's brevity and the vanity of riches and worldly honour.[113] His deliberate fusion of Stoic and Christian elements is already to be found here in his combination of passages from Seneca and Job.

Quevedo wrote the *aprobación*, or certificate of approval, for at least one work with Stoical overtones, and he had *aprobaciones* written for two of his Stoical works by a Jesuit with Neo-stoical leanings. Rodrigo Fernández de Ribera's *Mesón del mundo* (Madrid, 1631), a feebly contrived allegory of life whose title its author derives from Seneca, is described by Quevedo as consisting of 'burlas ejemplares y veras entretenidas', although he was shortly afterwards to make a suitably unkind reference to it in his *Perinola*.[114] The writer of the fulsome *aprobaciones* for *La cuna y la sepultura* and *Epicteto y Phocilides en español* was the Jesuit Juan Eusebio Nieremberg, whose own *De arte voluntatis* (Lyon 1631) aims at promoting Stoical attitudes towards such 'externals' as riches and poverty, pleasure and pain, honour and ignominy, life and death.[115] It is typical of the Jesuits' practical interest in Senecan constancy that, together with this erudite philosophical treatise, Nieremberg published an account of the martyrdom of three Jesuit missionaries in Uruguay.

---

[112] See *OP*, I. 113. For González de Salas, see E. C. Riley, 'The Dramatic Theories of Don Jusepe Antonio González de Salas', *HR*, xix (1951), 183–203.

[113] See *Obras de Don Luys Carrillo y Sotomayor* (Madrid, 1611), fols. ¶ ¶ ¶ 4ᵛ–¶ ¶ ¶ 5ʳ. That Quevedo was on close terms with Carrillo's brother, Alonso, is suggested by the fact that he lent him several books (see the first of two un-numbered pages at the beginning of the autograph MS. of *España defendida*, Real Academia de la Historia, Madrid, Colección Salazar y Castro, MS. L 76). Astrana Marín, *Vida turbulenta*, p. 136, states that the two men studied together at Valladolid.

[114] See *BP*, p. 1734b, and *Q*, II. 470a. For Fernández de Ribera's novel, see H. Schulte, *El Desengaño. Wort und Thema in der spanischen Literatur des Goldenen Zeitalters* (Munich, 1969), esp. pp. 135–6.

[115] See Blüher, *Seneca in Spanien*, esp. pp. 366–8. For Nieremberg's *aprobaciones*, see *Q*, II. xxvi–xxvii, III. 381 n. 1.

What information has come down to us concerning Quevedo's relations with his contemporaries suggests, then, that he was unusually well connected with the Neostoic movement in Spain as well as abroad. As we shall see, his attitudes to the Stoics and their philosophy qualify him as the movement's most powerful spokesman in Spain and as one of its most dedicated adherents anywhere in Europe.

# I

## THE *DOCTRINA ESTOICA*

### 1. *The Biblical Source of Stoicism*

ONLY one of Quevedo's works deals directly and exclusively with the Stoics and their philosophy. *Nombre, origen, intento, recomendación y descendencia de la doctrina estoica* (or, as it is conveniently abbreviated in the running head of the earliest editions, simply the *Doctrina estoica*) was first published in 1635 together with the *Defensa de Epicuro* and his translations of Epictetus and pseudo-Phocylides. If, as has been argued elsewhere, this brief essay is the work he sent his friend Tomás Tamayo de Vargas in 1612 as a fitting introduction to Epictetus' *Manual*, it is his first known Stoical work.[1] Be that as it may, the essay is based almost entirely on Lipsius' *Manuductio*. The idea of writing an introduction to Epictetus, however, may well have been inspired by Du Vair's *Philosophie morale des Stoïques*, which first appeared as a preface to the Lyons, 1594, edition of his translation of the *Manual* and is referred to by Quevedo as the *Doctrina de los estoicos*.[2] Apart from the translation of Lipsius' *De constantia*, the *Doctrina estoica* was the first Spanish introduction to Neostoicism.

From the outset Quevedo's concern is less with the Stoics themselves than with bringing them into the Christian fold. His essay takes as its starting-point the derivation of the name of the school from the portico at Athens where Zeno and his followers met. It begins, after a short dedication to the historian Rodrigo Caro, by borrowing from Lipsius two passages in Athenaeus and one in Tertullian which refer to porticos. The quotation from Tertullian is important because, as Lipsius had cited it out of context (one in which every authority but Christ and the Gospel was repudiated), Quevedo was able to present it as proof that

---

[1] See H. Ettinghausen, 'Acerca de las fechas de redacción de cuatro obras neoestoicas de Quevedo', *BRAE*, li (1971), 161–6.

[2] See *Q*, III. 386.

when he spoke of belonging to the Portico of Solomon, this Father prided himself on being a Stoic and lent his weight to Quevedo's theory of the origin of Stoic philosophy.[3] Prompted by a passage in which Seneca praises rulers who allow philosophers to live in peace, Quevedo goes on to dwell in lyrical tones on the secluded spots which have encouraged philosophy and, in particular, on 'aquel pórtico que guardaba el retiramiento para el logro de todas las horas', the Stoa Poikile.[4] Although he claims that his interpretation of Seneca's words is original, the really original part of his treatment of the Stoics' name lies in his linking the porticos and retreats of the philosophers with the tabernacles and courts of the Lord extolled in the Psalms. His conclusion to this first section of his essay juxtaposes those who walk in the counsel of the ungodly (Psalm 1) with the type of rulers censured by Seneca who mistrust scholars and philosophers. Although from the point of view of classical scholarship this discussion of the Stoics' name is hardly worthy of a disciple of Justus Lipsius, it is valuable as a first indication of the nature of our author's interest in the Stoa.

The concern to relate Stoicism to Christianity at almost any cost is still more apparent in the section on the origin of Stoic philosophy. On the title-page of the earliest editions the *Doctrina estoica* is mentioned as *El origen de los estoicos, y su defensa contra Plutarco*, the two least derivative parts of Quevedo's essay. As if to stress that he is making an original contribution to the history of philosophy, he begins now by making the intriguing claim that the Stoic school is older than its name and that its origin is nobler than has commonly been thought. The basis for this claim is the traditional assumption that any truth perceived by the ancients must have been divinely inspired: 'No pudieron verdades tan desnudas del mundo cogerse limpias de la tierra y polvo de otra fuente que de las sagradas letras. Y oso afirmar que se derivan del libro sagrado de Job, trasladadas en precepto de sus acciones y palabras literalmente.'[5]

In order to establish the biblical origin of Stoicism Quevedo sets out, first, to trace Epictetus' philosophy to the Book of Job

---

[3] See *Q*, III. 413. The quotations from Athenaeus and Tertullian are taken from *Manuductio*, I. xiv (see *Manuductionis ad stoicam philosophiam libri tres* (Antwerp, 1604), pp. 47, 48).

[4] *Q*, III. 414. The passage cited from Seneca is *Ep.* 73, 1–2.

[5] *Q*, III. 414.

and, secondly, to forge a link between Job and Zeno, the founder of the school. To begin with, he gives a concise account of some of the fundamental moral teachings of the Stoics drawn for the most part from Epictetus.[6] He then presents Job as the exemplar of the Stoic ethic, judiciously paraphrasing parts of the first two chapters of the Book of Job—those alone in which Job displays something like stoic resignation—and arguing that Job's reaction to the loss of his house, goods, health, sons, and wife epitomizes Epictetus' doctrine in the early chapters of the *Manual* that all such 'externals' be regarded as given on loan and that God must not be blamed for their loss. With this he considers his case as good as proven: '[¿]Quién negará que esta acción y palabras literalmente y sin ningún rodeo ni esfuerzo de aplicación no es, y son el original de la doctrina estoica, justificadas en incomparable simplicidad de varón, que en la tierra no tenía semejante[?]'[7] In his opinion the whole of the Book of Job is concerned with the Stoic distinction between 'internals' and 'externals', things within and beyond the individual's control—'todo su libro no se ocupa en otra cosa sino en enseñar a sus amigos, que los que él padece no son males'— and Job exemplifies the correct opinion of death better than Epictetus' hero, Socrates, who was himself inspired by Job. Epictetus' wish that God should rain down calamities upon him is derived from Job 6: 9–10; chapter 11 of the *Manual*, from Job 1: 21; and Epictetus' words in the final chapter, 'Si Deo ita visum fuerit, ita fiat', from Job's 'Sicut Domino placuit ita factum est'.[8]

The idea that Epictetus learned his philosophy from Job is probably less original than Quevedo would have his readers believe. When he introduced his second pair of parallel passages from Job and Epictetus he declared that he was following El Brocense's numbering of the chapters in the *Manual*. In his *Anotación* to the chapter from which Quevedo quoted, El Brocense cites the same text from Job that our author claims as its source, and this is not the only passage from Job cited in El Brocense's

---

[6] See *Q*, III. 414. Quevedo's explanation of the notions 'internals' and 'externals' is taken from the *Manual*, ch. 1; the statement that in order to live a peaceful life one must accommodate one's desires to the course of events, from ch. 8; the idea that children are given to their parents on loan, from ch. 11; and the injunction not to blame God, from ch. 31.

[7] *Q*, III. 415.

[8] Ibid.

commentary.[9] Remarking in *El Retraído* on the series of parallels drawn between Epictetus and Job in Quevedo's preface to *La cuna y la sepultura*, Juan de Jáuregui was to point to the precedent in El Brocense and to mock at Quevedo's claim to originality in this matter.[10] After the publication of the *Doctrina estoica* at least two Spanish works appeared which treat Job as a biblical Stoic: P. Jerónimo de la Cruz's *Job evangelico Stoyco ilustrado. Doctrina ethica, civil, y politica* (Saragossa, 1638), and the Jesuit José de Tamayo Velarde's *Job paciente en ambas fortunas* (Granada, 1648). Ultimately, no doubt, these too were inspired by the first Spanish translator of Epictetus.

Quevedo's demonstration of the chronological feasibility of his bid to derive Stoicism from Job is based entirely on Lipsius' *Manuductio*, I. x, which deals with the early leaders of the school. He takes from Lipsius the information that Zeno was a native of Citium who, although a pupil of Crates the Cynic, objected to the Cynics' way of life.[11] He also borrows Lipsius' quotations from Strabo, Diogenes, Suidas, Cicero, and Diogenes Laertius in order to prove that Zeno's birth-place had connections with the Phoenicians and, consequently, that the founder of the Stoa and his followers were natives of lands close to Judea.[12] Even his comment on these passages, including the remark that it is from Judea that the wisdom of all nations derives, comes from the *Manuductio*.[13] Although Lipsius provides evidence for only the most outside chance that there actually was any contact at all between Zeno and the Jews, carried away by typical polemical zeal Quevedo transforms this faintest of possibilities into the most incontrovertible certainty: 'no sólo es posible, sino fácil, antes forzoso el haber los cínicos y los estoicos visto los libros sagrados, siendo mezclados por la habitación con los hebreos, que nunca

---

[9] 'Siempre nos enseña Epicteto, que entendamos, que el cuerpo, y las otras cosas no son nuestras sino prestadas. . . . Bien conocia esto Iob, pues dixo: *Dominus abstulit, sit nomen Domini benedictum*' (Francisco Sánchez, *Dotrina del estoico Filosofo Epicteto* . . . (Madrid, 1612), fol. 25ʳ). In his *Anotación* to ch. 4 he writes: 'Traigamos siempre delante aquel dicho de Iob; *Dominus dedit, Dominus abstulit*' (fol. 12ᵛ).

[10] See *El Retraído* (Valencia, 1635), fol. 6ʳ.

[11] See *Q*, III. 415–16. Cf. *Manuductio*, ed. cit., p. 30.

[12] See *Q*, III. 416. Cf. *Manuductio*, ed. cit., pp. 30–1.

[13] Cf. *Manuductio*, ed. cit., p. 31: 'Illudunt, in quo iure glorietur ipse. è maioribus esse Syris, & Iudaeae finitimis, à quo tractu sapientia in alias oras, vt dixi, diffusa.'

los dejaban de la mano.'[14] Towards the end of his life he was to claim Job as the source of the myth of the phoenix, of Aristotle's theory of tragedy, of Sophocles' concept of decorum, and of Greek and Latin metre.[15] If his exposition of the biblical origin of Stoic philosophy is scarcely less fanciful, it earned the admiration of at least one learned contemporary. In his *aprobación* P. Juan Eusebio Nieremberg declares: 'Los Estoicos merecen el origen sagrado que aquí se les da. . . . De la doctrina Estoica, cuanto a la estima de la virtud, no fue hombre Autor.'[16]

## 11. *The Problems of Suicide and Apathy*

While Quevedo's account of the basic doctrines of Stoic moral philosophy was taken principally from Epictetus, his outline of the aims of Stoicism is primarily Senecan: to seek virtue for its own sake, to raise one's soul above ill fortune, to live with the body but not for it, to live with a view to dying, and neither to despise nor to fear death. His approving account of the Stoa's aims is, however, cut short by what he calls the scandal of Stoicism: the Paradox which permitted, and under certain circumstances even recommended, the sage to take his life. This doctrine has been named as one 'upon which the Stoics were occasionally taken to task by [seventeenth-century] English critics',[17] and it is one which no Christian, English or not, could very well condone. Pascal's scornful jibe, 'Oh! quelle vie heureuse, dont on se délivre comme de la peste!', was only to be expected.[18] Quevedo's reaction, however, was to consult Lipsius.

Quevedo takes from the *Manuductio* not only his formulation of the Stoic Paradox but also the information that Socrates' teacher was the philosopher Archelaus, that Sidonius Apollinaris named the Ionian school Socratic, and that Socrates developed philosophy from a primitive preoccupation with the stars into

---

[14] *Q*, III. 416.
[15] See *La constancia y paciencia del santo Job* (*Q*, II. 216a–218a, 240b–242b). Seneca, *Ep*. 42, 1, also compares the 'vir bonus' to the phoenix.
[16] *Q*, III. 381 n. 1 (p. 382).
[17] H. W. Sams, 'Anti-Stoicism in 17th- and Early 18th-Century England', *SP*, xli (1944), 66.
[18] *Pensées*, ed. C.-M. des Granges (Paris, 1955), p. 164. Cf. Augustine, *De civ. Dei* XIX. 4: 'O vitam beatam, quae ut finiatur, mortis quaerit auxilium!' (Migne, *Patrologia Latina*, xxxviii. 630).

concern with morals.[19] Unlike Lipsius, on the basis of these data he concludes that Socrates was a Stoic *avant la lettre*, but he again follows the *Manuductio* when he asserts that the deaths of Socrates and Seneca cannot be held to justify the Paradox, as they were simply carrying out their own death sentences.[20] In spite of this, he makes Seneca receive the brunt of his criticism. After borrowing from Lipsius two passages in which Seneca recommends suicide, he remarks: 'Ni el ser Séneca cordobés, ni el ser tales los escritos de Séneca, han podido acallarme para que en esta parte no diga, que con ellas [estas palabras] antes se mostró Timón que Séneca, tanto peor cuanto mejor hablado.'[21] His regret at condemning Seneca and his admiration for the Stoic's writings are plain to see, and he finds some consolation for having to censure the philosopher of Cordova (whom even here he addresses with the words '¡oh grande Séneca!') in the thought that another Spaniard, Martial, ridiculed the foolishness of killing oneself to avoid death. Referring to two passages from Seneca quoted in the *Defensa de Epicuro*, he expresses his surprise that Seneca favoured suicide in view of his repeated praise for Epicurus' heroic constancy in the face of an excruciating death.[22] Whereas in the *Defensa* he takes some trouble to defend Seneca's views on suicide, this is not the case in the *Doctrina estoica*. Indeed, he takes a passage in Epictetus borrowed from Lipsius as evidence that Seneca was an exception among the Stoics for his advocacy of suicide. Furthermore, he asserts that Epictetus' words are so true and pious that they might have been uttered by a Christian; and in support of this he quotes Augustine's scorn for the Paradox, which he likewise takes from Lipsius.[23]

Despite its indebtedness to the *Manuductio*, Quevedo's treatment of the Stoic Paradox differs greatly from the Fleming's. In the first place, although he takes over from Lipsius two of Seneca's recommendations of suicide, he omits all mention of Seneca's condemnations of suicide quoted by Lipsius, one of which follows directly on the passage from Epictetus that he had borrowed

[19] See *Q*, III. 416. Cf. *Manuductio*, title of III. xxii, and I. viii (ed. cit., pp. 199, 24, 25).

[20] See *Q*, III. 416. Cf. *Manuductio*, III. xxii (ed. cit., p. 203).

[21] *Q*, III. 417. Cf. *Manuductio*, III. xxii (ed. cit., pp. 199–200). The passages from Seneca are *Ep.* 69, 6, and *De ira*, III. xv. 4.

[22] See *Q*, III. 417. The passages referred to are *Ep.* 66, 47 and *Ep.* 92, 25.

[23] See *Q*, III. 417. Cf. *Manuductio*, III. xxiii (ed. cit., p. 207).

earlier.[24] In the second place, while he takes from Lipsius one instance in which Epictetus repudiates the Paradox, he glosses over passages cited in the *Manuductio* in which Epictetus recommends suicide no less heartily than Seneca.[25] His attempt at modifying his original declaration that the Stoa's attitude to suicide is the scandal of the entire school depends, then, on the suppression of evidence that he could not help having before his eyes. The difference between his approach and that of his model is made clear by a comparison of their conclusions. Lipsius had written: 'satis habeo vniuersè docuisse, Mortem arbitrij nostri non esse: nec Stoicis me, hac parte, suffragium dare';[26] Quevedo writes: 'Débame la doctrina estoica que la defiendo de la fealdad de este error, en que algunos estoicos se culparon.'[27] Characteristically, Lipsius had expounded the views of the Stoics without attempting to defend them against Christian censure. No less characteristically, our eminently polemical author made the attempt and did so by making a scapegoat of his favourite Latin author.

J. L. Saunders remarks of Lipsius' treatment of the question of suicide that it is 'an interesting introduction to the problems confronting any man who has such dual loyalties'.[28] Quevedo was clearly another such man, and one cannot but wonder why he did not simply follow Lipsius as closely here as he does elsewhere and censure Epictetus and the rest of the Stoics as much as Seneca, rather than condemn any one of them out of hand. The reason is not necessarily the one given by Marcilly, that he was more forcefully attracted to orthodox Stoicism than to the Senecan variety.[29] In an essay which sought to present Stoicism in the best possible light and to minimize its divergences from Christian dogma, the most convenient method of clearing the school of this notoriously

---

[24] Lipsius introduces this passage (*Ep.* 30, 12) with the words: 'sed & Seneca noster saepe temperat' (ed. cit., p. 207). For the view that Seneca was obsessed with the propriety of suicide, see J. M. Rist, *Stoic Philosophy* (Cambridge, 1969), esp. pp. 246–9.

[25] e.g. the passages from *Discourses* II. 16 and I. 24, which come immediately before and soon after the first passage from Seneca borrowed by Quevedo (see *Manuductio*, III. xxii (ed. cit., p. 199).

[26] *Manuductio*, III. xxiii (ed. cit., p. 209).

[27] *Q*, III. 417.

[28] *Justus Lipsius. The Philosophy of Renaissance Stoicism* (New York, 1955), p. xv.

[29] See C. Marcilly, 'L'angoisse du temps et de la mort chez Quevedo', *RMed*, xix (1959), 369.

un-Christian doctrine was to represent it as the view of one Stoic only. If the *Doctrina estoica* was intended as an introduction to Epictetus' *Manual*, this really left only Seneca. In his *Marco Bruto*, written in 1631, where his main concern is not with re-conciling classical philosophy and Christianity, Quevedo condemns Cato's suicide (the very reason for Seneca's admiration for him) but praises Porcia for the (Stoic) manliness he finds in her but not in other women.[30] As far as our author is concerned, it would seem that suicide is proof of weakness in men but strength in women.

The next section of the *Doctrina estoica* contains a defence of a number of Stoic Paradoxes against the strictures of Plutarch, whom Quevedo none the less treats with a respect reminiscent of Montaigne. Referring to him as 'el gran Plutarco', he states that all Plutarch's ethical works are Stoical, that his attacks on the Stoics were his only fault, and that one is only justified in contradicting him in order to come to the defence of the Stoa. His defence takes the form of a point-by-point refutation of the criticisms set out in the *Compendium Plutarchei libri perditi, cui argumentum et nomen fuit Stoicos quam poetas absurdiora dicere*, one of three anti-Stoic works of Plutarch's that he names. The Paradoxes ridiculed in this tract are all variations on the theme that the Stoic sage cannot be hindered or hurt, and Quevedo's defence, written in an antithetical style which anticipates that of his Senecan *De los remedios de cualquier fortuna*, relies on the Stoics' distinction between 'inter-nals' and 'externals' and, more especially, on the Senecan (and Christian) distinction between body and soul. For example, in defence of the first Paradox—that the sage is free even in prison— he writes: 'no su mejor parte, porque la cárcel cierra el cuerpo, no la mente, no el juicio, no el buen propósito, no los pasos del entendimiento, no los actos de la voluntad libre en las prisiones. Ningún tirano ha podido inventar cárcel para las potencias del alma, ni sus crueldades han sabido pasar de los sentidos, no pasa del cuerpo su poderío'.[31] On several occasions he introduces frankly Christian concepts and terminology, and in this, too, he looks forward to *De los remedios de cualquier fortuna* and his other

---

[30] See *Q*, I. 146b–147a, 150b.
[31] *Q*, III. 417–18. Part of one of Quevedo's imitations of Seneca's Epistles reads like a gloss on this Paradox: 'Tiénenme cerrado en una cuadra, mas a pesar de las vueltas de la llave estoy libre' (*Q*, II. 390a).

Stoical works. Thus, he declares that the sage knows that the soul tumbles to its ruin only if it sins; and he gives St. Laurence, 'el divino español', as an example of a Christian martyr who illustrates the Paradox that the sage does not suffer under torture, even though, on the grounds that it is unfair to use Christian examples in his reply to Plutarch, he also adduces the classical hero Anaxarchus.[32] However, he again brings in Christianity when he relates Anaxarchus' endurance of torture to Christ's words, 'No temáis a los que sólo pueden matar el cuerpo': '¿Quién negará que Anaxarco obedeció lo que no había oído (bien sin fe verdadera), y que Plutarco duda de lo que ve, y contradice la verdad que sabe?' And, in order to substantiate the sage's reputed ability not to be consumed by fire, he again refers to the martyrs.

Quevedo changes his tactics when he deals with Plutarch's mocking assertion that the sage could achieve whatever he desired. Far from defending it, he denies that the Stoics made any such claim and quotes Epictetus' injunction (*Manual*, chapter 8) to wish that things may come about as in fact they will. But, no more able to subscribe to this view than to the one ridiculed by Plutarch, he declares the former to be lacking in truth, the latter in reason. Although he leaves his own views on the matter undefined, the implication would seem to be that he advocates a prudent balance between fixed fate and free will. Finally, he deals with the Paradox that virtue of itself provides wealth, dominions, good fortune, and happiness with the argument, employed on a larger scale in *Providencia de Dios*, that goods cease to be goods in the hands of the wicked.[33]

With Plutarch's criticisms disposed of, Quevedo proceeds to grapple with the problem of apathy, like the Paradox concerning suicide, a traditional bone of contention with Christianity. Christian censure of the Stoics' ideal of the elimination of passions goes back as far as Paul, who holds that virtue is to be sought in their harmonization. Opposition to Stoic apathy was 'so universally professed in seventeenth-century England that it deserves to be called a commonplace.'[34] The same is true of Spain, where Alonso de Cartagena had left the problem of reconciling it with Christian

[32] See *Q*, III. 418. El Brocense cites the same example in similar terms (see Sánchez, *Dotrina*, fol. 21ʳ). In his sonnet on St. Laurence (*OP*, I. 329) Quevedo again treats him as an example of constancy.

[33] See *Q*, III. 419.

[34] Sams, 'Anti-Stoicism', p. 67.

dogma to 'altos ingenios';[35] and where Quevedo's contemporary, Gonzalo Correas, named 'lo duro de la Seta Estoika' as one of the school's main differences with Christianity.[36] The whole question was complicated by the fact that the Stoics themselves were far from clear on this point. While Epictetus forbids the sage to feel commiseration but allows him to feign it, Seneca rejects both the Peripatetics' view that apathy means allowing oneself to be affected by the passions in moderation and the Cynics' view that the sage feels no passions at all.[37]

Earlier in his essay, Quevedo had praised Stoicism for its concept of virtue, superior to that of any other school, which, thanks to its seriousness, manliness, and strength, 'tanta vecindad tiene con la valentía cristiana, y pudiera blasonar parentesco calificado con ella'.[38] However, he had qualified this eulogy by remarking that the Stoics erred in their excessive insensibility, and had referred to the criticism of Stoic apathy voiced by Aquinas and other Doctors of the Church. Now he states that the Pythagoreans and Peripatetics condemned the total exclusion of feeling implied in Stoic apathy and, once again without acknowledgement, takes from Lipsius one passage in Lactantius and two in Jerome condemning the doctrine.[39] It is only when he proceeds to inveigh against Lipsius for not emending Jerome as he was prepared to emend the classics that he mentions, for the first time in the essay, 'Justo Lipsio, varón doctísimo' and his 'Manuducción a los estoicos'.[40] As in his very first letter to the Fleming, he is not afraid to question his mentor's formidable scholarship. Here, by implication, he sets himself up as a superior textual critic, one who restores the text not of a pagan but of a saint.

After this somewhat surprising and unnecessary rebuff, Quevedo returns to Stoic apathy and, as earlier, names Aquinas as its principal Christian opponent. While admitting that any attempt to contradict the Church's condemnation of this doctrine would be tantamount to heresy, he feels free to 'interpret' the doctrine

---

[35] See Blüher, *Seneca in Spanien*, p. 104.

[36] *El Enkiridion de Epikteto*, p. 7. Augustine had contrasted 'duritiam Stoicorum' with 'misericordiam Christianorum' (see Migne, *Patrologia Latina*, xxxiii. 394).

[37] See, e.g., Epictetus, *Manual*, XVI, and Seneca, *Ep.* 85, 3 and 9, 3.

[38] *Q*, III. 414.

[39] See *Q*, III. 419. Cf. *Manuductio*, III. vii (ed. cit., pp. 159–60, 151).

[40] *Q*, III. 419 (with erratum 'Julio Lipsio').

and declares that he does so 'para mostrar que no se me ha cansado la afición con los estoicos'.[41] His interpretation follows the Senecan distinction between feeling and being overcome by feelings, and consists simply in assuming that when the Stoics said that passions should not be felt, what they meant was that one should not allow oneself to give in to them. This, he triumphantly announces, is the proper understanding of the Paradox and is partial repayment of his debt to the Stoa: 'No es cortesía descaminada entender bien lo que dijeron algunos de aquéllos que encaminaron todas sus acciones al bien; muchas cosas los debemos, débannos una.'[42]

In the first 'Fantasma' of the *Virtud militante* Quevedo sets out to clarify this interpretation. The 'Fantasma', presumably written shortly after the publication of the *Doctrina estoica* in 1635, is a reply to a query about his interpretation of Stoic apathy addressed to him by a certain Dr. Manuel Serrano del Castillo. As Quevedo records it, the query went as follows: 'Díceme vuesamerced que se convence de que se ha de sentir la muerte y los trabajos, y que en favor de las virtudes lo entiende así con los santos padres; y pregúntame vuesamerced qué calidad ha de tener aquel sentimiento para no ser reprehensible, antes loable.'[43] Apparently dissatisfied by the way Quevedo had neatly skated around the problem of reconciling Stoic apathy with Christian teaching, Serrano was still worried that the Stoic doctrine contradicted the Christian notion that suffering is a prerequisite of virtue. In *La cuna y la sepultura* Quevedo follows Seneca in considering death to be in general the thing most feared by man, arguing there, as in *De los remedios de cualquier fortuna*, that death 'hace mucho por hacerse amable, y aun digna de desprecio antes que de miedo.'[44] In the 'Fantasma' he is evidently thinking of the Stoics when he declares: 'Entre los gentiles, pretensiones tuvo más que de hombre quien pretendió que no se temiese la muerte ni los trabajos'.[45] The view he implies, that fear of death and adversity is natural, is put forward at greater length in one of his *Migajas sentenciosas* where, in reply to 'algunos hombres [again, obviously, the Stoics] que tienen más de prudencia dura que fuerte, los cuales no quieren

---

[41] *Q*, III. 419.

[42] *Q*, III. 420. When in his preface to *La cuna y la sepultura* he again mentions Aquinas' censure of Stoic apathy, he once more avoids confrontation and does so by naming Aristotle and Plutarch (as here, Pythagoreans and Peripatetics) as the saint's forerunners (see *Q*, II. 77).

[43] *Q*, II. 137a.          [44] *Q*, II. 84b.          [45] *Q*, II. 137a/b.

que el sabio tenga dolor', he quotes Seneca and cites the example of Job.[46] His solution of the problem of apathy in the 'Fantasma' is provided by the supreme example of Christ, who, as he seeks to establish in his undated *Declamación de Jesucristo* . . . *en el huerto*, 'temiendo la muerte, no la rehusó.'[47] What the Stoics taught, he asserts, 'entonces fue pretensión vana; hoy fuera más, pues la temió Cristo, que siendo hombre, fue Dios y hombre. No fue en agonía por no morir, que no podía rehusarlo quien encarnó para morir.'[48] Fear of death, although natural and in-evitable, is, however, surmountable. Despite the fact that not even Christian martyrs achieve apathy (for it is impossible not to feel pain and, in any case, suffering is necessary for virtue), they are enabled through the example of Christ's Passion to meet death joyfully:

Y aquel temor de Cristo y aquel sudor sangriento está animando de gozo en su muerte por su ley a todos los mártires, en quien el amor divino vence a la naturaleza humana . . . sólo al amor de Dios es per-mitida la victoria destos temores. En el mártir tiemblan con los tormen-tos los miembros; encógense con el fuego, desátanse con el cuchillo, enflaquécense desangrados, desfigúranse defuntos; y esto cuando el alma goza constante, como enamorada. . . . No tuvieran ejercicio la constancia y la fortaleza del espíritu si no tuvieran que moderar en la flaqueza del cuerpo. Naturaleza es, según esto, temer la muerte, y ella es temerosa al pecador, y por ser pena del pecado. Virtud y mérito es saber animar el espíritu contra este temor.[49]

All men feel pain, but only sinners need fear death. Elaborated and illustrated by the examples of Christ and the martyrs, Que-vedo's views here coincide with his interpretation in the *Doctrina estoica*, except for the introduction here of a Christian reason—fear of hell—to justify fear of death.

Marcilly is undoubtedly right to point out in connection with Quevedo's views on Stoic apathy 'une antinomie radicale entre l'éthique de Quevedo et celle des philosophes antiques qu'il pré-tend considérer cependant comme ses maîtres à penser'.[50] Con-flict was, however, inevitable at certain points for any Christian who took it upon himself to defend Stoic philosophy. What is more, perhaps unwittingly, Quevedo's interpretation of Stoic apathy is less fanciful than has sometimes been thought, for he

[46] *BP*, pp. 1002a–1003a.   [47] *Q*, II. 359a.   [48] *Q*, II. 137b.
[49] *Q*, II. 137b–138a.   [50] 'L'angoisse du temps', p. 370.

was in fact right when he said that the Stoics condemned only certain feelings.[51] But the significant thing, especially given the way Lipsius makes no attempt whatever to counter Christian criticism of Stoic apathy, is our author's determination, here and throughout his essay, to resolve this and other conflicts as best he can.

### III. *Quevedo* proficiens

The concluding section of the *Doctrina estoica* is a list of adherents to Stoicism drawn for the most part from the *Manuductio*. Beginning with the Greeks, Quevedo follows Lipsius' order but omits his learned comments, reducing three chapters of his source to a single sentence.[52] Even his statement that he is adding Homer to the list is false, for in this, as in his subsequent inclusion of Socrates, Demosthenes, Philo, and Plato, he is still following the *Manuductio*.[53] Few of the Greeks he mentions seem to have been more than names to him; if he had any interest in their teachings, about which Lipsius provides considerable information, this is not revealed in his works. Only Zeno among the early Stoics is referred to more than once outside this essay, and then merely as the founder of the Stoa or as the type of the philosopher.

With the exception of Virgil, included on the strength of a single quotation, Quevedo's list of Roman Stoics is likewise taken from Lipsius and provides evidence that he probably used the Paris, 1604 edition of the *Manuductio*, in which case he may have received the work from its author and probably read it soon after it first came out.[54] Again, few of the names in this list appear elsewhere in his works. The fact that he scarcely mentions Marcus Aurelius anywhere is perhaps due to the Stoic emperor's persecution of Christianity, though on one occasion he does, admittedly, call him 'el buen emperador'.[55] As for Seneca and Epictetus, they are

---

[51] See Rist, *Stoic Philosophy*, pp. 37–8.

[52] See *Q*, III. 420. Cf. *Manuductio*, I. x–xii (ed. cit., pp. 30–41).

[53] See *Q*, III. 420. Cf. *Manuductio*, I. xvii (ed. cit., pp. 54–5). For some reason, Quevedo omits Strabo, whom Lipsius mentions between Demosthenes and Philo.

[54] See *Q*, III. 420. Cf. *Manuductio*, I. xvii (ed. cit., pp. 55–6). The Paris, 1604 edition appears to be the only one that makes Thrasea Paetus two people by erroneously inserting a comma between his names. The same separation of the names occurs in the earliest editions of the *Doctrina estoica*.

[55] *Migajas sentenciosas* (*BP*, p. 1115b). A similar view is expressed by Tertullian, *Apologeticum*, V. 6.

treated in separate chapters of the *Manuductio* (I. xviii and xix) and are not even mentioned here by Quevedo. Nor does his list include any of the Silver Age Latin poets, several of whom were influenced by Stoicism and who were among Quevedo's favourite classical authors. However, in a note to his translation of one of Seneca's Epistles, he comments:

> Gran ventaja hacen a todos los filósofos y poetas los que dellos fueron en el tiempo de las persecuciones de los mártires cristianos; viéronlos despreciar la vida, triunfar en la muerte, predicar el Evangelio; pudieron oír a los apóstoles, y por esto excedieron en la doctrina a los demás. Son ejemplo Séneca, Epicteto, Juvenal y Persio . . .[56]

There and elsewhere he makes it clear that in his opinion the writers of Imperial Rome were superior to others by virtue of their contemporaneity with the first Christians. As far as he is concerned, it is no coincidence that the best authors of antiquity seem frequently to anticipate Christian thought.

Lipsius is still Quevedo's source when he lists those early Christians who thought well of the Stoics.[57] Only in the case of St. Charles Borromeo, the only modern Stoic mentioned by Lipsius, does he acknowledge his debt; but he goes one better than his model, preferring to regard the saint not simply as a Stoic, but as a super-Stoic.[58] He also makes his own additions to Lipsius' list. The first is St. Francis of Sales, Quevedo's translation of whose *Introduction à la vie dévote*, which he mentions here, was published the year before the *Doctrina estoica* with a preface stating that 'en sólo este libro se leen las dotrinas de los filósofos mejoradas y con enmienda; las proposiciones estoicas, cristianas y limpias; y tan católicamente corregidas, que si Sócrates, Zenón, Epiteto y Séneca vieran esta *Introducción*, leyeran lo que no acabaron de saber, y supieran lo que no pudieron alcanzar.'[59] The second (small return for Quevedo's indebtedness to him) is Lipsius who, he states, 'fue cristiano estoico, fue defensor de los estoicos, fue maestro de esta doctrina.'[60] The third is El Brocense, who is said by Quevedo to have prided himself on being a Stoic. The last is

---

[56] *Q*, II. 384b.

[57] See *Q*, III. 420. Cf. *Manuductio*, I. xvii (ed. cit., p. 56).

[58] 'Lipsio añade para lustre en nuestros tiempos de los estoicos, a San Carlos Borromeo, si bien fue más que estoico, pues no cabe en la doctrina suya lo que cupo en su santidad cristiana' (*Q*, III. 420).

[59] *Q*, II. 252.                                       [60] *Q*, III, 420.

Quevedo himself. In a remarkable profession of faith in Stoicism
he proclaims how much he has owed to its philosophy in adversity
and confesses his own inadequacy as a *proficiens*: 'yo no tengo
suficiencia de estoico, mas tengo afición a los estoicos: hame asis-
tido su doctrina por guía en las dudas, por consuelo en los trabajos,
por defensa en las persecuciones, que tanta parte han poseído
de mi vida. Yo he tenido su doctrina por estudio continuo; no
sé si ella ha tenido en mí buen estudiante'.[61] While it is impossible
to tell exactly when these words were written, it seems likely
that they date from Quevedo's second period of crisis. Early in
that period, confined to Villanueva de los Infantes in 1628 for
his attacks on the proposal to make St. Teresa co-patron of Spain,
he wrote a Stoical letter in Senecan Latin to a friend, Lucas van
Torre, telling him that, although banished from Court, he was
still a citizen of the world; that, so long as he lacked desires and
passions, he was not poor; and that he sought shelter from the
temptations of 'externals' in the haven of Stoicism.[62] In his last
period of crisis, after more than three years spent in a dungeon
in León, he was to proclaim his debt to Epictetus' *Manual* for
enabling him to prove for himself the truth of the first of the
Paradoxes defended in the *Doctrina estoica*: 'Ayer con la estafeta
vinieron cartas a la ciudad, diciendo unas que yo estaba libre.
Esto al Epicteto lo he debido en la prisión.'[63] It may have been
at the same period that he wrote, in a pastiche of a Senecan
Epistle: '¿Quieres saber al Pórtico lo que debo, y a su filosofía
varonil? Con ella hice maestro para mí al que sólo quiso ser mi
verdugo; hallé la misma usura en sus persecuciones que el niño en
los azotes, cuando le hacen que aprehenda lo que le importa
saber.'[64] All these statements, private and public, reveal clearly
his eagerness to regard himself and to be regarded by others as a
disciple of the Stoa.

Quevedo described the work he sent his friend Tamayo de
Vargas as 'esto, que tiene novedad y podría ser de algún provecho',[65] and it is surprising to find that, although the major part
of the *Doctrina estoica* is lifted from Lipsius, its author did in
fact write something new. As an introduction to the history and
teachings of the Stoics it is, of course, incomparably inferior to the
*Manuductio*. But Quevedo's intention was obviously not Lipsius'.

[61] *Q*, III. 420.    [62] See *EQ*, p. 208.    [63] *EQ*, p. 453.
[64] *Q*, II. 393b.                                  [65] *EQ*, p. 15.

He makes no attempt, as Lipsius had, to assess and compare the various contributions of the early adherents of the school or to distinguish its teachings from those of other ancient systems. His account of its moral precepts, presented largely in his reply to Plutarch, is typically polemical and unscientific. Although he knew of the *Physiologia* and had probably read it, he has not a word to say about Stoic logic or metaphysics and makes no attempt to reconcile Stoic fate and Christian Providence. However, whereas Lipsius had been prepared where necessary to admit differences between the Stoa and Christianity, Quevedo's main object, almost his sole purpose, is wherever possible to obliterate the differences altogether. To this end he is prepared to distort his source's balanced account of Stoic philosophy by tendentious selection and wishful interpretation, explaining away such un-Christian doctrines as the Stoic teachings regarding suicide and apathy. As the engraved title in the second edition shows most graphically, the *Doctrina estoica* transforms Lipsius' objective reconstruction of the Stoic system into what amounts to a plea for the adoption of Stoic ethics as a pattern for Christian living.[66]

Quevedo's elaboration of ideas suggested to him by El Brocense's translation of Epictetus is no less revealing. His greatest debt to the only Spaniard apart from himself whom he claimed as a Neostoic is his development of casual comparisons between the *Manual* and the Book of Job into the theory—or, as he would have it, fact—that Stoicism actually originated in Job and was, therefore, albeit indirectly, divinely inspired. Like so much else in this essay, this 'ennoblement' of the Stoa depends upon judicious selection of texts. As Jáuregui remarked about the similar demonstration in the preface to *La cuna y la sepultura*, passages like those chosen from Epictetus for comparison with Job could be found in a host of non-Stoic classical writers.[67] But Quevedo probably cared very little about this, if he cared at all. What mattered to him was that Stoicism should be seen to be a worthy precursor of Christianity. He shared the belief of his contemporary, the 'English Seneca', Bishop Hall, that 'by following those of Seneca's precepts which did not conflict with Christian teaching it would

---

[66] See H. Ettinghausen, 'Neostoicism in Pictures: Lipsius and the Engraved Title-page and Portrait in Quevedo's *Epicteto y Phocilides*', *MLR*, lxvi (1971), 94–100.
[67] See *El Retraído*, fols. *7ʳ–*8ᵛ.

be possible to have a minimum of unhappiness on earth while at the same time preparing one's way to heaven.'[68] What he does in the *Doctrina estoica* is exactly what he said he had set out to do in the work he sent Tamayo: 'seguir el parecer de los estoicos, en cuanto da lugar la fe cristiana.'[69]

[68] A. Chew, 'Joseph Hall and Neo-Stoicism', *PMLA*, lxv (1950), 1140.
[69] *EQ*, p. 15.

# II

## THE *DEFENSA DE EPICURO*

### 1. *Seneca and the First Draft of the* Defensa

ALTHOUGH it was only to find its Lipsius at the middle of the seventeenth century in Gassendi, the Renaissance revival of the philosophy of the Garden goes back at least as far as Lorenzo Valla's *De voluptate*, written in 1431.[1] While Quevedo was not the only writer of his time with a passionate interest in the Stoics to praise Epicurus, Menéndez Pelayo's bald statement, 'Surgieron partidarios de las diversas escuelas griegas en lo que no parecían hostiles al dogma, y hubo muchos estoicos, y Quevedo intentó la defensa de Epicuro', may seem a little strange.[2] Since Epicureanism and Stoicism are often regarded as practically opposites, it may well be wondered how Quevedo came to take up Epicurus' defence and why he published his *Defensa de Epicuro* together with a work in which he voiced his adherence to the philosophy of the Stoa. It is, however, no accident that the two were published in the same book.

At least two details in the *Defensa* point to the fact that Quevedo originally intended it to serve as a brief introduction to his essay on the Stoics. The first is his comment on a passage in which Seneca cites Epicurus' condemnation of suicide—'En pocas palabras condena con suma elegancia Epicuro la opinión de algunos estoicos, *que referiremos*, afirmando que el sabio puede y debe darse la muerte'[3]—which refers to his treatment of the Stoics' Paradox concerning suicide in the *Doctrina estoica* and was evidently written after that work. The second is his statement immediately following his remarks on two quotations from Montaigne: 'He procurado desempeñarme de las promesas desta introducción previa a la doctrina estoica',[4] in which the last two

---

[1] See B. Farrington, *The Faith of Epicurus* (London, 1967), p. 147.

[2] *Heterodoxos españoles*, v. 402.

[3] *Q*, III. 424 (my italics). The passage in Seneca is *Ep.* 24, 23.

[4] *Q*, III. 426. The passages quoted are from *Essais*, II. xi and II. x (see *Essais*, ed. A. Thibaudet (Bruges, 1958), pp. 464, 454–5).

words are obviously to be read as though italicized. This second statement, however, does more than lend support to the view that Quevedo's original intention was to make his defence of Epicurus precede and introduce the *Doctrina estoica*. It would also appear to imply that at this point, less than half-way through the *Defensa* as we know it, he considered that he had done what he could to restore Epicurus' reputation, and that his introduction to his essay on the Stoics originally ended here or shortly after. This hypothesis is borne out by the way he had introduced his two passages from Montaigne—'Dará fin a esta defensa la autoridad del Sr. de Montaña, en su libro, que en francés escribió, y se intitula *Essais* o *Discursos*'⁵—and by his remark prior to this that he would stop citing Seneca in order to prevent his pamphlet growing into a book. It is further supported by the appearance at this point of a list of the authorities upon which the *Defensa* up to here is based. Originally, then, Quevedo's defence of Epicurus was less than half its ultimate length and had been intended to preface the *Doctrina estoica*.⁶

That the *Defensa* originally ended less than half-way through the text as we now have it is more than a mere bibliographical curiosity. It points to the fact that, in its first state, the work was based on very little else than Senecan material. Whereas what appears to have been the original conclusion is preceded by the statement that in order to defend Epicurus it would have sufficed to mention Seneca's name,⁷ far from limiting himself in his first draft of the work to merely mentioning Seneca, our author had actually quoted some twenty-five passages from his works. What is more, the primitive draft probably opened, not as now by referring to previous defenders of Epicurus in general and to Andraeus Arnaudus in particular, but with Quevedo's reference to Epicurus' first champion, Seneca; and it is likely that at least some of the non-Senecan material in the first part of the work, as we know it, was added to the original draft at a later date.⁸

The object of the *Defensa* was to repair the damage to Epicurus' reputation wrought by his early defamers, who, Quevedo re-

---

⁵ *Q*, III. 425.

⁶ The comment on the second passage cited from Montaigne refers to Plutarch's criticisms of the Stoa and so also suggests that the *Doctrina estoica* had been written before the *Defensa*.

⁷ 'Grande es esta defensa donde bastaba nombrar a Séneca' (*Q*, III. 425).

⁸ See below, pp. 50 and 53–4.

peatedly claims, misled the Fathers of the Church, and so all Christendom, into thinking of the philosopher of the Garden as an arch-hedonist and an incorrigible atheist.[9] Commenting on Quevedo's statement that Epicurus figures more often in Seneca's works than any other philosopher, H. Iventosch surmised that, when he composed the *Defensa*, 'Quevedo probably had his eyes on an index of the Roman's works'.[10] He did, indeed, use an index to Seneca's references to Epicurus, and it was one that he drew up himself by writing 'Epicuro' in large letters in the margins of his copy of the first volume of Seneca's works published at Lyon in 1555.[11] References to and quotations from Epicurus marked in his copy of Seneca are pressed into service from the beginning. The Roman Stoic is first brought in to back up the claim that in Epicurus' philosophy virtue was the *sine qua non* of pleasure. Citing three passages in Seneca to prove this, Quevedo declares: 'Estas palabras por sí tienen soberanía, dichas por nuestro Séneca, ¡cuán grande estimación solicitan a Epicuro!'[12] Then, after quoting from Lucretius, Juvenal, and Pliny in answer to one of Epicurus' classical detractors, he cites another passage in Seneca to demonstrate that the latter speaks of Epicurus with the greatest respect.[13] His last introductory quotation from Seneca is prefaced by the following eulogy of both Seneca and Epicurus: 'Séneca, cuyas palabras todos los hombres grandes reparten por joyas en sus escritos, repartió en los suyos las de Epicuro, donde se leen con blasón de estrellas.'[14] The passage quoted, significantly enough, treats Epicurus' political philosophy as a corollary of Zeno's, and Quevedo does not fail to take the opportunity of equating the two.[15] Although, as Iventosch notes, this conclusion

---

[9] See *Q*, III. 422–3. For the contribution of Epicurus' philosophy to the rise of atheism in sixteenth- and seventeenth-century France, see ch. i, 'L'athéisme', of H. Busson, *La Pensée religieuse française de Charron à Pascal* (Paris, 1933).

[10] 'Quevedo and the Defense of the Slandered', p. 179 n. 44.

[11] See below, Appendix II. By means of a double *non sequitur* L. Astrana Marín, who first noticed the connection between the notes in Quevedo's copy of Seneca and the *Defensa*, ascribed the date 1632—itself apparently arrived at quite arbitrarily—both to the annotations and to the *Defensa* (see Quevedo, *Obras completas*, 'Prosa' (Madrid, 1932), p. 1315).

[12] *Q*, III. 422. The first passage quoted is a conflation of two sentences following a passage annotated by Quevedo (see Appendix II, no. 5). For the other two quotations, see nos. 79 and 80.

[13] See *Q*, III. 422. Cf. Appendix II, no. 81.

[14] *Q*, III. 423.

[15] Ibid. Cf. Appendix II, no. 85.

of Quevedo's is inaccurate,[16] this very inaccuracy reveals his urge to minimize the differences between the philosophies of Epicurus and the Stoics.

All but the first and the last of Quevedo's twenty quotations from Seneca's Epistles in the *Defensa* appear in the order in which he found them in Seneca's works. The first, from *Ep.* 8, is taken out of order so as to introduce the rest with Quevedo's comment: 'Más frecuente es Epicuro en las obras de Séneca, que Sócrates y Platón, y Aristóteles y Zenón. . . . Por esto en veinte epístolas Séneca le cita todas las veces que necesita de socorro en las materias morales que escribe'.[17] Quevedo's string of passages from Seneca is a miscellany of comments on and sayings of Epicurus. Since they reflect Seneca's tastes and prejudices, and he obviously took pleasure in shocking Lucilius by championing Epicurus in the same breath as he preached Stoicism, they give the impression that the philosopher of the Garden, far from being what is commonly meant by Epicurean, was a kind of Stoic sage *malgré lui*. In the order in which they appear in the *Defensa*, they cover the following topics: Epicurus' personal impact upon his followers; his teaching that wealth cannot be absolute and that one should concern oneself only with what is one's own; his censure of those who never start living properly—on this occasion Seneca praises him effusively and Quevedo in his turn praises Seneca; Epicurus' practice of fasting in order to discover just how little he required in order to be happy; his greater interest in those he ate with than in what he ate; the fame promised Idomenaeus, and achieved by him, by virtue of the letters written to him by Epicurus; Epicurus' saying that the way to make a man rich is to remove his cupidity, and Seneca's praise for this; Seneca's statement that he likes to quote Epicurus so as to confound those who use his name as a cover for vice—to which Quevedo adds that he is quoting Epicurus for the same reason; another declaration by Epicurus deploring those who never manage to get down to the business of right living; his scorn for those who seek and for those who fear death—

---

[16] See 'Quevedo and the Defense of the Slandered', p. 182.

[17] *Q*, III. 423. Cf. Appendix II, no. 16. The remark that Seneca cites Epicurus in 20 of his Epistles is not quite accurate: he is cited or referred to in 26, and in the *Defensa* passages from only 15 are quoted by Quevedo. The number 20 is probably based either on the fact that Quevedo quotes that number of passages relating to Epicurus in these 15 Epistles or else on a rough count of the Epistles (in fact 21) that he had marked 'Epicuro'.

Quevedo praises Seneca here for quoting Epicurus against himself;
Epicurus' injunction to act as though one were constantly being
watched; his recommendation to retire into oneself when in a
crowd—Quevedo asserts that this implies recognition of the
notions of conscience and a vigilant God; Seneca's praise for a
book written by Lucilius which he compares with the works
of Epicurus and Livy; Epicurus' distinction between those who
find the truth for themselves and those who need help to do so;
and Seneca's assurance that Epicurus taught what amounted to
the fundamental Stoic doctrine of the division of things into
'internals' and 'externals', and his admiration for Epicurus'
constancy in death—Quevedo stresses the fact that Seneca
regarded Epicurus as a Stoic on the first count and declares that
he himself regards him as the greatest of Stoics on the second,
quoting yet another passage in Seneca in support of this claim.
This stream of Senecan quotations is finally brought to a close by
a passage from the pseudo-Senecan *De paupertate*, included in the
Lyon 1555, edition of Seneca's works, in which Epicurus praises
poverty.[18]

There was still, however, one last quotation from the Epistles
in the early version of the *Defensa*. It occurs in what has been
argued was the original conclusion, and it is a passage which neatly
rounded off Quevedo's attempt to depict Epicurus as a Stoic and,
no less neatly, brought up the subject of the essay on Stoicism
which was to follow. Quevedo introduces the quotation by praising
the Stoa in the following terms: 'La secta es fuera del común
sentir, mejor diré contraria; los términos con que se declara
son forasteros a los espíritus vulgares, más altos de lo que puede
percibir la oreja'.[19] Then, after quoting the passage (*Ep.* 13, 4)
which justifies this praise, he goes on to equate Epicurus with
Epictetus, defies anyone to dare ignore Seneca's admiration for
the former, and makes public his own indebtedness to Epicurus'
first defender:

Es lengua no sólo diferente, sino extraña la de la verdad; es amarga,
óyese, y en vez de aprenderse se teme: en esta lengua escribió Epicteto,
en ésta escribió Epicuro, no en la que le achacaron a la gula y embria-
guez: los que conocieron su culpa en no obedecerla, disfamáronle los
torpes filósofos idólatras. Admiróle Séneca, admiróle: con él deshonra

---

[18] See *Q*, III. 423–5. Cf. Appendix II, nos. 14, 18, 19, 21, 23, 24, 27, 29, 30,
32, 34, 35, 36, 39, 42, 47, 68, 70.                          [19] *Q*, III. 426.

al grande cordobés, quien no le creyere en esto, quien no le siguiere. No soy quien le defiende, oficio para mí desigual; soy quien junta su defensa, porque no pueda blasonar el vicio, que fue tan admirable filósofo su secuaz.[20]

Since virtually all the quotations from Seneca in the early draft of the *Defensa* appear in the same order there as in Seneca's works, Quevedo, it appears, originally relied simply and very nearly solely upon the number of Senecan passages he cited, that is, on the weight he attached to the Stoic's authority. His failure even to arrange his Senecan quotations thematically bears this out. He was, clearly, guided in his choice of passages by one criterion only: to portray Epicurus as essentially in agreement with, and even (in his views on suicide) superior to, the Stoics both in his life and in his teachings. While Quevedo may well have considered that the addition of any more quotations from Seneca would make the *Defensa* impossibly diffuse, it is curious to find that several of the passages marked 'Epicuro' in his copy of Seneca's works but omitted from his defence are ones in which Seneca is something less than eloquent in Epicurus' praise.[21] While, as its author admits, the *Defensa* in its primitive form was not the most original of works, it is certainly a revealing one. It demonstrates his assumption that to follow Seneca's depiction of Epicurus as a Stoic in disguise would, with the help of the *Doctrina estoica*, be sufficient to restore the maligned philosopher's reputation. Although he knew both Andraeus Arnaudus' *Apologia* for Epicurus and El Brocense's declaration that he considered Epicurus' philosophy, properly understood, superior to those of the Peripatetics and the Stoics,[22] it seems almost certain that the initial inspiration for his *Defensa* came from Seneca.

## 11. *Cicero Attacked and Seneca Interpreted*

Quevedo took up and added to the original draft of the *Defensa* on several occasions. The various stages of its composition can be

---

[20] *Q*, III. 426.

[21] See Appendix II, e.g., nos. 17 (at the beginning of *Ep.* 9 Seneca mentions Epicurus' criticism of the Stoic teaching that the sage is self-sufficient), 26 (in *Ep.* 20 he doubts whether Epicurus' poor man would despise riches if they were offered him), and 33 (in *Ep.* 24 he ridicules Epicurus' arguments against fear of death).

[22] See *Q*, III. 431, where Correas' praise for Epicurus is also cited. Cf. Sánchez, *Dotrina*, fol. ¶4ᵛ, and Correas, *El Enkiridion*, p. 115.

followed with very little trouble thanks to his lack of concern to maintain an integrated structure for the work by interpolating all his additions in the early version. Three successive extensions are distinguishable by two further lists of authors cited in Epicurus' favour. The first extension is an attempt at rebutting Cicero's criticisms of Epicurus and was prompted by a desire to stress further the point made in the primitive *Defensa* that the philosopher's ill repute among Christians was due to the unscrupulous slanders of his classical detractors.[23] After citing passages in which Cicero praises Epicurus' concept of virtue, Quevedo quotes the orator's statement that Epicurus' notion of God as immovable and unmoving amounted to a denial of Providence, and proceeds to interpret this as meaning that God is not bound by his own Providence: 'Si esto ha de ser verdad, es forzoso que se regule con la fe santa y católica, entendiendo que Dios, aunque cuida de todo, él no padece cuidado ni ocupación de toda su providencia, que le embarace o sea molesta, achaques de los que los hombres llaman negocios, cuidados y ocupaciones.'[24] Noting Cicero's frequent contradictions of Epicurus, he takes the opportunity to quote Quintilian's statement that Cicero often contradicts himself and to assert on his own account that Cicero was a bigot and, in any case, not primarily a philosopher but a lawyer. Not content with this, he declares that Cicero's philosophical works show the marks not of wisdom but of his profession—a profession for which, incidentally, Quevedo repeatedly expresses his contempt in his satirical works. Commenting on Cicero's horror that Epicurus should have held that the gods are similar to men, rather than vice versa, Quevedo goes so far as to call him an ignoramus, maintains that Epicurus' view is perfectly compatible with Christian teaching as illustrated by the cult of sacred images, and refers to Cicero's rejection of the same view in Homer, apparently the better to abuse him: 'Pues Cicerón repite esta (a su parecer) advertencia, preciado estaba de ella, o empeñado en acreditarla, cosa aún a su elegante persuasión difícil.'[25] In fact, in so far as Cicero's point that man is made in the image of the gods (so that Epicurus should have said that men are similar to the gods) is reconcilable with Christianity, Quevedo could be held to be as unjust to him as any of the defamers he attacks were to Epicurus. Despite this

---

[23] See *Q*, III. 426. Cf. *Q*, III. 422–3.
[24] *Q*, III. 427.     [25] Ibid.

spirited critique, Cicero's name is included in the second list of
authorities which brings this first extension to the *Defensa* to a
close.

The first list of authors cited in Epicurus' defence had consisted
of Diogenes Laertius, Seneca, Petronius, and Juvenal. The second
includes the first two names, omits the second two, and adds,
besides Cicero, Aelianus and Arnaudus. Aelianus is added by
virtue of a quotation from *De varia historia* in this first extension,
but Arnaudus is only mentioned at the very beginning of the early
version. The fact that he appears there and also in the second list
of authorities but had not figured in the first suggests that the first
paragraph of the *Defensa* in its final form was probably added at
the same time as Quevedo wrote the first extension to his original
draft. Arnaudus' brief defence of Epicurus, dedicated to Du Vair,
had appeared together with his *Apologiae* for Bacchus and Phalaris
at the end of his *Ioci* (Avignon, 1600). Although he inevitably cites
some of the classical testimonials for Epicurus given in Quevedo's
*Defensa*, the fact that he has a good deal of information about the
philosopher's life which our author does not mention would seem
to suggest that the latter came across the *Ioci* after he had written
the first version of his defence. The omission of Petronius and
Juvenal from the second list of authorities—it is surprising to
find that Montaigne is not mentioned either here or in the first—
may well have been made in order to keep the number of authors
mentioned down to a bare minimum so that Quevedo could add
his own name to those of a select few:

> Yo no califico a Epicuro, refiero las calificaciones que hallo escritas
> de su doctrina y costumbres, en los mayores hombres de la gentilidad;
> diligencia hecha primero por Diógenes Laercio, por Eliano, por Séneca,
> por Cicerón, y en nuestros tiempos por Arnaudo, en que yo que los
> junto soy el sexto, que no pudiendo añadir autoridad a esta defensa,
> la añado un número.[26]

The second extension made to the primitive *Defensa* seems
again to have been prompted by Quevedo's desire to contest
the traditional Christian condemnation of Epicurus—'Clemente
Alejandrino stromatum I, llama a Epicuro príncipe de los autores
impíos, y San Agustín en muchas partes'— and it includes the
modern example of Juan del Encina as another writer whose

[26] *Q*, III. 427.

reputation had suffered unjustly at the hands of the *vulgus*.[27] However, it soon develops into a sustained and characteristically satirical attack, not now on Cicero alone, but also on contemporary Ciceronians:

Temo, escarmentado, que unos hombres que en este tiempo viven de hazañeros del estudio, cuya suficiencia es gestos y ademanes, han de ladrar el haber osado yo moderar a Cicerón las alabanzas en la filosofía . . . Consideren estos doctores en tropelía, que si en la arte oratoria, que fue su blasón y su oficio, y toda su presunción, fue tan reprensible, que no es considerable que lo sea en la filosofía . . .[28]

Calling the Ciceronians 'estos censores avinagrados, que apoyan lo auténtico de sus embustes en las rugas de su frente', Quevedo refers them to two anti-Ciceronian works written a century earlier by Ortensio Landi and M. A. Majoragius.[29] While his views in the *Defensa* are no doubt coloured by his main purpose of restoring Epicurus' reputation, the contrast between his attitudes towards Seneca and Cicero in this work is too extreme not to reflect a real and deep-seated prejudice for the former and against the latter. The bitter sarcasm to which he treats Cicero and his followers places him undeniably within the anti-Ciceronian movement, led by Montaigne, Lipsius, and Bacon, which in the sixteenth and seventeenth centuries was instrumental in setting up Seneca in Cicero's place as the model for Latin and vernacular style as well as for moral philosophy.

After a third, and final, list of authorities, preceded by quotations from Sextus Empiricus and the statement that our author condemns everything in Epicurus to which the Church could take exception, and followed by a passage which clearly echoes the conclusion to his primitive draft, Quevedo begins his third extension with a lengthy quotation from Diogenes Laertius which 'reminds' him of a passage he had marked in his copy of Seneca.[30]

---

[27] See *Q*, III. 427–8. For Quevedo's treatment of Encina, see Iventosch, 'Quevedo and the Defense of the Slandered', pp. 99–103, 177.

[28] *Q*, III. 428.

[29] These are, respectively, *Paradossi, cioè, sententie fuori del comun parere*, printed several times, the earliest edition in the British Museum being of 1543, and *Anti-paradoxon, libri sex, in quibus M. Tullii Ciceronis omnia paradoxa refelluntur* (Lyon, 1546). Both authors' names were mis-spelt in the first edition ('Laudio' and 'Mayaxio'), the latter being corrected in the *fe de erratas* to 'Mayoraxio'.

[30] See *Q*, III. 429. The third list of authorities includes all those in the second, reinstates Juvenal, and adds Torquatus and Montaigne.

This passage takes him back once more to the problem of Epicurus' ideas on Providence. His interpretation here of Epicurus' notion of God's unconcern for his Creation—an important source of deism and atheism from the sixteenth century onwards—is developed from the marginal note he had made to this passage in Seneca. When, says Quevedo, Epicurus holds that God does nothing, what he means is that what God does requires nothing of him, is nothing to him: 'nuestra manera de hablar en español me declara: decimos de quien hace algo sin cuidado, parece que no hace nada, nada hace en hacerlo.'[31]

Having once returned to his copy of Seneca, Quevedo quotes the passage he had marked immediately before the one just mentioned, and this takes him on to the question of the difference between Epicurus and his followers.[32] The passage he cites from *De beneficiis* condemns the Epicurean doctrine that virtue is subservient to pleasure, a view which shocked Christian writers as much as it had Seneca. On this occasion Seneca fails to make his usual distinction between Epicurus and his followers. Taking him up on this, Quevedo does his best to deny that this doctrine is imputable to Epicurus, attributing to him the belief, also referred to here by Seneca, that there can be no pleasure without virtue, and to the Epicureans the statement to which Seneca objects. Earlier, in his first draft, when he had quoted the same passage from Seneca, he had attributed both statements to Epicurus apparently with no qualms at all.[33] Now, however, not only does he argue that only one of them represents Epicurus' views, but he also rejects Seneca's objection to any attempt at associating pleasure with virtue. Furthermore, he points out that, whereas Seneca had unpleasant things to say about the Epicureans, he called Epicurus a sage and his philosophy holy.

Surprisingly enough, when he came to his final conclusion Quevedo did not make out a new list of authorities, but he did take up again the belligerent tone of the earlier, abortive endings, describing opponents of Epicurus who rely on Cicero (who speaks of Epicurus 'con discursos, unos desmentidos de otros') as 'hombres . . . graduados por sí propios . . . catedráticos de su ignorancia, que pasan lo lego por profeso, sin saber otra facultad

[31] *Q*, III. 430. Cf. Appendix II, no. 6.
[32] See *Q*, III. 430. Cf. Appendix II, no. 5.
[33] See *Q*, III. 421.

que la de que usan, para juzgar y reprender'.[34] Although he again
defies critics of Epicurus to scorn the corpus of defenders of the
philosopher's reputation that he has assembled, he appeals to
the historian Rodrigo Caro, to whom both the *Defensa* and the
*Doctrina estoica* are dedicated, to bear with the calumnies that
he himself expects from his critics, 'mastines de los libros, que,
asalariados de la rabia contra el estudio, ponen la suficiencia
en el veneno de sus dientes, en tanto que la verdad, saludador
efectivo, los mata a soplos.'[35]

### III. *Epicurus Christianized*

The reason why Quevedo started making additions to his first
draft of the *Defensa* may be inferred from two passages in the
first draft which are almost certainly interpolations. The first is
the series of quotations from Jerome, Ambrose, and Augustine
criticizing the kind of sophistry that had been repudiated by
Epicurus.[36] His purpose in adding these quotations was to lend
the weight of Christian authority to the opinion of Petronius
Arbiter, of which he states, 'poco es para esta defensa voz elegante',
before introducing the Fathers with the exclamation: 'oigamos
voz elegante, doctísima y sagrada.' Originally, it would seem, he
had been quite content with simply citing his classical critic of
sophistry, for the passage from Petronius Arbiter is preceded
by the words: 'Con felicísimo estilo le [i.e. Epicurus] defiende el
primer fragmento de Petronio Arbitro; mucho pierde quien me
obliga a traducir sus palabras'.[37] It is curious that, whereas he
felt that he should not have recourse to Christian authority in
order to defend the Stoic Paradoxes against Plutarch's strictures,
Quevedo has no scruples about doing so in defence of Epicurus.
The reason for this difference is very likely that, while on the
whole Christianity had looked with favour upon the philosophy
of the Stoics, it had in general thought of Epicurus as scandalously
heathen. Quevedo seems to have been keen to stress any similarities

---

[34] *Q*, III. 432.    [35] Ibid.
[36] See *Q*, III. 421. The reason for considering this an interpolation is that all
three names are absent from the first (and subsequent) list of authorities. While
it might be argued that this is because none of the three quotations refers specifically to Epicurus, the same is true of the quotation from Petronius Arbiter,
whose name is none the less included in the list.
[37] *Q*, III. 421.

he could find between Christianity and Epicureanism even when, as here, they amounted to no more than the somewhat negative coincidence of common opposition to sophistry.

The second probable interpolation in the early version of the *Defensa* is the discussion of Epicurus' writings which develops out of Cicero's description of one of them as a book fallen from heaven. As the *Defensa* now stands, the sentence which comes immediately before the first quotation from Seneca's Epistles does not follow logically on the preceding sentence: 'Más frecuente es Epicuro en las obras de Séneca, que Sócrates y Platón, y Aristóteles y Zenón. El se precia mucho de hacerlo, y da la razón en la epístola VIII'.[38] The only sentence on which it does follow logically is the one preceding the quotation from Cicero: 'Séneca, cuyas palabras todos los hombres grandes reparten por joyas en sus escritos, repartió en los suyos las de Epicuro, donde se leen con blasón de estrellas.' The first of these three sentences would appear to have been added at the end of the interpolated quotation from Cicero in an unsuccessful attempt to reintroduce the passage from Seneca which had become separated from Quevedo's original introductory sentence.[39] Although this second interpolation brings in a classical, not a Christian, author, it draws from Quevedo the significant comment that Epicurus' works were as holy as one could expect of a pagan and that one of them, by its title alone, can be seen to have been Stoical: 'los títulos de todos son útiles, son decentes, son, como es lícito decir en un gentil, santos: entre otros, escribió el libro de *Apetencia y fuga*, que es toda la doctrina estoica, que Epicteto abrevió en las dos palabras *Sustine, et abstine*.'[40]

These two probable interpolations confirm the impression that Quevedo's motive in adding to the original *Defensa* was, initially at least, concern to suggest Epicurus' compatibility with Christianity. As has already been noted, he began all three of his extensions by seeking to persuade his readers that Epicurus' evil reputation in Christian eyes was the fault of his classical defamers. In the first extension he had begun by defending the philosopher

---

[38] *Q*, III. 423.
[39] Like the three Fathers (see above, p. 53 n. 36), Cicero does not appear in the first list of authorities, despite the fact that two further passages from his works appear (also interpolated?) between the two quotations from Montaigne (see *Q*, III. 425).
[40] *Q*, III. 423.

against the charge, quoted from St. Peter Chrysologus, that he rejected immortality; and he had then dealt with the problem posed by Epicurus' alleged denial of Providence.[41] At this stage he had referred his readers to what was probably an early draft of *Providencia de Dios*[42] and, while conceding that Epicurus denied Providence, had excused him on the basis of Augustine's statement that Faith alone provides insight into the truth. Iventosch sees here evidence that Quevedo 'is unquestionably engaged in a mortal inner struggle to reconcile his reason and his faith'.[43] But it is perhaps less with his reason that his religious faith has to struggle here than with his faith in Epicurus. The point he is intent upon making is that there is no more contradiction between Christian teaching and that of Epicurus than is to be expected in the necessarily inferior, but remarkably little inferior, thought of one of the best of the pagan philosophers:

Por esto no vió Epicuro a Dios y a su providencia; porque su mente no alcanzó la vista, que a nosotros nos da la fe que alcanzamos. Y, pues, por misericordia de Dios tenemos la luz que le faltó a él, y a todos los filósofos gentiles; estimemos lo que vieron, y no les acusemos lo que dejaron de ver; cuando lo condenáremos no disfamemos su memoria, si contradijéremos sus escritos.[44]

Quevedo's chief contributions to the defence of Epicurus, apart from the mere collecting and glossing of passages from the works of previous defenders, are his rejection of Cicero's criticisms, his efforts to interpret a rare criticism of Seneca's so as to save Epicurus himself from the Stoic's censure, and his attempt throughout to break down Christian hostility towards the philosopher of the Garden. He was evidently not particularly attracted to Epicureanism, at least not as a philosophy distinct from Seneca's. However, it is something of an exaggeration to say that in the *Defensa* he makes 'a distinct attempt at a Stoic–Epicurean fusion'.[45] It is not that he develops a philosophy of his own based on Stoicism and Epicureanism, but rather that he seeks to identify the latter with the former by adopting Seneca's

---

[41] See *Q*, III. 426.
[42] '. . . yo trato este punto en mi libro que intitulo: *Historia teologética, política de la divina providencia*' (ibid.). In *Providencia de Dios* he writes: 'Cuanto a Epicuro, me remito a mí en lo que escribí en su defensa en el *Epicteto*, que traduje' (*Q*, II. 167b).
[43] 'Quevedo and the Defense of the Slandered', p. 187 n. 58.
[44] *Q*, III. 426.                                        [45] Iventosch, p. 179.

ready-made assimilation to his brand of Stoicism of certain sayings of Epicurus, by equating Epicurus' and Zeno's political philosophies, by relating the title of one of Epicurus' works to Epictetus'
Stoic slogan, and by asserting that these two philosophers 'spoke
the same language'. In this work, as Iventosch notes, Quevedo
is 'seeking a place in the pan-European movement toward the
adjustment of the ancient philosophies to Christianity'.[46] Epicurus'
philosophy is adjusted by way of Stoicism; and, particularly in
the primitive *Defensa*, this adjustment is the continuation of the
task undertaken by Seneca. By its reliance on Seneca and its
efforts to make a Stoic of Epicurus, the *Defensa* helps to enhance
the standing not only of Epicurus but also of Seneca and of
the philosophy of the Stoics. In its first draft especially, it was a
fitting introduction to the *Doctrina estoica*.

[46] Iventosch, p. 184.

# III

## *EPICTETO ESPAÑOL* AND *DE LOS REMEDIOS DE CUALQUIER FORTUNA*

### 1. *The Sources of Quevedo's Translations*

WHEN Quevedo published them in 1635, the *Doctrina estoica* and the *Defensa de Epicuro* were placed, in that order, after his translations of pseudo-Phocylides and Epictetus, his version of the *Manual* being given pride of place as well as a separate, engraved title-page. The only other translation of a classical (or, better, pseudo-classical) work that he published, *De los remedios de cualquier fortuna*, appeared three years later and was, ironically enough, the last work he published before his imprisonment in León in the following year. It may seem strange at first sight that his two Stoical translations did not appear together. *De los remedios* had, after all, been completed in the summer of 1633 and might well be considered a more appropriate companion-piece for his version of the *Manual* than pseudo-Phocylides' *Carmen admonitorium*. However, unlike Epictetus' *Manual*, *De remediis fortuitorum* is not a digest of Stoic moral philosophy but a work made up of *sententiae* designed to prove that what the *vulgus* considers ills are really *indifferentia*. Nor is it, like pseudo-Phocylides' *Carmen*, a didactic poem which only required translating in order to turn it into a pendant for Quevedo's verse translation of the *Manual*. But the main reason why Quevedo published *De los remedios* on its own was probably a desire to encourage comparison between his translation—the first to appear in Spanish[1]—and the original, as well as between this and his own additions. Nevertheless, his two Stoical translations have much in common, and considering them together should help throw light on both. To begin with, the preliminary matter of

---

[1] Blüher, *Seneca in Spanien*, p. 100 n. 26, lists several fifteenth-century Spanish MSS. which contain translations of *De remediis* and mentions (p. 105) a translation with glosses by Alonso de Cartagena. He also refers (p. 182) to a mid-sixteenth-century version by Martín Godoy de Loaisa.

both translations gives clues to the texts on which they are based and so allows us to appreciate the accuracy achieved in each and the extent to which Quevedo modified the original works.

Two items in the preliminaries to the translation of the *Manual* derive from the second Spanish translation, published by Gonzalo Correas in 1630, and cannot therefore have been written much before *Epicteto español* appeared in print. In his brief *Vida de Epicteto*, inspired by Correas' *De la vida de Epikteto*, Quevedo refers to Correas' statement that he believed there were some letters by Epictetus in Florence, includes several details to be found in Correas' Life but not in El Brocense's, and does not include the one point in El Brocense's omitted by Correas.[2] For some reason, however, he omits Correas' observation that Epictetus' birth-place, Hierapolis, was the scene of Philip the Apostle's martyrdom, and he takes from Lipsius' *Manuductio* (I. xix) the fact that Epictetus was lame and the discussion of the date of his death. The other item in the preliminaries which derives from Correas is the *Razón de esta traducción*, inspired by the latter's *De la traduzión*. Both here and in the dedication of his translation to Olivares' equerry, Juan de Herrera, Quevedo compares the various versions of the *Manual* that he had consulted, especially those of El Brocense and Correas. While acknowledging Correas' claim that his is the more faithful, he maintains that El Brocense's translation reads better. It is 'docta y suave, y rigorosa en lo importante, no en lo impertinente.'[3]

A third item in Quevedo's preliminaries owes its origin either directly or indirectly to El Brocense. In his undated and probably unfinished commentary on the Wisdom of Solomon, Quevedo quotes chapter 31 of the *Manual* and remarks: 'Parece doctrina expresada deste primero capítulo de la *Sabiduría*, y recogida en vaso idólatra, cuyo sabor se conoce solamente en la pluralidad de dioses.'[4] Epictetus' habit of referring to the gods in the plural, for Quevedo his only un-Christian trait, is dealt with at greater length in the brief prefatory essay to his translation entitled

---

[2] See *Q*, III. 388–9. The point in El Brocense's Life omitted by Correas is Aulus Gellius' testimony that Epictetus was a slave (see Sánchez, *Dotrina*, fol. ¶6ᵛ). D. Castellanos, 'Quevedo y su *Epicteto en español*', *Boletín de la Academia Nacional de Letras* (Montevideo), i (1947), 195, misunderstands the reference to Florence, taking it that Quevedo is talking about a MS. of the *Manual* which he used for his translation.

[3] *Q*, III. 385.    [4] *Q*, II. 344a.

*Prevención a la pluralidad de los dioses.* Correas' censure of Epictetus' 'hablar de la multitud de Dioses i Xupiter' was doubtless inspired by El Brocense's passing criticism of his 'hablar de los dioses en plural',[5] and one or both of these remarks evidently gave rise to Quevedo's attempt at 'interpreting' Epictetus' apparent polytheism. Although on another occasion he asserts uncompromisingly that the pagan gods were the invention of the Devil,[6] here he sets out to prove that the classics referred to gods in the plural merely in order to conform to popular taste. The word gods, he says, is 'tan repugnante a la razón y al discurso, que me persuado no creyeron pluralidad de Dioses algunos de los antiguos, sino que juzgando que en Dios todo era Dios, le multiplicaron por sus atributos ciegamente, llamando Dios a su Poder, a su Amor, a su Sabiduría, a su Piedad, y a su Enojo, y así en los demás.'[7] Among other examples in the classics of 'God' in the singular, he cites Seneca's view that God is synonymous with Nature, his statement that Liber, Hercules, and Mercury are all names of one and the same God, and his comment that, whether he is addressed as Lucius, Annaeus, or Seneca, these names all refer to the same person.[8] It is only surprising—unless he thought it too daring a parallel—that Quevedo does not compare this last passage from Seneca with the Christian concept of the Trinity.

The chief novelty in Quevedo's translation, compared with those of El Brocense and Correas, lies in the fact that he put the *Manual* into verse. As he twice declares, he did so with a view to creating the maximum possible effect upon his readers: 'Hícela en versos de consonantes, porque el ritmo y la armonía sea golosina a la voluntad y facilidad a la memoria.'[9] The fact that his intention was not merely to provide a crib for Spanish students of the classics but to make Epictetus' teachings strike the ordinary reader as forcibly and lastingly as possible goes a long way to explaining his preference for El Brocense's less stilted translation

---

[5] Correas, *El Enkiridion*, p. 7; Sánchez, *Dotrina*, fol. ¶6ʳ.
[6] See *Providencia de Dios* (*Q*, II. 193a/b).        [7] *Q*, III. 387.
[8] See *Q*, III. 387–8. The passages he quotes are from *De benef.* IV. vii. 1, IV. viii. 1, and IV. viii. 3. The last is one that he annotated in his copy of Seneca (see Appendix II, no. 7). For the Stoics' acceptance of the popular notion of the gods, see W. L. Davidson, *The Stoic Creed* (Edinburgh, 1907), p. 215.
[9] *Q*, III. 385. Cf. Quevedo's dedication (*Q*, III. 382). On the engraved title-page in the second edition the translation is entitled: 'Epicteto Spañol en verso con consonantes.'

over Correas' more literal one. It also helps one understand why his own version, despite his express concern with accuracy, is far freer than either of the earlier translations. He himself states in his *Razón de esta traducción*: 'en mi versión seguí la mente y disposición de Sánchez.'[10] Where it is possible to tell, for his verse adaptation naturally forced him frequently to diverge from his source, he does indeed follow El Brocense, not only in adopting his renumbering of the chapters and his practice of prefixing them with descriptive titles, but also in the text itself, preferring his translation both to Correas' and to the Latin version and the Greek original. Being one of the very few chapters in which he made no additions of his own, one of the best for comparison with El Brocense and Correas is his chapter 39 (Loeb, chapter 33, 14–16). The only stage at which his version differs from the sense of the Greek is when he translates the sentence, 'It is dangerous also to lapse into foul language', by 'Y debes excusarte / De oir obscenas pláticas lascivas'.[11] Whereas Correas' version renders this sentence faithfully, 'Tanbien es peligroso el adelantarse a hablar torpes razones', El Brocense's is clearly the model Quevedo used: 'Tengo por peligroso que oyas, ó aprueues platicas suzias, y obscenas.'[12] His apparently total dependence, here and throughout his translation, on the first Spanish translator of Epictetus suggests that, as in his translation of the *Introduction à la vie dévote* and his *Anacreón castellano*, he relied less on the original text than on a previous translation.[13] Here, where, unless he made his translation before 1630, he had the choice of two, he seems deliberately to have chosen to follow the less literal one.[14]

[10]  *Q*, III. 386.

[11]  *Q*, III. 401b.

[12]  Correas, *El Enkiridion*, p. 62; Sánchez, *Dotrina*, fol. 54ʳ.

[13]  Other striking instances of his dependence on El Brocense are his avoidance of the suggestion of homosexuality in ch. x (cf. Quevedo, ch. xii) and his transformation of the injunction not to spend too much time in 'much evacuating of the bowels, much copulating' into an attack on jewelry and horse-riding (ch. xli—cf. Quevedo, ch. xlvii). In ch. xlix (Quevedo, ch. liv) he follows El Brocense in adding the name of Aristotle to that of Chrysippus on the first occasion that Epictetus cites the latter as an example of a difficult writer, and then substituting Aristotle for him  on subsequent occasions. For Quevedo's reliance elsewhere on earlier translations, see R. Lida, 'Quevedo y la *Introducción a la vida devota*', *Letras hispánicas*, pp. 124–41; Castanien, 'Quevedo's *Anacreón castellano*', pp. 569 ff.; and Bénichou-Roubaud, 'Quevedo helenista', *passim*.

[14]  For a discussion of the date of Quevedo's translation, see H. Ettinghausen, 'Acerca de las fechas', pp. 166–7. A. Vilanova, 'El tema del gran teatro del mundo', *BRABLB*, xxiii (1950), 174, argues that Quevedo based his translation

The question of the authenticity of *De remediis fortuitorum* is discussed in Quevedo's prefatory *Juicio* to his translation, and it is curious to find that he appears to have changed his mind about this question between the publication of the first and the second edition. In both, his point of departure is Lipsius. Referring to the Fleming's edition of Seneca, which he admiringly describes as 'mejorado con sus enmiendas, ilustrado con sus notas',[15] he observes that it includes *De remediis* even though Lipsius rejected this work as spurious on stylistic grounds. However, he is careful to tone down Lipsius' comments, which included the remark that even a blind man could see that the treatise was not written by Seneca.[16] In both of the first two editions of *De los remedios* Quevedo sets out to contest Lipsius' opinion, referring none the less to his erstwhile mentor as 'varón doctísimo y lleno de religión y piedad', significant epithets in view of Lipsius' notorious 'lapses' into Protestantism. In opposition to the great editor of Seneca's works, he maintains that *De remediis* is not only made up of Senecan *sententiae*, but that its style, too, is that of the Roman, 'porque en Séneca hallamos, primero que en el Petrarca, el estilo de repetir una palabra muchas veces, y consolarla, y declararla repetidamente de diferentes maneras.'[17] It is in what now follows that the first two editions diverge. Whereas in the first, Madrid, edition Quevedo flatly rejects Lipsius' repudiation of the work—'Por esto no sigo la censura de Lipsio: empero añado que, quando no fuera el tratado (digo la disposicion del) de Seneca, es cierto que todas las razones y sentencias lo son'—in the second, printed at Barcelona in the same year, he turns his rejection of Lipsius' opinion into something like qualified acceptance: 'Yo sigo la censura de Lipsio; empero añado, que quando no es el tratado . . .'[18] The reason for this change of heart may very well be that, on reflection, he realized

---

of *Manual*, XVII on Marino's sonnet, 'Eugenio, è di Comedia, et è di Gioco'. Marino's only examples are a king and a soldier. Quevedo's 'pobre', 'esclavo', 'rey', and 'tullido' are taken from those given by El Brocense: 'medico', 'coxo', 'Principe', and 'vn particular' (in text), and 'Rey', 'labrador', 'matrona', 'esclaua', and 'Conde' (in *Anotación*).

[15] *Q*, II. 370.
[16] See Seneca, *Opera quae extant omnia* (Antwerp, 1652), p. 840.
[17] *Q*, II. 370. In support, Quevedo cites *Ep.* 47, 1 and 17.
[18] *De los remedios de qualquiera fortuna* . . . (Madrid, 1638), fol. a6ᵛ; ibid. (Barcelona, 1638), fol. 1ᵛ. The Barcelona edition contains the same *censura*, *aprobación*, and *imprimatur* as those made for the Madrid edition.

that his own view was not incompatible with that of Lipsius and relented of needlessly dissenting from so eminent and admired a scholar. One may wonder, in fact, whether his concession that, if not actually written by Seneca, *De remediis* is made up out of thoughts and sentences of his was not actually inspired by Lipsius' title to the work: *Excerpta quaedam e libris Senecae.*[19] He may also have thought that his compromise solution to the authorship problem had the additional virtue of justifying his making so bold as to add to his translation Senecan *sententiae* of his own.

Quevedo's comments on Lipsius in his *Juicio* must not lead one to assume that he necessarily made his translation of *De remediis* from Lipsius' text. In point of fact, while a few passages in *De los remedios* are influenced by Lipsius' edition, for the most part Quevedo follows Erasmus' text in the Lyon 1555, edition which he used for his *Defensa de Epicuro*. Thus, while other texts, including Lipsius', have 'Unde ergo primum incipimus? Si tibi videtur, à morte', this one reads 'Vnde ergo incipiendum tibi uidetur? A morte', and is, clearly, the source of Quevedo's '¿De dónde pues te parece que debo empezar? De la muerte.'[20] Similarly, when Quevedo writes 'Necio eres, pues lloras los sucesos de los mortales', he is not following, for example, Lipsius' 'Stultus es, qui defleas mortem mortalium', but Erasmus' 'Stultus es, qui defleas casus mortalium'.[21] There are only two instances in which he appears to have preferred Lipsius' reading, and these occur in successive paragraphs.[22] That it is possible to determine which text Quevedo followed at any point in his translation gives some idea of its fidelity. Here he was not bothered by the kind

[19] See Seneca, *Opera*, ed. cit., p. 837. Quevedo's view is still a respectable one (see R. G. Palmer, *Seneca's* De remediis fortuitorum *and the Elizabethans*, Inst. of Elizabethan Studies Publications, no. 1 (Chicago, 1953), p. 20 n. 99). Blüher, *Seneca in Spanien*, p. 348, notes that Erasmus still treated *De remediis* as genuine and that Quevedo took from him his sub-title, *Diálogo entre el sentido y la razón*.

[20] *Q*, II. 371a. Cf. Seneca, *Opera, quae extant omnia* (Lyon 1555), i. 653–4.

[21] *Q*, II. 377b. Cf. Seneca, ed. cit., i. 658.

[22] Quevedo has 'Saque el dolor clamores' (*Q*, II. 375b); cf. Lipsius' 'Dolor clamorem exprimat' (Seneca, *Opera* (Antwerp, 1652), p. 839) and Erasmus' 'Dolor clamorem exprimit' (Seneca, *Opera* (Lyons, 1555), i. 656). Compare: Quevedo, 'Antes tú molestas a la pobreza' (*Q*, II. 376a), Lipsius, 'Imò tu paupertati', Erasmus, 'immo tu gravior paupertati'. P. U. González de la Calle, *Quevedo y los dos Sénecas* (Mexico, 1965), compares Quevedo's translation with a nineteenth-century edition, marvels at what he calls Quevedo's mutilation of the text (p. 222), and unjustly condemns him for committing 'con tanta profusión tantos disparates' (p. 229).

of problems he had to face when putting Epictetus' *Manual* into Spanish verse. Nor did he have to worry about any modifications he might wish to make, for he could introduce as many as he liked in his own additions to *De remediis*.

## 11. *Epictetus Senecanized and Seneca Imitated*

Senecan echoes in *Epicteto español* are first to be found in its dedication to the soldier and courtier, Juan de Herrera, in which Quevedo treats the *Manual* as an admirable guide to right living— 'No es lección para entretener el tiempo, sino para no perderle. No detiene el camino de la hora, mas lógrale, y esto porque a la dirección de la vida humana está escrito con tantos nortes como letras'—and a haven from 'las borrascas del siglo, que se ven feas, y se oyen roncas.'[23] Although he contends that the *Manual* helps the soul free itself from servitude to the body and that it teaches that wealth consists in scorning Fortune's goods, that virtue is its own reward, that only the sage is rich, free, and invincible, and that, while only God can stand outside the realm of evil, the sage can raise himself above it, these are all Senecan and Senecan-Christian, rather than Epictetan, doctrines. So, too, are his exhortations to self-sufficiency, to live 'como quien cada instante muere, y cada día puede morirse', to live a good life rather than a long one, and to be prepared for death. And one topic, the recommendation not to hide behind closed doors, is a direct paraphrase of Seneca.[24]

More reminiscences of and borrowings from Seneca occur when Quevedo tells his friend of the two aspects of 'miseria humana' that he most deplores. The first, that where 'bienes de fortuna' are concerned we envy those whom we ought to pity, and

---

[23] *Q*, III. 383. Pedro Fernández Navarrete had made very similar claims for Seneca: 'podra sacar à tu animo del peligroso golfo del mundo, colocandole en la tranquilidad de apacible pueto [*sic*]' (*Siete libros de L. Æ. Seneca* (Madrid, 1627), fol. ¶3ᵛ).

[24] 'Ajustemos la república de nuestros sentidos y potencias, para atrevernos a vivir en público. Los porteros y las clausuras mañosas las inventó el miedo de la conciencia, no la vanidad de la soberbia: puédense aventurar muchos malos a llamarse buenos, mirando a los testigos; empero muy pocos mirando a las conciencias' (*Q*, III. 383). Cf. *Ep*. 43, 4–5: 'Rem dicam, ex qua mores aestimes nostros: vix quemquam invenies, qui possit aperto ostio vivere. Ianitores conscientia nostra, non superbia opposuit; sic vivimus, ut deprendi sit subito adspici. . . . Bona conscientia turbam advocat, mala etiam in solitudine anxia atque sollicita est.'

vice versa, is simply a statement of the basic Stoic doctrine that if
'externals' do not seem to be *indifferentia*, this is because we do
not hold the 'correct opinion' of them, and Quevedo's gloss on
this doctrine is another Senecan paraphrase.[25] The second thing
Quevedo deplores, a corollary of the first, is that good qualities
are commonly held to 'devalue' things and that the absence of
good qualities raises the esteem in which they are held. Employing
one of his favourite Senecan arguments against avarice, he maintains that it is an act of ingratitude to God to dig up the gold,
valued simply because of its weight, which God, in his wisdom,
buried under mountains.[26]

Senecan influence is apparent in the translation itself as well
as in its dedication. Whereas, unlike Seneca, Epictetus had no
place in his more orthodox Stoic system for the concept of Fortune,
Quevedo frequently introduces it into his *Epicteto español*. On one
occasion he adds 'la adversa suerte' and on another 'la sinrazón
de la fortuna' to lists of ills; and elsewhere he associates 'externals'
in general with the 'arbitrio de fortuna' and adds the recommendation to concern oneself with 'internals' 'en cualquiera
fortuna'.[27] While one critic notes in Quevedo's attitude to death
in this work 'un hondo patetismo que contrasta con la glacial
indiferencia que enseña la doctrina de Epicteto',[28] he fails to notice
that this is largely due to Seneca's influence. At one point Quevedo
adds a line censuring the *vulgus* for imagining 'que no se muera,
quien nació muriendo',[29] a clear echo of Seneca's 'cotidie morimur'.
At another, when Epictetus compares life to a stop on shore and
death to the captain's call to re-embark, his translation confuses
the symbols, equating the ship with life and describing death as
'piloto de tu vida', again suggesting that life itself is part of the

---

[25] 'Diga el rico que no duerme, y padece el oro que junta, ¿a quién gasta el
dinero, que no gasta, si merece la envidia que le tiene el pobre, o la compasión
que él tiene de sí? ¿Diga el poderoso, a quién puede quitar la fortuna cuanto le
dió y le envidian, si tiene envidia al ignorado, a quién no puede quitar nada,
porque no se lo dió; si fue dichoso, porque no lo recibió; si fue cuerdo, porque
lo despreció; si lo tuvo, si fue sabio?' (*Q*, III. 383–4). Cf. *Ep.* 115, 17: 'Utinam
qui divitias optaturi essent, cum divitibus deliberarent! Utinam honores petituri
cum ambitiosis et summum adeptis dignitatis statum! Profecto vota mutassent,
cum interim illi nova suscipiunt, cum priora damnaverint.'

[26] See *Q*, III. 384. Cf. *Ep.* 90, 15 and 110, 9–10.

[27] *Q*, III. 391b, 392a, 397b. In his ch. lvii, Quevedo translates LIII. 3 in two
lines and then adds another eleven introducing the Senecan themes of constancy and, again, Fortune.

[28] Castellanos, 'Quevedo y su *Epicteto*', p. 205.          [29] *Q*, III. 394b.

process of dying.[30] And he again talks of life in terms of death when he describes the body here, as elsewhere in his prose and verse, as 'sepulcro que portátil me acompaña'.[31] Time and again he adds the adjectives 'ciego', 'loco', and 'burlado' to Epictetus' references to the *vulgus*. Attracted as he was by Epictetus' brief compendium of Stoic ethics, he evidently missed in it the pathos with which Seneca speaks of Fortune, death, and the plebs, and did not hesitate to make amends.

If in *Epicteto español* Quevedo introduces Senecan sentiments surreptitiously, in *De los remedios* he makes no secret of his attempt at imitating Seneca. In his dedication of this work to another friend, the Duke of Medinaceli, he writes modestly of his attempt:

Atrevíme a traducir y a imitar a Séneca; por eso invío a vuestra excelencia que estime en él y que enmiende en mí. El que bien leyere, no pasará de su texto; quien no se cansare de leer, verá mis adiciones. No se me debe reprehender el imitarle, menos el no saberle imitar: porque como aquello es conveniente; saber imitarle, para mí es imposible, para todos difícil. Yo conozco que sirvo sólo de hacer a Séneca prolijo.[32]

His preface 'Al más desdichado hombre' is imbued with the pathos which he describes to the Duke as 'la docta y bien intencionada melancólica de Séneca'.[33] Proclaiming the *miseria* of life's brevity in unmistakably Senecan language, he recalls the dedication of *Epicteto español* when he again deplores man's aberration in envying those he should pity, and declares in the paradoxical style dear to Seneca: 'No sabe la lástima lo que se hace en este mundo; pues la que se ha de tener al fortunado, se tiene al infeliz. Más descanso es en el trabajo esperar descanso, que en el descanso temer trabajos. Dieta saludable es para la salud del seso humano la falta de dicha.'[34] But, more striking than his success at imitating Seneca's prose is his self-identification here with the unhappiest of men, to whom his preface is addressed. Having told Medinaceli that 'Dar consuelos quien

---

[30] See *Q*, III. 393a.   [31] *Q*, III. 395b.
[32] *Q*, II. 369–70. In view of this passage it is a little difficult to agree with González de la Calle, *Quevedo y los dos Sénecas*, p. 218: 'no podremos absolver a nuestro autor de una cierta ligera confusión entre sus propios conceptos y los del autor traducido, confusión ni legítima, ni, por ende, justificable, ni a todas luces conveniente.'
[33] *Q*, II. 370.   [34] Ibid. Cf. pp. 63–4, above.

los ha menester, es liberalidad de buena casta', he now declares: 'Si crees a Séneca por docto, y a mí por desdichado, la lástima que los muy afortunados te tuvieren, en lugar de agradecérsela, se la tendrás; y enseñaráslos en quién han de gastar la compasión.'[35] We know that Quevedo considered that Epictetus had taught him the truth of the Stoic Paradox that the sage is free even in prison. From the pseudo-Senecan *De remediis* he may well have tried to teach himself, as well as his readers, how to deal with misfortune in general.

Like pseudo-Seneca, Quevedo treats in turn the 'externals' death, illness, exile, pain, poverty, weakness, and the loss of wealth, sight, children, friends, and wife; and his additions to Reason's polemic against the vulgar, common-sense fears and complaints of the Senses follow closely the pattern of his model both in substance and in style. For the most part his arguments are either variations on those he found in pseudo-Seneca or else are based on Seneca himself. Thus four of his eighteen replies to fear of death take up pseudo-Seneca's argument that death is universal, two being practically identical;[36] another, the argument that death is natural; and three, the argument, again used by his model, that death is inherent in the process of living; while three more employ the argument found in Seneca, but not in *De remediis*, that death brings an end to vice and to life's miseries. An unusually large number of Senecan, as opposed to pseudo-Senecan, arguments is to be found in his treatment of poverty. First, he includes the saying of Epicurus quoted from Epistle 21 in the *Defensa de Epicuro* and paraphrased in *La hora de todos y la Fortuna con seso*;[37] his recommendation to despise all goods is practically identical with Seneca's comment on Demetrius in Epistle 62; his argument that by lacking wealth one avoids ills worse than poverty recalls the Senecan topic of ills avoided in poverty borrowed in the second *Sueño*;[38] and, when called upon

---

[35] *Q*, II. 369, 370.

[36] Pseudo-Seneca (in Quevedo's translation): '"Morirás." Ni el primero ni el postrero. Muchos murieron antes de mí; todos después' (*Q*, II. 371b); Quevedo: '"Morirás." No podré de otra manera seguir a muchos y ser seguido de todos' (*Q*, II. 372a).

[37] See *Q*, II. 376a. Cf. the second Danish *arbitrio* proposed in *La Fortuna con seso*: 'Para tener inmensas riquezas en un día, quitando a todos cuanto tienen, y enriqueciéndolos con quitárselo' (*Q*, I. 391b).

[38] '"Soy pobre." De oro y de ladrones, de oro y de invidiosos, de oro y de aduladores; no tengo hacienda ni miedo, no tengo hacienda ni desvelo. Más

to reply to the complaint that others are rich, he uses the Senecan arguments that money owns its owners and that, as they cannot be absolute, riches are in fact poverty.[39] Just occasionally, his replies are inspired by Epictetus.[40]

The logical absurdity of the kind of argumentation imitated by Quevedo is seen very clearly when, in more than one instance, his replies to the senses contradict each other. For instance, in his section on illness he first asserts that, far from preventing good works, illness actually encourages them in those who tend the sick; but he then contends that those who tend the sick suffer from anger, lack of charity, and cupidity, which he considers worse ills than those suffered by their patients;[41] and, when he replies to the fear of being maligned, he argues both that one should do one's best to convince one's detractors that they are wrong and that detractors are impossible to placate.[42] His eagerness to imitate his model can also be seen in the fact that he cites classical authorities for the first time in the section in which pseudo-Seneca first introduces them;[43] and he borrows such characteristic stylistic devices as the rhetorical question, the formula 'Not A, but B', and the method of dealing with a problem by dividing it up into two or more alternative propositions. Mérimée's quip— 'Il est impossible de dire plus spirituellement des sottises; les stoïciens et Quevedo doivent en partager la responsabilité[44]— has the merit of recognizing Quevedo's success. Like pseudo-Seneca, and Seneca himself, Quevedo is less concerned to build up a reasoned case against common opinion than to invent ingeniously paradoxical *sententiae* whose very preposterousness, as in the *conceptista* style for which our author is renowned, is an essential part of their effect.

rico eres en no tener esto que en tener aquello' (*Q*, II. 376a). Cf., e.g., *Ep.* 20, 7 and 42, 9–10; and *El alguacil endemoniado*: '¿Hay diablo como un adulador, como un envidioso, como un amigo falso, y como una mala compañía? Pues todos éstos le faltan al pobre, que no le adulan, ni le envidian, ni tiene amigo malo ni bueno, ni le acompaña nadie' (*Q*, I. 307a).

[39] See *Q*, II. 376b. Cf., e.g., 'nostri essemus, si ista nostra non essent' (*Ep.* 42, 8); 'Neminem pecunia divitem fecit, immo contra nulli non maiorem sui cupidinem incussit' (*Ep.* 119, 9).

[40] e.g. the last answer to fear of dying young (see *Q*, II. 373a) is a précis of *Manual*, XVII; and the notion which Quevedo noted as common to Job and Epictetus, that children are given on loan, is implied at least twice (see *Q*, II. 378a).

[41] See *Q*, II. 374b.

[42] See *Q*, II. 375a.    [43] See *Q*, II. 373a/b.    [44] *Essai*, p. 283.

## III. *Epictetus and Seneca Christianized*

Quevedo's preface to *Epicteto español* ends with Jerome's statement of the compatibility of Stoicism and Christianity: 'San Jerónimo, en el capítulo II sobre Isaías: *Stoici vita et moribus cum christiana disciplina haud parum concordabant.*'[45] In his dedication to Juan de Herrera, referring to those who never get down to the business of living virtuously, he declares: 'Estos errores corrige la filosofía estoica, si los perficiona la cristiana.'[46] The notion that Christianity crowns and brings to perfection the moral philosophy taught by the Stoics is treated at length in *La cuna y la sepultura*, the final draft of which was taking shape some two years before Quevedo published his translation of the *Manual*; and we have already seen the principle applied to Epicurus that the best among the writers of antiquity intuited part of the truth revealed in its totality by Christ. However, the readers of the composite work he published in 1635 would first have come upon this principle in his dedication of *Epicteto español*, in which he regrets that the author of the *Manual* was unable to benefit from the illumination of Christianity: 'No saliera defectuosa la doctrina de nuestros estoicos si, como Epicteto la escribió a la luz de su pobre candil, la hubiera estudiado a los rayos puros de la vida y palabras de Jesucristo Nuestro Señor, de quien como el Sol de justicia precede día privilegiado de noche y escuridad.'[47] Since Epictetus and his fellow Stoics only reached as far as reason could take them, his philosophy should be supplemented 'con asistencia de la Cruz de Cristo, meditada por la doctrina de los Santos Padres, nivelándole para el ejercicio por la *Introducción a la vida devota* del Beato Francisco de Sales'.[48]

In his verse translation of the *Manual*, however, Quevedo himself undertook to 'perfect' Epictetus. While Castanien maintains that 'evidence of any intention on the part of Quevedo to Christianize Epictetus, as he did [the *Carmen*] in his version of the pseudo-Phocylides, is very slight',[49] Castellanos had earlier attributed part of Quevedo's additional material in his translation to 'interferencia cristiana'.[50] Although many of Quevedo's interpolations in *Epicteto español* seek to stress the fundamental

---

[45] *Q*, III. 386.      [46] *Q*, III. 383.      [47] *Q*, III. 384.      [48] Ibid.
[49] D. G. Castanien, 'Quevedo's Version of Epictetus' *Encheiridion*', *S*, xviii (1964), 76.                    [50] See 'Quevedo y su *Epicteto*', pp. 200–3.

Stoic division of things into 'internals' and 'externals', things within and outside our control, on one occasion he equates control over the former with free will, on another he describes these as 'los santos bienes', on a third he adds that it is 'la voluntad de Dios' which determines what is within man's control, and on yet another he describes the Christian virtues of patience and humility as man's surest arms against 'externals'.[51]

Quevedo frequently avoids translating literally Epictetus' rationalist Stoic goal 'to keep your moral purpose in a state of conformity with nature'. In one case he replaces it by the Senecan precept to be prepared for adversity, and in another he enlarges upon Epictetus' ideal of 'making progress' in two lines which suggest a Christian end: 'Y si con mi doctrina / Quieres atesorar la paz divina . . .'[52] Elsewhere he adapts the Stoic's aim to the Christian notion of perfecting the soul, addressing the aspiring sage as 'Tú, pues, que a la verdad del alma atiendes' and counselling his readers to listen to 'la voz de la verdad divina'.[53] His exhortation at the end of his translation,

> . . . no pases
> De lo que la razón te aconsejare,
> O la santa verdad te declarare,[54]

can scarcely have been taken by his readers as anything but an injunction to observe the doctrines of the Church. It is also noteworthy that he frequently introduces the idea that goods are given to man on loan, the point of contact most strongly stressed in the *Doctrina estoica* between Epictetus and the Book of Job. By this means, he makes the *Manual* appear to be far closer to Job than in reality it is. For example, he adds the line 'pues da la vida cuanto da prestado', and, in the chapter on which he based virtually the whole of his demonstration that Epictetus was influenced by Job, he inserts the lines 'Que el hombre en tierra y lodo fabricado, / Cuanto tiene es prestado.'[55] The reader of his essay on the Stoics who took the trouble to verify his thesis that Stoicism had as its source the Book of Job would thus be likely to be satisfied by what he found.

Since Quevedo's additions to *De los remedios* also contain an important admixture of Christian elements, it is perhaps surprising

---

[51] See *Q*, III. 394b, 395b, 397a.     [52] *Q*, III. 394a.
[53] *Q*, III. 395b, 397b.     [54] *Q*, III. 405b.     [55] *Q*, III. 393b.

that he makes no comment there, as he does in his *Vida de San Pablo*, on the question whether the dedicatee of *De remediis*, Seneca's brother, Gallio, is to be identified with the proconsul of Achaea who refused to hear the Jews' case against Paul. In his Life of the Apostle, probably written during his imprisonment in León and published in 1644, he does not merely support the identity of the two Gallios, but regards them (or him) as the lost link between Paul and Seneca, and surmises that, through his brother, Seneca may have asked Paul to visit Spain.[56] Based as it is on the wildest of hypotheses, this view of Quevedo reveals a desire on his part to link the apostle with Spain via Seneca and to suggest that the Roman Stoic held both Spain and Paul dear, neither of which notions can in any sense be inferred from Seneca's writings.

In his version of the *Manual* Quevedo was eager to explain away Epictetus' apparent polytheism and generally followed El Brocense in translating 'gods' in the singular. In *De los remedios* he shows a similar wariness of using terms which clash with Christian dogma, but here he is content to warn his readers of their presence in the work without, on the whole, changing them in his translation. Christian 'interference' in *De los remedios* is first noticeable in the preface, where he gives Christ as the example of 'la majestad de los desprecios'.[57] In his additions, Christ is made the supreme exemplar of the correct attitude towards poverty and tyranny; in answer to the Senses' complaint at exile we find his remark that no one is a prophet in his own land; 'Blessed are the poor of spirit' is cited in Quevedo's section on poverty, where he also gives a curious Senecan twist to the metaphor of the camel and the eye of a needle, refers to Lazarus and the miser, and quotes one of his favourite Fathers, Peter Chrysologus. Christ's words are again turned into arguments for Stoical consolation in reply to the complaint at loss of sight; Paul's authority is adduced in the section on the loss of a wife; and, on one remarkable occasion, Quevedo declares that he is 'canonizing' a passage in Virgil— 'autor . . . que mereció en la filosofía estoica ser citado de mi Séneca',[58] he says, with little apparent appreciation, here or elsewhere in his works, for Virgil's qualities as a poet—with another quotation from Paul. Each of these direct appeals to Christian authority occurs at the end of his additions to *De*

[56] See *Q*, II. 33b.          [57] *Q*, II. 370.          [58] *Q*, II. 379a.

*remediis* and provides a Christian conclusion to round off and 'perfect' his own pseudo-Senecan arguments.

Direct reference to Christian authority is not, however, Quevedo's only method of Christianizing pseudo-Seneca. He also intermingles Christian concepts into his Senecan polemics. For example, when he combats fear of death he introduces the notion that the death of the body opens the way to true life, and he states that the soul leaves the body at the moment of death. This Christian–Platonic (and also Senecan) distinction between the fates of the body and the soul is maintained in his treatment of the complaint at being left unburied, where he argues that non-burial is not a threat to the soul but only to the body, the 'sepultura de mi alma', and it is made still more explicit when, referring to the Last Judgement, he states that the body will be resurrected whether it is buried or not.[59] More striking still is the Christianiza-tion of one of his favourite Senecan ideas when he implies that, if life is part of the process of dying, this is due to Original Sin: 'Después que el pecado enfermó la naturaleza, mi propia naturaleza es enferma, y yo soy una enfermedad viva.'[60] What is more, in this work we again find Anaxarchus set up as an example to counter fear of pain, and, just as in the *Doctrina estoica* he was coupled with St. Laurence, here the ability to withstand pain learned by pagans from (Stoic) philosophy is compared with the positive delight in pain displayed by Christian martyrs; and the example of the Stoics, who achieved so much by the use of reason unaided by grace, is put forward as one which may put Christians to shame:

'Padezco dolor.' Si le padezco como Anaxarco, bien le padezco. Martillábale en una pila de piedra el cuerpo Nicocreonte tirano, y decía estas animosas palabras: 'Muele, muele el costal; que Anaxarco está más allá de donde llega tu martillo.' Quebrábanle los martillos los huesos, y parecía que los huesos eran los que atormentaban a los martillos. . . . Los gentiles idólatras alcanzaron de la filosofía esfuerzo para saber padecer los dolores; empero los mártires de Jesucristo nuestro Señor tuvieron gracia para gozarle en ellos, descansar en el fuego, coronarse de los martirios. Cristiano, será afrenta no igualarme a los idólatras; será delito no imitar a los cristianos.[61]

Of the three classical texts translated and published by Quevedo, two (the *Manual* and *De remediis*) are Stoic and the third (pseudo-Phocylides' *Carmen*) is said to have impressed him by 'its similarity

---

[59] See *Q*, II. 373b, 374a.      [60] *Q*, II. 374a.      [61] *Q*, II. 375b.

to Stoic doctrine'.[62] To the *Carmen* he added 'items that emphasize the apparent Christian philosophy of the poem',[63] and he declares in his dedication to the Duke of Osuna that its author 'evangelizó (si así se puede decir) en medio de la gentilidad'.[64] He translated the *Manual* persuaded that it was inspired by the Book of Job and that Epictetus, like Seneca, had received further inspiration through his contemporaneity with the earliest years of Christianity; and he was to argue the identity of the dedicatee of *De remediis* and Paul's protector. The words he used to recommend pseudo-Phocylides—'Su gloria de este autor es que, siendo tantos años antes de Cristo, dejó en qué aprendiesen conforme a sus preceptos, los que tenemos su ley, y nacimos tanto después'[65]—express a view that he obviously held with regard to Seneca and Epictetus also. No less than in the *Doctrina estoica*, the *Defensa de Epicuro*, and his translations and imitations of Seneca's Epistles, in *Epicteto español* and *De los remedios* he was determined to treat his favourite classical authors as more than mere pagans. If Licenciado Pedro Blasco could say that *De los remedios* contained 'sana y pía doctrina' and that the translations of Epictetus and pseudo-Phocylides were of 'evidente utilidad, por ser moralmente tan émula de la Evangélica',[66] this was due in no small part to our author's ability as a Christianizing translator.

[62] Castanien, 'Quevedo's Translation of the Pseudo-Phocylides', *PQ*, xl (1961), 44.

[63] Ibid., p. 50.          [64] *EQ*, p. 10.          [65] *Q*, III. 407.

[66] *Censura* for *De los remedios* (*BP*, p. 954a); *aprobación* for *Epicteto y Phocilides* (*Q*, III. 381 n. 1 (p. 382)). Similarly, Juan Eusebio Nieremberg remarks in his *aprobación*: 'Cuan cerca andaban [the Stoics] de la doctrina Cristiana, veráse en estos avisos de Epicteto, y en su sentimiento' (ibid.).

# IV

## *LA CUNA Y LA SEPULTURA*

### 1. *The Stoical Chapters*

ALTHOUGH *La cuna y la sepultura* was the first work published by Quevedo after his name appeared on the 1632 Index, the first five chapters, which make up the greater part of it, had been written by 1628. When these five chapters were published in Barcelona and Zaragoza in 1630 under the title *Doctrina moral del conocimiento propio y del desengaño de las cosas ajenas*, they became the first of his Stoical works to reach the public.[1] Apart from minor modifications to this early version, *La cuna* contained new preliminary matter and added titles to the original chapters, three prayers, and the short treatise *Doctrina para morir*, which was subtitled *Muerte y sepultura*. The primitive part of the work, together with the prayers, was now headed *Cuna y vida*. These were certainly important changes, but Fernández-Guerra's statement, repeated by Astrana Marín, that 'años adelante (en la primavera del de 1633) hizo [Quevedo] de esta obra moral y filosófica una cristiana y ascética' overstates the contrast between the two versions.[2] The first three chapters anticipate *Epicteto español* and *De los remedios de cualquier fortuna* by their reliance on the Stoics' division of things into 'internals' and 'externals' in order to suggest that what the *vulgus* desires is to be feared or scorned, and vice versa; and the polemic in which Quevedo engages in order to convince his reader of this paradoxical view of life is strongly marked by his familiarity with the writings of Seneca and Epictetus. While Luisa López Grigera appears to hold that they are descended exclusively from Epictetus' *Manual*, these early chapters also contain many close parallels

---

[1] For an attempt at refuting the view that *La cuna* is the work Quevedo sent Tamayo de Vargas in 1612, see Ettinghausen, 'Acerca de las fechas', pp. 161–6. *La cuna* and the *Doctrina moral* can now be compared in *CS*, whose variants from the edition in BAE are noted in the present chapter.

[2] *Q*, II. 75 n. (a). Cf. *La vida turbulenta*, p. 191.

with Seneca.[3] However, as we shall see, these essentially Stoical chapters are Christianized even in the early version, and the overtly Christian additions to the text of the *Doctrina moral* correspond in a number of ways to a Stoical view of life.

The first chapter opens with the idea that one must live virtuously and bring body and soul into a state of harmony by eschewing 'externals'. If the notion that the body's desires weigh down the soul has biblical as well as Senecan antecedents, the prescription for the correct attitude to adopt towards the body is a direct paraphrase of Seneca:

Has de tratarle, no como quien vive por él, que es necedad, ni como quien vive para él, que es delito; sino como quien no puede vivir sin él. Trátale como al criado: susténtale y vístele y mándale; que sería cosa fea que te mandase quien nació para servirte, y que nació confesando con lágrimas su servidumbre; y muerto, dirá en la sepultura que por sí aun eso no merecía.[4]

The remainder of the chapter is an exposition of *miseria hominis* in Senecan and Epictetan terms. It begins by employing the Senecan topic that life is part of the process of dying, not, as in Seneca's works, ostensibly to minimize the pathos of death, but to maximize that of life, an attitude emphasized by Quevedo by fusing the Senecan equation of life with death with Job's comparison of life to the days of a hireling:

Es, pues, la vida un dolor en que se empieza el de la muerte, que dura mientras dura ella. Considéralo como el plazo que ponen al jornalero, que no tiene descanso desde que empieza, sino es cuando acaba. A la par empiezas a nacer y a morir, y no es en tu mano detener las horas; y si fueras cuerdo, no lo habías de desear; y si fueras bueno, no lo habías de temer. Antes empiezas a morir que sepas qué cosa es vida, y vives sin gustar della, porque se anticipan las lágrimas a la razón.[5]

To underscore further the wretchedness of the human condition Quevedo has recourse to the Senecan idea that the very sources of life are a danger to the body and, again exaggerating Seneca's

---

[3] See *CS*, p. xv. For a detailed examination of the parallels with Seneca, see Rothe, *Quevedo und Seneca*, chs. 4 and 5.

[4] *Q*, II. 79a. Cf. *Ep.* 14, 1–2: 'Fateor insitam esse nobis corporis nostri caritatem; fateor nos huius gerere tutelam. Non nego indulgendum illi; serviendum nego. . . . Sic gerere nos debemus, non tamquam propter corpus vivere debeamus, sed tamquam non possimus sine corpore.'

[5] *Q*, II. 79b. Cf., e.g., *Ep.* 24, 19–24, and Job 7: 1–3.

thought, argues that man's sustenance is a continual reminder of his predicament:

Si quieres acabar de conocer qué es tu vida y la de todos, y su miseria, mira qué de cosas desdichadas ha menester para continuarse. . . . ¿Cómo puede dejar de ser débil, y sujeta a muerte y miseria la que con muertes de otras cosas vive? Si te abrigas, murió el animal cuya lana vistes; si comes, el que te dio sustento. Pues advierte, hombre, que tienen tanto de recuerdos y memorias como de alimento. Por otra parte, mira cómo en todas esas cosas ignoras la muerte que recibes; pues los manjares con que (a tu parecer) sustentas el cuerpo (y es así), en su decocción, por otra parte, gastan el calor natural (que es tu vida) con el trabajo de disponerlos.[6]

Although the comparison of life to a candle ultimately derives from the same source, Seneca's fire symbol had been transformed into a candle by several writers before Quevedo, and has a close parallel in Luis de Granada.[7] The same is true of the argument that even health-giving things can bring death to man's frail body.[8] The idea that human nature is diseased is expressed in a way which implies both, as in *De los remedios de cualquier fortuna*, that the cause is Original Sin, and the Senecan topic that life is part of the process that leads up to and is consummated in death: 'no puede dejar de estar enfermo quien siempre en su misma vida tiene mal de muerte. Con este mal naces, con él vives, y dél mueres.'[9] Quevedo's list of 'sucesos desdichados', however, is reminiscent of those suffered by Job and compared in the *Doctrina estoica* with those dealt with in Epictetus' *Manual*. Their description as 'estas cosas que no están en tu mano' is, likewise, clearly Epictetan; and so, too, is Quevedo's illustration of man's 'mayor miseria'.[10] Even the idea that human misery is the result of lack

[6] *Q*, II. 79b. Seneca, *Ad Marc*. XI. 3, describes the body as 'alimenta metuens sua, quorum modo inopia deficit, modo copia rumpitur'.

[7] Rothe, p. 56, compares 'Vela eres: luz de la vela es la tuya, que va consumiendo lo mismo con que se alimenta; y cuanto más apriesa arde, más apriesa te acabarás' (*Q*, II. 79b) with *Ad Marc*. XXIII. 4. Cf. Luis de Granada, *Libro de la oración y meditación*, I. ix (BAE (Madrid, 1848), viii. 26): 'Según esto, ¿qué es nuestra vida, sino una candela que siempre se está gastando, y mientras más arde y resplandesce, más se gasta?'

[8] See the passage which Rothe, p. 55, compares with *Ad Marc*. XI. 4, and Granada, p. 29: 'Un aire basta muchas veces, y un sereno, y un sol recio para despojarnos de la vida . . . Si preguntas de qué murió Fulano, o Fulana, responderte han que de un jarro de agua fría que bebió, o de una cena demasiada que cenó'.

[9] *Q*, II. 79b.　　　　　　　　　　　　　　　　　[10] *Q*, II. 80a.

of self-knowledge, and the definition of this knowledge as 'usar bien de lo que te dio el que te crió', have clear precedents in the Stoics' insistence on the need for correct opinion and in the attitude to life which both Epictetus and Seneca express in terms of acting out the role allotted to one. It is because man holds false opinions that he confuses the *miseria* of the body with the *dignitas* of the soul and is undeceived too late. By depicting life's wretchedness with what has been described rather too strongly as philosophical pessimism,[11] Quevedo seeks to bring about *desengaño* in time.

While the very leitmotiv of this and the following chapters—'Todo lo haces al revés, hombre'[12]—implies the Stoic doctrine of the need to distinguish those things which are in man's control from those which are not, clearly Christian ideas about the nature and purpose of life appear already in the first chapter. Memories of the Old Testament and the long tradition of Christian ascetic literature, as well as of the Senecan *brevitas vitae* topic, come together to produce the pointed, antithetical account of man's ultimate misery: 'Vuelve los ojos, si piensas que eres algo, a lo que eras antes de nacer; y hallarás que no eras, que es la última miseria. Mira que eres el que ha poco que no fuiste, y el que siendo eres poco, y el que de aquí a poco no serás: verás cómo tu vanidad se castiga y se da por vencida.'[13] And Quevedo's recapitulation of the first chapter skilfully Christianizes Stoic teaching: self-knowledge (man's correct opinion of himself) includes the Senecan equation of life with death, the Senecan–Christian notions of the soul's imprisonment in the body and its immortality, the Epictetan idea of life given on loan, the transformation of the Stoics' division of things into 'internals' and 'externals' into those of the soul and those of the body, and the combination of the Stoics' insistence on concern with what is proper to man with the Christian concept of Judgement.[14]

The definition of man presented in chapter one is developed in chapters two and three into a detailed exposition of the correct

[11] See Blüher, *Seneca in Spanien*, esp. p. 338.

[12] *Q*, II. 80a. Cf. 'Y ha de ser al revés' (81a), 'Al revés lo entiendes todo' (84b), and 'antes lo entiendes todo al revés' (86a). Blüher, p. 431, notes similar expressions in Gracián.

[13] *Q*, II. 80a.

[14] See *Q*, II. 80b–81a. Seneca, too, sometimes associates 'internals' with the soul (e.g. *Ep*. 74, 16).

attitude to adopt towards both attractive and unattractive 'externals'. From the beginning, however, the Stoic idea of correct opinion is expressed in terms of the proper use of the Augustinian attributes of the soul: understanding, memory, and will. Memory, in particular, should remind man of his *miseria*, and the will should make him desire eternity, (spiritual) wealth, peace, and truth.[15] Anticipating the dedication of *Epicteto español* and the preface to *De los remedios de cualquier fortuna*, Quevedo remarks on the deceptiveness of appearances: 'De verdad te digo, hombre, que no tuvieran los hombres vanos deseos si usaran del entendimiento como debían; no los vencieran las apariencias de las cosas, no por cierto, ni se les atrevieran. Si de todas las cosas que te faltan y ves en otro hicieras tal examen, en vez de desearlas, tuvieras lástima a quien tienes envidia'; and his injunction, 'Debías considerar para qué cosas te hace falta a ti, cuál es en sí la cosa, y qué provecho da su uso al dueño della', recalls the opening chapters of the *Manual*.[16] Chapter two takes the 'externals' of beauty, palaces, wealth, and worldly honour, and sets about stripping them of their false appearance by means of the correct use of understanding. Our poet, who at other times penned courtly complaints at being unrequited in love, here calls on his readers to take a Stoical look at 'la mujer hermosa, y al mancebo poseído de su belleza', arguing not merely, as in *De los remedios de cualquier fortuna*, that sex debilitates but (as with the digestive process in chapter one) that it actually accelerates the process by which life leads to death, 'pues engañada con el placer la salud, sin dejar saber a los más qué es vejez, los llega a la muerte'.[17] Seneca, too, had argued against over-indulgence by warning of its effects on the body, and Epictetus had contrasted pleasure before sex with remorse afterwards.[18]

Seneca's influence is unmistakable in Quevedo's paradoxical contrasting of the advantages of a 'pobre casa' or 'cabaña' with

[15] See *Q*, II. 81a. For the Stoical sources of Quevedo's concept of peace of soul and view of the soul's attributes, see Rothe, *Quevedo und Seneca*, pp. 72–4, 79–80.

[16] *Q*, II. 81b.

[17] Ibid. Cf. *De los remedios* (*Q*, II. 378b): 'La mujer propia con su hermosura y su compañía te hurta las fuerzas y la salud.' In his copy of Flaminio Nobili, *Trattato dell'amore humano* (Lucca, 1567), now in the British Museum, Quevedo marked with the word 'stoicos' the passage: '& gli Stoici, quando vogliono diffinire Amore, espressamente pongono, che nasca da bellezza' (fol. 7r).

[18] See, e.g., *Ep.* 95, 21, and *Manual*, XXXIV.

the disadvantages of 'grandes palacios'. His answer to those who envy the powerful inhabitants of palaces reads like a gloss on passages in which Seneca had contended that in the Golden Age only slaves had lived under roofs of gold and marble, had pointed out that one cannot live in more than one room at a time, and had enumerated the ills avoided by cottage-dwellers.[19] Anticipating words he was to write from prison in 1642, Quevedo adds as his final argument the contention, consonant with the Stoic precept to be prepared for death, that living in a hovel is good practice for facing death without fear and for the need eventually to accommodate oneself to the confines of the grave: 'y en cierto modo va el cuerdo ensayando el cuerpo para la sepultura, que hecho a tales habitaciones, no se le hará angosto el ataúd ni le espantará el forzoso hospedaje de la muerte.'[20] The attack on wealth is, similarly, rich in Senecan ideas. Like the Stoic himself, Quevedo asserts that riches are merely a burden; that, since they must be given up at death, they are not worth acquiring; that Nature, which wisely buried 'precious' metals and stones beneath mountains, bountifully supplies the necessities of life; that wealth is only such when used virtuously; that the poor enjoy the advantage of not being deceived by flatterers; that poverty alone ensures freedom; that the rich do not own their wealth, but are owned by it; and that the acquisition and possession of riches is a constant worry.[21] While the mere enumeration of his Senecan arguments misses entirely the force of Quevedo's rhetoric, his Senecan style can easily be appreciated by comparing passages in *La cuna* and *De los remedios de cualquier fortuna*. Often, for instance in his onslaught on gold, with its puns on the various meanings of 'gastar', Quevedo's Senecan polemics come close to the *conceptista* satire of the *Sueños*.[22]

---

[19] See *Q*, II. 82a. Cf. *Ep.* 8, 5; 17, 3; 89, 21; 90, 10; and Rothe, pp. 90–1.

[20] *Q*, II. 82a. Cf. letter to P. Pedro Pimentel: 'Yo, señor, quedo vivo en este sepulcro, ensayándome de muerto, ocupado en el ejercicio de la paciencia' (*EQ*, p. 450).

[21] See *Q*, II. 82a/b. Cf., e.g., *Ep.* 104, 34; 102, 25; 90, 10; 94, 72; 20, 7; 17, 3; 119, 12; 115, 16.

[22] '¿Cómo puede ser bueno quien, como tú, oro poderoso, se parece tanto a los males y enfermedades, que lo mejor dellos y de los malos humores es gastallos? Y si no, ellos gastan la vida, y tú en gastalla eres más pródigo que ellos' (*Q*, II. 83a). Cf. *De los remedios*: '"Tiene otro mucho dinero." . . . Si tiene el dinero, no le gasta; si no le gasta, no le goza; si le gasta, no le tiene' (*Q*, II. 376b); and the puns on 'guardar' in Quevedo's treatment of a miser in the first *Sueño* (*Q*, I. 300b).

As for the last 'externals' dealt with in chapter two, worldly honour and power, Quevedo again treats attachment to them as a matter of false opinion—'¿Qué opinión tienes de esas grandezas, que así mueres por alcanzallas?'[23]—and employs Senecan arguments to correct the views of the *vulgus*. His contention that power, far from giving freedom, enslaves the powerful is essentially the same as that used earlier to combat the desire for wealth; and the notion that in order to rid oneself of illusions about power one need only look at the fate of the powerful is, similarly, to be found in Seneca.[24] With a view to belittling the ruler's power to sentence his subjects to death, he adapts the Senecan equation of life with death, used to the same end in *De los remedios de cualquier fortuna*, to show that all men are condemned to death by Nature from the day they are born. As the ultimate ambition of those who seek after power he takes the office of royal favourite, whose insecurity he had pointed out before the appearance of the *Doctrina moral* in his *Discurso de todos los diablos*; and here, too, he is indebted to Seneca and to pseudo-Seneca. One passage added in *La cuna* to the earlier version of the work recalls Seneca's comments on Stilbo's dictum, 'Omnia mea mecum sunt', and borrows the Senecan example of the horse weighed down and made powerless by its heavy gold harness.[25] Another takes up again the device of alternative conditions, employed in *De los remedios de cualquier fortuna*, in order to prove that it is impossible for the *privado* to please his subjects: 'si eres bueno, te aborrecen los malos; si eres malo, los buenos; tu día postrero todos le desamparan. Si no eres culpable, serás inocente, mas por esto más envidiado; y debes considerarlo.'[26] The favourite's chief fault is that he holds incorrect opinions and is unable to tell things in his control from those which are not: 'Al revés lo entiendes todo, pues tienes soberbia de los méritos ajenos y que no son tuyos.'[27] Among Christian elements in this chapter we find the remark that gold may take pride in the fact that, since it is abandoned only by those who seek God, he is its only rival; the contradiction of Stoic faith in reason and self-reliance by Job's words that wisdom lies in fear of God; Christ's

---

[23] *Q*, II. 83b.     [24] Ibid. Cf., e.g., *Ep*. 94, 73.
[25] 'No es dichoso aquél a quien la fortuna no puede dar nada más, sino aquél a quien no puede quitar nada. . . . Aprende de un caballo, que cargado en su propio adorno de inmensa cantidad de oro, desea que le descarguen, y no que le alaben' (*Q*, II. 84b). Cf. *Ep*. 9, 19 and 41, 6.
[26] *Q*, II. 84a. (*CS* reads 'te desampararán'.)     [27] *Q*, II. 84b.

'Judge not that ye be not judged'; and the reference here, as in *De los remedios de cualquier fortuna*, to Christ's scorn at his trial for the justice of this world.[28]

Having turned the objects of man's desires into *indifferentia* or worse, Quevedo sets out in chapter three to persuade his readers that what they fear most is not merely 'indifferent' but desirable. Like Seneca and Epictetus he devotes most attention to fear of death and, like them, he combats the opinion of the *vulgus*:

> Conviene que te certifiques de que la opinión hace medrosos muchos casos que no lo son; sea por todos el de la muerte. ¿Qué cosa más terrible, así representada, más fea ni más espantosa? Y si dejas la opinión que della tiene el pueblo, verás que en sí no es nada de eso, y antes hallarás que hace mucho por hacerse amable, y aun digna de desprecio antes que de miedo.[29]

Here again his method consists in glossing arguments to be found in Seneca and pseudo-Seneca. Death is inevitable and necessary, an end to life's ills, exempting no one, not a punishment but a law of life, part of the very fact of living and growing older which all desire.[30] Even the recommendation to learn from philosophers and virtuous men how to live and die well, and to make oneself familiar with death has parallels in the Stoic. As in *De los remedios de cualquier fortuna*, arguments are accumulated with little apparent concern for their mutual compatibility: at one point Quevedo borrows the Erasmian argument that fear of the agony of dying is an *engaño* of Nature designed as a deterrent to suicide; and then a few lines later, once again in a style reminiscent of pseudo-Seneca, he gives as the ultimate answer to life's misery the Stoic solution of suicide:

> Dirás que es dolorosa y llena de congojas y parasismos. Pues dime, si eso no hubiera en la muerte, siendo tan desdichada la vida, ¿quién no la tomara por sus manos? Prevenida la naturaleza la cercó de congojas, y la hizo parecer temerosa, para que los hombres viviesen algún tiempo. . . . Si has vivido contento y todo te ha sucedido bien, harto de vida despídete della. Y si todo te ha sucedido mal, ¿para qué quieres añadir cada día más trabajo? Vete enfadado. Y si te ha sucedido unas veces mal y otras bien, no hay más que experimentar; cánsate de repetir una misma cosa. Poca honra tienes, pues sabiendo

---

[28] See *Q*, II. 82b, 83b, 84a.
[29] *Q*, II. 84b. Cf., e.g., *Ep.* 78, 5 and *Manual*, V.
[30] See *Q*, II. 84b–85a, and Rothe, *Quevedo und Seneca*, pp. 94–5.

que te ha de dejar a ti la vida, aguardas ese desprecio della, y no la dejas antes, pudiéndolo hacer.[31]

Both arguments have in common, however, the tinge of Senecan melancholy on which Quevedo remarks in the dedication of *De los remedios de cualquier fortuna*, each implying as it does that the sufferings involved in dying are preferable to those of life.

Further parallels with Seneca, Epictetus, and *De los remedios de cualquier fortuna* occur in the second half of the chapter. Quevedo's treatment of slanderers contains at least two passages which anticipate his additions to pseudo-Seneca;[32] his remedy for fear of robbers employs the question–answer device which he regarded as typically Senecan; to provide consolation for the death of close relatives he borrows the Senecan concept that death is the natural end of life's journey; and he replies to the complaint at loss of money and like calamities with Epictetan insistence on correct opinion.[33] His most direct borrowing from the Stoics in *La cuna* is, however, his attack on anger, which is paraphrased from *De ira* and in which we find the first of the only two references to Seneca in the entire work. Quevedo's reason for mentioning him is his determination to show that he can go one better than the Stoic by proving that anger is not merely not natural but actually contrary to Nature.[34] His demonstration that the causes of anger are all 'external', however, relies on the Epictetan example of the master enraged by his servant's ineptitude; and there are further reminders of the *Manual* in his repeated emphasis on the doctrine of correct opinion and the contrasting of things which are 'en tu mano' with those that are 'fuera de tu poder'.[35]

[31] *Q*, II. 85a. For the Erasmian argument, see M. Bataillon, *Erasmo y España. Estudios sobre la historia espiritual del siglo XVI*, trans. A. Alatorre, 2nd ed. (Mexico/Buenos Aires, 1966), p. 567.

[32] 'Si oyes que dicen malas cosas de ti en tu presencia, te enojas . . . ¿No miras que si son verdad las cosas que te dicen, era justo enojarte contigo, porque haciéndolas diste ocasión al otro de decirlas; y que siendo así, habías de agradecer tor [*sic*] reprehensión lo que aborreces?' (*Q*, II. 85b–86a); cf. '"Tiénen de ti mala opinión los hombres." Lo que me importa es no sacarlos verdaderos. . . . "Hablan mal de ti." Si dicen verdad, no hablan mal; si mienten, hacen mal' (*Q*, II. 375a). 'Dijo uno mal de ti; no digas tú mal dél, siquiera por no parecerte a él y por no imitarle' (*Q*, II. 86b); cf. '"Hablan mal de ti." Por no imitallos hablaré bien dellos' (*Q*, II. 375a).

[33] See *Q*, II. 88a.

[34] See *Q*, II. 86b–87a, and Rothe, pp. 91–2.

[35] *Q*, II. 87b. For the example of the irritated master, see *Manual*, XII and XXVI.

Once again, even in the early, *Doctrina moral*, version of this nominally Stoical chapter Christian elements are not lacking. Among the most obvious are the passage cited from Ecclesiastes in reply to fear of death,[36] the quotation from Fr. Cristóbal de Fonseca's *Tratado del amor de Dios*, the gloss on Christ's exhortation to love one's enemies and the assertion that revenge is God's prerogative,[37] and the reference, anticipating that in *De los remedios de cualquier fortuna*, to Christian martyrs as well as the heroic example of the Stoics in support of the view that fear of death arises out of false opinion:

> ¿Dirás que no se puede quitar este sentimiento propio de la naturaleza? Engáñaste. ¿Qué hicieron dél, si sabes, aquellos filósofos antiguos que o codiciaban la muerte o la despreciaban; aquellos soldados que no hallaron en ella cosa fea ni temerosa, y se ofrecieron a ella y la buscaron? ¡Cuántos millares de valerosos mártires, soldados católicos, la pasaron con risa y contento! ¿Qué te parece? Pues en éstos naturaleza humana había, mas tenían diferente opinión de la vida y de la muerte que tú . . .[38]

It is largely thanks to the Christianization of Stoicism in these first three chapters that the pathos of Senecan argumentation and the cold rationalism of Epictetan insistence on correct opinion do not, as has been suggested by more than one critic, add up to mere pessimism.[39] As will become clear later in the present chapter, Quevedo's Stoicism in this work represents not so much his own view of life as a preparation for his 'perfected' Stoicism.

## ii. *The 'Sceptical' Chapter*

Chapter four of *La cuna* may be said in a sense to return to the *miseria hominis* theme of the first chapter, which, according to the title added in the later version of the work, 'amanece con el desengaño la noche de la presunción'. Quevedo's 'sceptical' chapter four also aims at combating man's false opinions of himself: 'Resta ahora desengañarte del estudio vano y de la presunción

---

[36] See *Q*, II. 85b. The passage cited is Eccles. 7: 3.
[37] See *Q*, II. 86b.
[38] *Q*, II. 88a. For *De los remedios*, see above, p. 71.
[39] It is difficult to agree with Blüher, *Seneca in Spanien*, p. 340, that Quevedo's attitude to death in *La cuna* is coloured above all by 'pessimistischen Zügen senecaischer Lebensentwertung' and that 'der auf die innere Freiheit der sittlichen Entscheidung gegründete Todesheroismus der Stoa bleibt ihm dagegen fremd'. Rothe, *Quevedo und Seneca*, p. 52, makes the unlikely suggestion that the Christian ideas in the first four chapters arose unconsciously.

de la ciencia, y enseñarte cómo es ninguna tu sabiduría'.[40] This is an important chapter, showing Quevedo as it does in a sceptical, and more particularly, anti-Aristotelian light not untypical of the Neostoic movement as a whole.[41] His critique of human knowledge is, like those of Seneca and Epictetus, an attack on academic curricula; but he goes further than either Stoic in actually putting in doubt the very possibility of knowing. He begins by censuring the pretensions of the non-specialist and of the bogus philosopher. He apparently considers mathematics, at least, a reasonable field of study, at any rate for mathematicians; and his satire on scholastic university syllabuses is, as Rothe has shown, based on Seneca's mockery of so-called 'liberal' studies.[42] However, even early in the chapter natural philosophy is treated not as natural at all but as 'fantástica y soñada',[43] although it is not clear whether this is because Quevedo considers that there is no such thing as science or merely because he finds Aristotelian science a waste of time. While it is not long before we find him declaring that 'la [hipocresía] de la sabiduría, como no hay ninguna, no se funda sino sólo en presunción', and recalling Francisco Sánchez the Sceptic with his bald statement, 'nadie sabe nada',[44] he is evidently unwilling to commit himself to scepticism. Just as in the revised, *Juguetes de la niñez*, version of the fourth *Sueño* (in which he actually mentions Sánchez's *Quod nihil scitur*) he specifically excludes theologians, philosophers, and jurists from his earlier wholesale rejection of study as a 'vano ejercicio', so in *La cuna* the bold contention, 'Toda nuestra sabiduría es presunción acreditada de la ignorancia de los otros', is followed not by a demonstration of the pointlessness of grammar but merely by the example of the *incompetent* grammarian.[45]

It is probably impossible to determine exactly the sources of Quevedo's sceptical attitudes. While they have parallels in *Quod nihil scitur*, even the notion that man's ignorance is such that he is ignorant even of his own ignorance can be found in other writers

---

[40] *Q*, II. 88b.
[41] See Levi, *French Moralists* (*passim*). Blüher, pp. 283 ff., links El Brocense's anti-Aristotelianism with his interest in the Stoa and relates his sceptical attitudes to the Erasmian tradition.
[42] See *Q*, II. 89a, 90a/b, and Rothe, esp. pp. 65–6.
[43] *Q*, II. 88b.
[44] *Q*, II. 89a.
[45] Ibid. Cf. *Q*, I. 325, and Rothe, p. 59.

known to our author.[46] Indeed, it is difficult to accept the view that his brand of scepticism is as far removed from Montaigne's as it is from Sánchez's.[47] On the contrary, his qualified and equivocal scepticism is far closer to that of the *Apologie de Raimond Sebond* than to the methodical doubt of the doctor of Toulouse. The passages from the *Essais* quoted in the *Defensa de Epicuro* are taken from the two essays immediately preceding the *Apologie*, in which Montaigne marvels no less than Sánchez at the profundity of human ignorance.[48] Among parallels between the *Apologie* and chapter four of *La cuna* the following may be cited: the argument for the impotence of human reason from the disagreements between the various philosophical schools of antiquity; the attack on the mind's ability to deal with natural phenomena; and dismay at the sway of scholasticism, in which Aristotelian natural philosophy is singled out for the harshest censure.[49] However, such points of similarity as these are less important than the function to which both writers put sceptical arguments and attitudes. The *Apologie* has been described as 'a detailed attack on human presumption, directed at its very foundation, human reason'.[50] Overtly, at least, it is also motivated by the aim of making its readers come to accept the authority of God, 'leur faire sentir l'inanité, la vanité et deneantise de l'homme; leur arracher des points les chetives armes de leur raison; leur faire baisser la teste et mordre la terre soubs l'authorité et reverence de la majesté divine.'[51] Scepticism is a useful tool because it can be employed to persuade the rejection of human wisdom for faith in the wisdom of God.[52]

[46] For possible reminiscences of *Quod nihil scitur*, see Rothe, pp. 60–3. Blüher, p. 222, cites the following from Antonio de Guevara, *Epístolas familiares*: 'Que no sabía otra cosa más cierta sino saber que no sabía nada' and 'no ay en este mundo cosa más cierta que ser todas las cosas inciertas.'

[47] See Rothe, *Quevedo und Seneca*, p. 58.

[48] e.g. 'L'homme qui présume de son sçavoir, ne sçait pas encore que c'est que sçavoir' and 'm'en partiray d'icy plus ignorant toute autre chose que mon ignorance' (*Essais*, ed. A. Thibaudet, pp. 494, 600). While Rothe, p. 58 n. 42, holds that evidence of Montaigne's influence on Quevedo is not found before the *Defensa*, it should be noted that the date of that work is uncertain and that its quotations from the *Essais* occurred in its first draft (see above, p. 43).

[49] See *Q*, II. 89b–90b. Cf. *Essais*, ed. cit., pp. 599–600, 604–5, 611.

[50] A. J. Krailsheimer, *Studies in Self-interest from Descartes to La Bruyère* (Oxford, 1962), p. 26.       [51] *Essais*, ed. cit., p. 493.

[52] The fideist scepticism of another Neostoic is studied by J.-B. Sabrié, *De l'Humanisme au rationalisme: Pierre Charron (1541–1603), L'homme, l'œuvre, l'influence* (Paris, 1913), esp. pp. 291 ff.

In much the same way as in chapter one *miseria hominis* is balanced, at least in passing, by *dignitas hominis*, the scepticism of chapter four leads up to a positive, fideist conclusion. Even early in the chapter, instead of being supported by a philosophical proof of the impossibility of knowing, such as was attempted by Francisco Sánchez, the thesis that 'todo es opinión y los más cuerdos sospechan' rests on a series of Christian tenets linked in such a way as to give a superficial impression of logical demonstration: 'la sabiduría verdadera está en la verdad, y la verdad es una sola, y esa verdad una es Dios solo, que por eso le llaman Dios verdadero'.[53] Wisdom, the object of 'tantos antiguos filósofos', is placed outside man's reach by a quotation from Job the proto-Stoic: 'Así debes tener por cierto que la primera lección que lee la sabiduría al hombre es en el día de su muerte . . . ¿Quieres ver cuánta sabiduría se enseña en aquel postrer suspiro? Que él solo desengaña al hombre de sí mismo, y él solo confiesa claramente lo que es el hombre y lo que ha sido.'[54] The only practicable object of study is active virtue ('la consideración y ejercicio de las virtudes'), the Stoics' *summum bonum*, which Quevedo expresses in Christian terms. Man can reach God by the right use of things and, above all, by the exercise of constancy in adversity, which Quevedo links with Christian humility: '¿Qué cosa más digna de estudio y de alabanza que el ejercicio del sufrimiento, armado de prudencia y modestia contra las insolencias de la fortuna? ¿Qué mayor riqueza que una humildad atesorada de tal suerte, que ni desprecies a nadie ni sientas que te desprecien todos?'[55] All efforts to comprehend the universe are doomed to failure, and its workings can safely be left to Providence. Divination (as Epictetus had taught) is impossible and, in any case, unnecessary for 'los sabios que saben despreciar lo próspero y sufrir lo adverso', who, like the Stoic sage, are omniscient and at liberty under all conditions.[56]

Towards the end of the chapter the same ideas are given a more distinctively Christian flavour, but we still find the largely Stoical notions that the only worthwhile object of study is to be sought 'dentro de ti mismo', that the only worthwhile aim is

[53] *Q*, II. 89a.
[54] Ibid. The quotation is from Job 28: 14, 22. Quevedo's views are very close to those of Vives (see Rice, *The Renaissance Idea of Wisdom*, p. 158).
[55] *Q*, II. 90a.
[56] Ibid. Cf. *Manual*, XXXII. Rothe, p. 66, cites parallels in Seneca, *Ep.* 88, 14–17.

*desengaño*, and that one can only begin to become a sage when one
has rid oneself of fear of adversity and desire for worldly honour,
when nothing surprises one, and when one learns truth by studying
one's own nature. Life itself, Quevedo holds, teaches the Senecan
lesson that 'Cada día y cada hora que pasa es un argumento que
precede para tu desengaño a la conclusión de la muerte.'[57] However, if earlier he quoted Job, here he cites Ecclesiastes to repeat
the quite un-Stoical idea that wisdom is granted by God to the
righteous only after death; and the very author of Ecclesiastes
is cited as proof that wisdom is lost 'en llegándose a las cosas de
la tierra.' None the less, 'las cosas espirituales y eternas' can be
learned in this life through 'escarmiento' and 'desengaño'. These
can be obtained by concerning oneself with the afflicted, the
lonely, and the dead, by being suspicious of flattery and wary of
the evidence of the senses, and by being humane, forgiving, and
content with one's lot.[58] The Stoic–Christian synthesis to which
the entire work is directed is epitomized in the reading-list given
at the end of the chapter. After vituperating petty critics, as in
the *Defensa de Epicuro*, Quevedo recommends Seneca's works,
Epictetus' *Manual*, pseudo-Phocylides' *Carmen*, and Theognis
alongside the Wisdom of Solomon and the Book of Job and the
writings of Paul and the saints.[59] Quevedo's 'sceptical' chapter
resolves itself in Stoical fideism.

### III. *Stoicism 'Perfected'*

When in chapter three Quevedo claimed to outdo Seneca in
stigmatizing anger, he confessed that he was unequal to rivalling
the Stoic in *agudeza*.[60] The implication of this remark—that he
was attracted not only by Senecan attitudes and ideas but, as in
*De los remedios de cualquier fortuna*, by the witty *sententiae* that
had won Senecan style its European prestige—becomes quite

[57] *Q*, II. 90b. Cf. *Ep.* 101, 1: 'Omnis dies, omnis hora quam nihil simus
ostendit et aliquo argumento recenti admonet fragilitatis oblitos; tum aeterna
meditatos respicere cogit ad mortem.'
[58] *Q*, II. 90b.
[59] See *Q*, II. 91a. It is curious that the *Panegirico al Exmo . . . Duque de
Medina Sidonia* (?Seville, ?1629) of Pedro Espinosa, in whose *Flores de poetas
ilustres* (Valladolid, 1605) Quevedo's first published poems had appeared, gives
an almost identical reading-list (see F. Rodríguez Marín, *Pedro Espinosa.
estudio biográfico, bibliográfico y crítico* (Madrid, 1907), p. 232 n. 6).
[60] 'Más mostramos nosotros, que [la cólera] es contra naturaleza, no tan aguda-
mente, pero con más facilidad' (*Q*, II. 87a). (*CS* reads 'Mas mostramos . . .')

clear in the final chapter. Headed in *La cuna* 'Perficiona los cuatro capítulos precedentes de la filosofía estoica con la verdad cristiana, acompañándolos con tres oraciones a Jesucristo nuestro Señor', it opens with the startlingly frank admission that he had employed the *engaño* of ingenious argumentation in order to achieve his object of *desengaño*: 'Ya que moralmente quedas advertido, quiero que en lo espiritual oigas con más brevedad lo que te puede ser provechoso y no molesto; que estas cosas son las que más te convienen y menos apacibles te parecen, y es menester a veces disfrazártelas, o con la elocuencia o variedad o agudeza, para que recibas salud del engaño.'[61] In the preceding Stoical–sceptical chapters he had been holding up to nature the less flattering of the two mirrors—the one in which you see 'solas las cosas desaliñadas y mal puestas y las faltas que tienes'—mentioned in chapter three.[62] His Senecan melancholy had been, as he said of *De remediis fortuitorum*, the '*bien intencionada* melancólica de Séneca'.[63]

If the first four chapters of *La cuna* use Stoical and sceptical arguments to bring its readers to a state of willingness to accept the truth of Christianity, the final, Christian, chapter is itself coloured by Stoical ideas. It adapts the Stoical topic of the 'indifference' of exile in a Pauline sense by applying it to 'un alma eterna (que está cumpliendo un destierro en el cuerpo)'. It contends that alms-giving affords the only happiness attainable in this life, thus extending the attack on avarice in chapter two. It recommends, 'no te hagas juez de tu prosperidad ni adversidad, ni de los bienes ni de los males', recalling the Stoics' scorn for popular opinion. It states that God gives more than man could ask for, and this may be read as a Christian version of Seneca's praise for Nature's bounty. Finally, it gives a formula for becoming a *proficiens* in Christian philosophy which recalls Seneca as well as Juvenal and Persius: 'Entonces serás buen principiante en la filosofía cristiana cuando no rezares escondido y entre los dientes, y pidieres por los rincones a solas a Dios aquellas cosas que te da

---

[61] *Q*, II. 91a. (*CS* has 'ser más provechoso'.) In 1633, in the preface to *La cuna*, Quevedo expresses the same paradox in different terms, but terms which again imply the idea of using the intellect to trick the intellect: 'he querido (viendo que el hombre es racional, y que desto no puede huir), valiéndome de la razón, aprisionarle el entendimiento en ella. Y para fabricar este lazo, en que consiste su verdadera libertad, me he valido en los cuatro primeros capítulos de la dotrina de los estoicos' (*Q*, II. 77).

[62] *Q*, II. 86a/b. For the mirror as a symbol of *desengaño* and its use by Seneca, see Schulte, *El desengaño*, pp. 157–60.     [63] *Q*, II. 370 (my italics).

vergüenza que las oigan los hombres.'[64] While his exhortations to give up one's judgement and to rely solely on God's wisdom contradict Stoic rationalism and Senecan self-reliance, the advice not to pray for property, gold, honours, or revenge recalls the Stoical 'devaluation' of these 'externals' in chapters two and three. What is more, the succession of epigrammatic conceits that makes up much of this chapter—particularly the gloss on the hypocrite's version of the *Pater noster*, 'esta oración, donde está toda la retórica y dulzura y eficacia del cielo'—is, once more, reminiscent of the Senecan rhetoric imitated in *De los remedios de cualquier fortuna*.[65] The final paragraphs contain a masterly fusion of Stoical means directed towards a Christian end: 'en el temor de Dios empieza la sabiduría, crece el amor y se deshace el miedo de las demás cosas que nos hacen terribles las opiniones recibidas. . . . Tú, que a Dios te encaminas en todo, para ir a él fía dél solamente, y usa de las demás cosas sin hacer dellas más confianza de la que ellas dicen con sus fines y sucesos que merecen.'[66] The way to God begins with correct opinion.

The additions made by Quevedo to the *Doctrina moral* undoubtedly changed the balance of the work by bringing to the fore the ideas of repentance, Judgement, and salvation. However, if there were many clearly Christian features even in the professedly Stoical and sceptical chapters, Stoical overtones also run through the explicitly Christian additions to the early version. Probably through Senecan influence, the very title of *La cuna y la sepultura* transforms Job's wish (quoted on the engraved title-page in the earliest known editions) that he had been delivered straight from the womb to the tomb (Job 10: 19) into a general statement of *brevitas vitae* implying that man's only hope is to be found hereafter.[67] The three prayers added in *La cuna* to round off the

---

[64] See *Q*, II. 91b–92a. Cf. *Ep.* 10, 5: '"Tunc scito esse te omnibus cupiditatibus solutum, cum eo perveneris, ut nihil deum roges, nisi quod rogare possis palam." Nunc enim quanta dementia est hominum! Turpissima vota dis insusurrant; si quis admoverit aurem, conticescent.'

[65] See *Q*, II. 92b–93a. Quevedo has an even more satirical version of the *Pater noster* in his *Cartas del Caballero de la Tenaza* (*Q*, I. 454a). For the Erasmian source of the passage in *La cuna*, see A. Alatorre, 'Quevedo, Erasmo, y el doctor Constantino', *NRFH*, vii (1953), 681–3.

[66] *Q*, II. 93b.

[67] For the engraved title-page, see *CS*, plate facing p. xxxviii. Cf. *Ad Marc.* X. 5: 'mors enim illi denuntiata nascenti est; in hanc legem erat satus, hoc illum fatum ab utero statim prosequebatur.'

section *Cuna y vida* ask for deliverance from passions and ills and profess calm acceptance of the 'externals' poverty, illness, and death whenever God may think fit to send them:

Dame lo que sabes dar, quítame lo que no sé poseer. Si para asegurar las insolencias de mi maldad conviene ninguna hacienda, poca salud, corta vida, vengan de tu mano por tu misericordia la pobreza, la enfermedad y la muerte, y deje las lágrimas en la sepultura quien las estrenó en la cuna. . . . Te ruego que me guíes y defiendas de la maldad de mis apetitos, de la debilidad de mi naturaleza, de las insolencias de mi voluntad, de la malicia de los pecadores, del ejemplo de los malos, del poder de los tiranos, de la venganza de mis enemigos, de la invidia de los espíritus amotinados. . . .[68]

They also give the first hint that the Senecan paradox that life is part of death can be turned into the Christian one, developed in the section *Muerte y sepultura*, that life begins at death.

In view of the fact that the *Doctrina para morir*, added in *La cuna*, borrows heavily from Erasmus' *Praeparatio ad mortem*, it seems likely that the second section of the work as published in 1634 is to be identified with a *Prevención para la muerte* which Quevedo is known to have written, and was said to be about to publish, by 1632.[69] Whether or not it was originally intended as a sequel to the *Doctrina moral*, the *Doctrina para morir* has much in common with the work to which it was joined and, like the three prayers added in *La cuna*, it too contains Stoical ideas. Indeed its opening words—'Recelar decir a vuestra merced que se muere, es acusarle el discurso de hombre y negarle la razón. Bien claro se lo dijo el primer instante de su nacimiento. ¿Qué día se lo ha callado? ¿Qué hora, qué instante no ha sido cláusula con que el tiempo ha pronunciado a vuestra merced esta ley, que llama sentencia?'—are an ingenious variation on a passage in Seneca paraphrased in chapter four, and put forward the Senecan idea that death is a law, not a punishment.[70] There are echoes of Stoic fatalism in the *sententia*, 'Necedad es temer lo forzoso, y delito negar lo debido'; and, especially in the light of the early chapters of the work, it is difficult to read 'la hacienda se queda, la salud nos fatiga, la vida nos deja' without being reminded of the

[68] *Q*, II. 94a/b.
[69] See Juan Pérez de Montalván, *Para todos* . . . (Huesca, 1633), fol. 25ᵛ. The *Para todos* was first published in 1632. For the borrowings from Erasmus, see Alatorre, pp. 674 ff.
[70] *Q*, II. 94a. Cf. above, p. 86.

Stoic concept of 'externals'.[71] As for the passages taken from Erasmus, there can be little doubt that part of their attraction for Quevedo lay in the striking similarity in ideas and rhetorical forms of *De remediis fortuitorum* and Erasmus' altercation between the Devil and the dying man. It is curious to find that, ignoring Erasmus' advice not to enter into disputation with the Devil, he set out to gloss, among others, the Stoical themes of death, the end of worldly pleasures, and the loss of friends, wife, and children.[72] As the following example suggests, if many of his imitations of pseudo-Seneca Christianized Stoicism, several of his additions to Erasmus Senecanize Christianity:

<table>
<tr><td>La cuna</td><td>De los remedios</td></tr>
<tr><td>'Desdichada cosa es morir.'<br>Bienaventurados los que mueren en el Señor. En todo mientes; morir es descanso del cuerpo y justa restitución a la tierra de la parte que me ha prestado; es libertad del alma, que en cierta manera resucita. Tú me engañaste cuantas veces he creído que nací a vivir, pues en naciendo empecé la muerte. Hoy no me engañarás, que espero que muero para nacer a la que solamente es vida. (Q, II. 96b)</td><td>'Morirás.' No viviera con esperanza de descansar, si no esperara morir. (Q, II. 372a)<br>'Morirás lejos.' En todas partes mi cuerpo pisa la tierra y ve el cielo: a la una debo el cuerpo, y al otro el alma. ¿Cómo es posible que me aparte de mis acreedores? (Ibid. 372b)<br>'Morirás.' No hay otro camino para pasar a vida sin muerte. (Ibid. 372a)<br>'Morirás.' No dices bien; di que acabaré de morir, y acertarás, pues con la vida empecé la muerte. (Ibid. 371b)<br>'Morirás.' Si he vivido bien, empezaré a vivir; si mal, empezaré a morir. (Ibid. 371b–372a)</td></tr>
</table>

Although his answers to the Devil's attempt at making the dying man either despair of salvation or rely on the efficacy of his works alone are supported entirely by biblical and patristic authority, especially Peter Chrysologus, his style of argumentation is distinctly Senecan. Even the final gloss on the *Pater noster* contains reminiscences of *De remediis fortuitorum*.

Méndez Bejarano's statement that *La cuna* 'no pasa de exposición popular, siguiendo a Séneca, de la moral estoica, sazonada

---

[71] *Q*, II. 94b–95a. (*CS* has the apparent error 'tener' for 'temer'.)
[72] For Erasmus' advice, see *CS*, p. 184, note to line 86.

con referencias teológicas'[73] fails to bring out the relationship which exists between its Stoical and Christian elements. In his preface to *La cuna* addressed to the court preacher Fr. Cristóbal de Torres, Quevedo describes the moral philosophy of the Stoics as, apathy apart, 'en lo demás útil y eficaz y verdaderamente varonil y robusta, y que aun en la idolatría animó con esfuerzo hazañoso las virtudes morales: dotrina que en aquel siglo, que no había amanecido Jesucristo nuestro señor, Dios y hombre verdadero, tuvo por séquito las mayores almas que vivieron aquellas tinieblas.'[74] Neither here, nor even in the early version of the work itself, does he treat Stoicism as anything more than the nearest approximation arrived at by the ancients to the truth revealed in Christianity. As its function within the work makes clear, the philosophy of the Stoa, and especially that of Seneca, appealed to him first and foremost because he found it useful and efficacious. Like the 'scepticism' of chapter four, the Stoical ideas and arguments in *La cuna* serve the purpose of preparing the way for the Christian message to which the whole work is directed: the consolation depicted as attainable solely through knowledge of God, charity, faith in Providence, prayer, and obedience to the Roman Catholic Church.[75] In his petty, yet often perspicacious, satire on *La cuna*, Juan de Jáuregui makes the book describe itself, aptly, as a 'Devocionario'.[76] While nowhere in it is Stoicism presented as the philosophy to follow, the Christian attitudes to which it leads are themselves affected by Stoic thought. If, as has been claimed, the role allotted to the ethical books of the Bible and the absence, at least in the early version, of theological speculation and references to forms of worship and the sacraments are Erasmian,[77] these characteristics may also be seen as the result of a Stoicizing attitude to Christianity. As Juan Eusebio Nieremberg noted in his *aprobación*, in *La cuna* Quevedo made it seem that Epictetus had turned Spaniard and Seneca Christian.

---

[73] M. Méndez Bejarano, *Historia de la filosofía en España hasta el siglo XX* (Madrid, n.d.), p. 329.

[74] *Q*, II. 77.  [75] See *Q*, II. 93a/b.  [76] *El Retraído*, fol. 2ᵛ.

[77] See Rothe, *Quevedo und Seneca*, p. 103, and Blüher, *Seneca in Spanien*, p. 340. R. O. Jones, 'Some Notes on More's *Utopia* in Spain', *MLR*, xlv (1950), 480 ff., provides evidence that Quevedo (although he borrows from him in *La cuna*) was highly critical of Erasmus.

# V

## THE *VIRTUD MILITANTE*

### 1. *The Stoical–Christian Dilemma*

THE *Virtud militante* is made up of two parts: a critique of *Las cuatro pestes del mundo*—envy, ingratitude, pride, and avarice—and four epistles on death, poverty, scorn, and illness entitled *Las cuatro fantasmas de la vida*. Although they were not published until six years after their author's death, the four *Pestes* existed at least in a first draft by spring 1634; and at least the first three of the four *Fantasmas* had been written by the autumn of 1635.[1] That they were intended to form a single work is clear from the autograph manuscript in the Biblioteca Menéndez Pelayo. The first part of the work makes very clear just how delicately balanced Quevedo felt the rival attractions of classical and Christian authority to be. The four *Pestes* show him apparently attempting to break with the classics but, thanks to the *afición* for the Stoics to which he confessed in the *Doctrina estoica*, failing spectacularly to do so.

'Invidia', the first of the *Pestes*, begins with a scornful repudiation of pagan authority which comes as something of a shock after his earlier works: 'La Iglesia católica nos ha enriquecido con la doctrina de tantos santos padres y doctores, que no tenemos ocasión de mendigar enseñanza de los filósofos; mejor y más segura escuela es la de los santos.'[2] What follows, however, is far less startlingly unequivocal. Indeed, Seneca, the only pagan philosopher mentioned by name, is actually praised for his pithy *sententiae* and the concentrated wisdom of his philosophical writings more glowingly here than anywhere else in Quevedo's works. And, as in *La cuna y la sepultura*, what is stressed above all is his *agudeza*: 'Agudísimo y admirablemente docto fue Séneca; su estilo, con la brevedad de las sentencias, tiene obras de estrecho, que ciñe en pequeños espacios corrientes de profundos mares de

---

[1] See Ettinghausen, 'Acerca de las fechas', pp. 167–70.
[2] *Q*, II. 101a.

ciencia.'³ When, after alone being excepted from Quevedo's summary rejection of the classics, Seneca too is repudiated, it is noteworthy that Peter Chrysologus is named as the chief authority for the *Peste* on the grounds that he emulated the Stoic's 'dignidades de espíritu sublime, que fulmina con las razones, que hace hablar cada letra de por sí'.⁴ The first *Peste* is, in fact, little more than an extended gloss on passages taken from this Christian Seneca, whom, just as he frequently refers to 'nuestro Séneca' and even 'mi Séneca', Quevedo calls 'nuestro santo' and, on at least one occasion, 'mi santo'. However, although he adopts the saint's definition of envy, his commentary plays on the Stoic division of things. Having wittily defined the envious man as 'adúltero de los bienes, pues deja los propios por los ajenos', he gives as his remedy for envy 'ten tanto contentamiento de los bienes ajenos como de los propios; tanta misericordia de las calamidades de los otros como de las tuyas';⁵ and his remark, 'pocos juicios hay a prueba de prosperidades', implies the Senecan paradox, developed at length in *La constancia y paciencia del santo Job* and in *Providencia de Dios*, that good fortune is more to be feared than ill.⁶ Elsewhere he puts forward other propositions which, while not peculiarly Stoical, are no less paradoxical.⁷ Even in this first *Peste*, despite its initial wholesale rejection of the classics, he is overcome by the desire to add the weight of Antiquity to Christian doctrine. With the excuse 'porque oigan los redimidos con la sangre de Cristo cómo detestaron la invidia los idólatras', he proceeds to cite Plutarch, and, in what may well be an addition to an early version of the *Peste*, quotes a classical comparison of the envious with Etna.⁸

Early in the second *Peste*, 'Ingratitud', Quevedo again states his resolve to follow the 'más seguro camino' of the saints and

---

³ *Q*, II. 101a/b.      ⁴ *Q*, II. 101b.      ⁵ *Q*, II. 102b, 106b.
⁶ *Q*, II. 105a. Cf. Seneca, e.g. *Ep.* 66, 50 and 91, 4.
⁷ e.g. 'Ninguno invidia en otro la virtud; proposición que sacaré de paradoja, mostrando la verdad manifiesta' (*Q*, II. 102b); 'Muchos hombres hay invidiados de otros, y muchos que invidian a otros, y muchos más que se invidian a sí mismos. Parece esta invidia nuevamente hallada, y es la más antigua' (ibid.); and 'Poco he dicho en decir que el hombre es invidioso de sí mismo: oso afirmar que todo el hombre está compuesto de invidias' (*Q*, II. 103a).
⁸ *Q*, II. 105b, 106a. It seems probable that the original draft ended after the quotations from Augustine and Bonaventure, introduced with the remark: 'Rematen sagradamente mi antídoto a esta peste las soberanas plumas de san Agustín y de san Buenaventura' (*Q*, II. 105b).

Scripture at least 'en todo lo substancial'.[9] However, he borrows
the Stoic doctrine of correct opinion as the means whereby real
goods may be distinguished from those which only seem good,
identifying the Stoic concept of 'internals', as in *La cuna y la
sepultura*, with the Christian one of things which benefit the soul:

Conviene por esto, para ser verdaderamente agradecidos y para no
ser ingratos, conocer cuáles son bienes verdaderos, cuáles aparentes;
el mal que se disimula en algunos bienes, el bien que yace secreto en
algunos males; la felicidad que encierran las desdichas, y las desdichas
que ocultan las felicidades. . . . Ello es cierto que sólo son bienes y
beneficios los que enriquecen el alma y disponen el cuerpo a la obediencia
del espíritu.[10]

What is more, he treats Seneca as the undisputed authority on
benefits, and refers his readers to the philosopher himself rather
than risk misrepresenting his teachings: 'Séneca dice que las
riquezas ni las honras no son beneficio, sino señales visibles por
donde se conocen los beneficios, los cuales están radicalmente en
la intención del que los da. En esta materia mejor es remitirme a
Séneca que desaliñar su doctrina con mis palabras.'[11] Not only
does he adopt the Stoic's definition of a benefit, but he also takes
over from him the notion that, as far as giving benefits is concerned,
wild beasts are superior to man;[12] and his demonstration that
Christ's incarnation is the supreme instance of a benefit is introduced by the statement, again reminiscent of Seneca, that God,
the supreme benefactor, bestows his gifts upon the wicked and the
righteous alike.[13] Other ideas which seem to have been inspired
by *De beneficiis* are: that the ungrateful are the first to complain
of ingratitude in others, that ingratitude is an essential ingredient
of all other vices, and that (in the form of greedy heirs) ingratitude plagues even the dead.[14] However, all Quevedo's examples of
man's ingratitude are biblical, not, he tells his readers, because he

[9] *Q*, II. 108a.
[10] *Q*, II. 109b. See above, p. 76.
[11] *Q*, II. 110a. Cf. *De benef.* I. v. 6, I. vi. 2. Quevedo's only qualification—
'Sólo añadiré que no puede ser beneficio, aunque lo agradezca el que lo recibe,
aquella dádiva que sirve al apetito o al pecado'—is a point made also by Seneca
(*De benef.* II. xiv).
[12] See *Q*, II. 108b–109a. Cf. *De benef.* I. ii. 5. Quevedo changes Seneca's
example of the elephant to a serpent in order to make it conform to the passage
he cites in support from Psalm 90: 13.
[13] See *Q*, II. 111a. Cf. *De benef.*, esp. IV. xxviii.
[14] See *Q*, II. 115b–116a. Cf. *De benef.* III. i. 1, I. x. 4, IV. xx. 3.

despises classical authors, but because the true doctrine of benefits was only revealed in Christianity:

Esta doctrina, en razón de los beneficios, siempre estuvo remontada de la mente de los filósofos; por eso no los nombro en este tratado, no porque los desprecio para él, sino porque no los hallo en él. Algunos crepúsculos desta luz se divisan en mi Séneca, algunos en el doctísimo Campano; empero participan debilidad de la voz humana: son luz dudosa; aquí solamente amanece colmada de divinidad, sin confinar con las sombras de la noche.[15]

If none of the ancients was capable of perceiving the light of Christian teaching, 'mi Séneca' at least saw as much of it as was possible for a pagan to see.

When, at the outset of 'Soberbia', the third *Peste*, Quevedo seeks again to define his position *vis-à-vis* the classics, he appears at first to be in agreement with the opinion he cites from Chrysologus that, in view of the superiority of Christianity, the pagan philosophers may safely be dispensed with: 'Teniendo por sospechosa toda la doctrina de los filósofos, me valdré de las sacrosantas escrituras y de los santos padres, sabiendo que, como en aquéllos hay algo bueno, en éstos no hay algo que no lo sea.'[16] However, his quarrel is not with those who make use of the classics but with those who do so to the exclusion of Christian authority, 'aquéllos que para la verdad cristiana *solamente se valen de doctrinas de idólatras*, mal guarecidas de su contagio, y dejan las que, aseguradas en el Espíritu Santo, o establece por canónicas la Iglesia en los dos Testamentos, o aprueba en la santidad iluminada de los padres.'[17] Furthermore, noting that the Fathers themselves often cite 'los grandes filósofos', he states that he, too, may from time to time cite the classics in order to teach bad Christians that even pagans who lacked the benefit of Christian doctrine were better than they.

Given Quevedo's admiration here and elsewhere for 'mi gran Pedro Crisólogo', his comments on the passage he cites from this Christian Seneca (as he was established in the first *Peste*) are most revealing. In the passage in question the saint says of those philosophers—obviously the Stoics—who spoke of the goodness of death that, although they managed to overcome their feelings,

---

[15] *Q*, II. 117a. For Campano, author of *De ingratitudine fugienda*, see *Q*, II. 108 n. (a).

[16] *Q*, II. 118a.    [17] *Q*, II. 118b (my italics).

they could provide no hope of eternal life. After citing a selection of Senecan arguments against fear of death which were more than familiar to our author, he concludes: 'Sed haec talia cum dixerint, dicunt totum de sententia, non de vita.'[18] Translating 'sententia' by 'agudeza' and identifying the 'sentencias' cited by Chrysologus as 'literales de Séneca', Quevedo proceeds to take one of his favourite Christian Fathers to task for what he regards as an attack on his favourite philosopher. In Seneca's defence Quevedo develops three arguments: that the saint does not oppose him in 'lo sólido de la moral'; that, in order to spare the Stoic's good name, Chrysologus attributed the Senecan arguments vaguely to the ancients in general; and that Seneca and Epictetus were not just any pagans but, as we have seen he says in the note to his translation of Epistle 41, were influenced by the apostles and the first martyrs:

> Séneca y Epicteto, que vivieron en tiempo de los apóstoles, y veían las hazañas de la fe de los cristianos y la perfección de la vida, y que la daban al fuego y al cuchillo, no sólo con valentía, sino con gozo enamorado, confaccionaron [*sic*] con lo que veían lo que escribieron; de tal manera, que su doctrina, con resabios de aquella atención, es en muchas cosas bien parecida a nuestra verdad: tuvieron por maestros en la primitiva Iglesia a los mártires, y oyeron la doctrina de sus triunfos.[19]

Having turned his repudiation of pagan authority into a spirited defence of Seneca and Epictetus, Quevedo resolves to follow Chrysologus and to 'desconfiar de los filósofos'. Yet, although he bases much in the *Peste* on 'mi Santo, que con cada palabra excede en precio todas las doctrinas de los filósofos',[20] he eventually quotes from both Juvenal and Seneca.[21]

Seneca's name had been brought to his mind by the passage recounting Nero's persecution of the Christians which he had quoted from Pope Leo I. This had turned his thoughts back to the comments he had made earlier on the inspiration derived by the Stoic from Christian example. Now he declares that Seneca's motive in writing his philosophical works was to counter Nero's evil influence. In particular, he holds that Seneca addressed *De ira*

---

[18] Sermon CI (Migne, *Patrologia Latina*, LII. 482B). Seneca himself refers to this type of charge in *Ep*. 24, 15.

[19] *Q*, II. 119a.             [20] *Q*, II. 120a.

[21] See *Q*, II. 127a. The passages from Seneca are *De ira*, II. xxi. 1, III. iii. 1.

to his brother Novatus (the Gallio to whom *De remediis fortuitorum* is dedicated), in order to disguise the fact that it was intended as criticism of the proud and irate emperor; and he considers that the dedication of *De clementia* to Nero was an 'estratagema muchas veces bien lograda, para reprehender a los monarcas, alabarlos de lo que no hacen ni tienen ni quieren'. As for the remainder of the Stoic's writings, 'todas fueron antídotos para defender los ánimos opresos de los romanos, de tan inhumana opresión . . . todas son medicina a la tolerancia de las últimas calamidades.'[22] Seneca was inspired by resistance to the same angry pride which sent early Christians to martyrdom.

In 'Avaricia', the last of the four *Pestes*, although he takes his definition of avarice from 'la escuela escolástica', Quevedo begins his attack on the vice itself by borrowing Senecan arguments previously used by him in *La cuna y la sepultura*: 'al avaro tanto le falta lo que tiene como lo que no tiene . . . él no tiene la hacienda, sino la hacienda a él', and he cites the Senecan *exemplum* of Euripides' character whose praise of wealth roused an audience to righteous indignation.[23] However, although he later refers to the myth of Midas and paraphrases an epigram to prove that the ancients 'no ignoraron que los avarientos morían ahorcados', he also declares that 'para salir bien de todo conviene no salir del Evangelio sacrosanto' and, commenting on a passage from Chrysologus, asks: '¿En cual filósofo se pudo hallar rastro de tan alta doctrina?'[24] In this, as in the previous *Pestes*, he appears to be equally attracted by two contradictory ideas: the first, that Christian authors have no need to go begging to the ancients; the second, that what all Christians ought to know was already common knowledge among the best of the pagans. His remarkable string of contradictory statements on the value of classical authority in moralizing literature suggests that, perfectly aware as he was that more than enough for his purposes had been written on the subjects of the *Pestes* by Christian authors, he was unable to bring himself to abandon at least his favourite classical writers. In particular, despite his efforts to persuade himself that Seneca is 'perfected' in Chrysologus, he praises the Stoic in every one of the *Pestes*, and quotes from his works in all but the first. In the

[22] *Q*, II. 127a.
[23] *Q*, II. 130a, 130b. Cf. above, p. 78, and *Ep*. 115, 14–15.
[24] *Q*, II. 132a, 133b, 134a.

letter to the Duke of Medinaceli in which he refers to what was probably his final draft of the four *Pestes*, he claimed that they were written 'sin valerme en ellos de otra cosa que de las Sagradas Escrituras y santos padres, y teología escolástica'.[25] The fact that, in spite of his efforts to make it so, this statement is not strictly true implies that his attempts at synthesizing classical and Christian thought involved the reconciliation of rival claims. However, Quevedo was not the only Spaniard of his time who felt that it was wrong to yield to Seneca's appeal as moralist and stylist to the exclusion of Christian writers: Gracián protested against the kind of affectation criticized by Quevedo at the beginning of the third *Peste*: 'Comenzaba el otro afectado su sermón por un lugar de Séneca, como si no hubiera San Pablos . . . dejando la sólida y sustancial doctrina, y aquel verdadero modo de predicar del Boca de Oro, y de la Ambrosía dulcísima y del néctar provechoso del gran prelado de Milán.'[26] While sharing this view, Quevedo was obviously as powerfully attracted by Seneca as any *afectado*.

## 11. *Seneca and the Four* Fantasmas

The four *Fantasmas* which make up the second part of the *Virtud militante* are not, as one critic has claimed, arms provided by God to combat the *Pestes*.[27] As has recently been pointed out, in his translation of chapter four of the *Manual* El Brocense used 'fantasma', 'imaginación', and 'fantasía' to render the Stoic term φαντασία.[28] In *Epicteto español* Quevedo takes over from El Brocense both 'fantasía' and 'fantasma', and declares in *Providencia de Dios*: 'Lo que se llama fantasma o fantasía es la imaginación.'[29] In the *Fantasmas* he sets out to teach the correct opinion of things whose appearance has been distorted by the imagination. If their title is inspired, apparently, by Epictetus, the letter-form in which they are written is reminiscent of Seneca's Epistles.

We have already seen that the first *Fantasma* was prompted by a request to clarify the interpretation of Stoic apathy in the *Doctrina estoica*.[30] It develops, however, into an attempt to do for his reader

[25] *EQ*, p. 376.          [26] Baltasar Gracián, *El Criticón*, III. x.
[27] See J. Juderías, *Don Francisco de Quevedo Villegas: la época, el hombre, las doctrinas* (Madrid, 1922), p. 212.
[28] See Blüher, *Seneca in Spanien*, p. 288.          [29] *Q*, II. 183a.
[30] See above, p. 36.

what Quevedo claims love of God did for the martyrs, and there is no question here of his doing without Senecan *agudeza*. Indeed, the *Fantasma* has many parallels with *De los remedios de cualquier fortuna, La cuna y la sepultura*, and Quevedo's consolatory letter to Antonio de Mendoza on the death of a friend.[31] The only quotation in the second half of the *Fantasma* is a passage from Seneca which had twice been paraphrased in *La cuna y la sepultura*, and is one of three quotations from the Stoic in the letter to Mendoza.[32] However, while the notion of immortality is strong in the letter, in the *Fantasma* it is almost lost amid the welter of Senecan polemics against fear of death. Above all, like the first chapter of *La cuna y la sepultura*, the *Fantasma* imprints upon its readers the idea of *miseria hominis* by an accumulation of *conceptista* variations on Seneca's equation of life with death:

| *Virtud militante* | *La cuna* |
|---|---|
| ¡Oh miseria humana, no sólo fugitiva, sino instantánea e invidiosa de algún momento de reposo y consuelo; que si llegas, te vas; que si pasas, no vuelves; que antes de venir molestas; venida huyes, y pasada no tornas! Vivimos tiempo, sin poder decir cuál antes que se pase, sin poder decir cuánto antes que se acabe. En un propio instante se vive y se muere. Ninguno puede vivir sin morir, porque todos vivimos muriendo. (*Q*, II. 138a) | A la par empiezas a nacer y a morir, y no es en tu mano detener las horas . . . Antes empiezas a morir que sepas qué cosa es vida . . . (*Q*, II. 79b) |
| Ninguno se ha quejado de no haber sido tantos siglos antes que naciese, y todos se quejan de dejar de ser despuésde haber sido . . . (Ibid. 138a) | Vuelve los ojos, si piensas que eres algo, a lo que eras antes de nacer; y hallarás que no eras, que es la última miseria. Mira que eres el que ha poco que no fuiste, y el que siendo eres poco, y el que de aquí a poco no serás . . . (Ibid. 80a) |
| ¿Qué codicia el hombre en la vida más larga, sino más muerte? Cada día que pasó fue enfermedad del que ha de venir, y en cada día que vive, cuenta tantas enfermedades | En ninguna cosa tienes segura salud; y es necedad buscarla, pues no puede dejar de estar enfermo quien siempre en su misma vida tiene mal de muerte. Con este |

31 For the Stoical ideas in this letter (*EQ*, pp. 253–60), see Blüher, pp. 343–7.
32 See *Q*, II. 138b. Cf. above, p. 86, and *Ep*. 101, 1.

mal incurables como horas, tantos pasos hacia la muerte como instantes. Todo le es maestro para este desengaño, y siempre será rudo dicípulo de las aves y animales, que murieron para darle sustento, de las que murieron para darle abrigo. (*Q*, II. 138b)

Pues ¿cómo llamo vida una vejez que es sepulcro, donde yo propio soy entierro de cinco difuntos que he vivido? ¿Por qué, pues, deseré vivir sepultura de mi propia muerte, y no desearé acabar de ser entierro de mi misma vida? (Ibid. 138b)

¿Quién desde que tiene razón no desea pasar de unas edades a otras? ¿Quién no desea que a la edad varonil no se añada la vejez? De manera que todos deseamos llegar a viejos, y todos negamos que hemos llegado. Queremos que se alargue la vejez y tememos la muerte, y cuando estamos peleando con ella, la rehusamos, y antes se padece que se cree. Tememos que vendrá la que no tememos habiendo venido. La vida es toda muerte o locura; y pasamos la mayor parte de la muerte, que es toda la vida, riendo, y gemimos un solo instante della, que es la postrera boqueada. (Ibid. 139a)

No se puede aprender la doctrina de la muerte, de los muertos, porque no tenemos con ellos comercio los vivos. Hase de pedir a los viejos, que vivos, todo el tráfigo de sus personas le tienen con la muerte. (Ibid. 139a/b)

naces, con él vives, y dél mueres. (*Q*, II. 79b)

¿Qué yerbecilla, qué animalejo, qué piedra, qué tierra, qué elemento no es parte o de tu sustento, abrigo, reposo o hospedaje? (Ibid. 79b)

¿Tú piensas que pasan en balde los días? Pues dígote que no hay hora que pase por ti, que no vaya sacando tierra de tu sepultura. (Ibid. 85a)

Tú temes la muerte, y tu mayor deseo es que se llegue. ¿Quiéreslo ver? ¿En qué otra cosa gastas la vida que en desear, siendo niño, verte mancebo y que llegue el tiempo de verte mayor, y luego de verte hombre? . . . ¿De qué sirve pues huir de lo que deseas, y temer el llegar adonde a toda diligencia caminas y te llevas a ti mismo? ¿Por qué tienes miedo a la última obra de naturaleza? Lo menos de la muerte temes, que es aquel punto, y lo más della (que fue toda tu vida) pasaste riendo. (Ibid. 85a)

Trata con los afligidos y estudia con ellos, comunica a los solos; oye a los muertos, por quien hablan el escarmiento y el desengaño . . . (Ibid. 90b)

'Pobreza', the second of the four *Fantasmas*, consists chiefly of glosses on passages in the Scriptures and the Fathers and on events in the life of Christ. Throughout, paradoxical *conceptista* arguments abound again. Quevedo cites Croesus and Tantalus as

paradoxical examples of poverty in wealth, sets out to prove
the truth of the 'paradoja . . . que todos nacen más pobres que
mueren', and contests the popular division of worldly things into
'unos muebles y otros raices' by contending that the only immovable goods are those provided by God.[33] Indeed, while a
large part of the *Fantasma* is given over to exhorting the miserly
rich to perform Christian charity, it relies from the beginning
on the Stoical-Christian paradox that the only true riches are
those of the soul: 'Novedad tiene mi estudio en este discurso.
He aprendido qué cosa sea la pobreza de las ansias de los ricos,
y lo que es la riqueza de la paz de los pobres.'[34] Many specifically
Senecan arguments against the 'common-sense' view of poverty
in the *Fantasma* recall similar arguments in *De los remedios de
cualquier fortuna* and *La cuna y la sepultura*:

| *Virtud militante* | *De los remedios* and *La cuna* |
|---|---|
| Al opulento, a pesar de lo que tiene, le hace mendigo lo que desea; porque no se juzga rico el que tiene mucho, si no lo tiene todo. Cierto es que nadie puede en este mundo tenerlo todo, empero despreciarlo todo puede cualquiera. (*Q*, II. 140a) | 'Soy pobre.' De lo necesario ninguno es pobre; de lo supérfluo ninguno es rico. 'Soy pobre.' Nadie lo puede tener todo, y cualquiera lo puede despreciar, para tenerlo todo. (*Q*, II. 376a) |
| Con lo necesario ruega la naturaleza; lo supérfluo no es caudal, sino demasía; no es hacienda, sino carga. . . . Hacienda que da codicia de más hacienda, no es más hacienda, sino más codicia. Lo mucho se vuelve poco con desear otro poco más. (Ibid. 145b) | Ves . . . gran cantidad de hacienda y posesiones . . . dime ¿qué otra cosa es eso que desigual carga al que aun desnudo camina cargado de sí propio? (Ibid. 82a) Epicuro dijo: Si quieres ser rico, no añadas dinero, quita codicia. (Ibid. 376a) ¿Ves cómo la hacienda es pobreza, pues siempre tiene con necesidad de más al que más tiene? (Ibid. 376b) |
| Si te afliges porque tu aposentillo no es grande palacio, considera cuánto espacio dél sobra a tu persona y dejas desocupado, y le darás gracias por lo que te sobra, y | Si tuvieras muchos cuerpos y tu grandeza te necesitara de mayores espacios, perdonárate los sentimientos; mas siendo uno solo, tal, que no hay aposento tan estrecho |

---

[33] See *Q*, II. 141b (Croesus), 142a/b, 146b (Tantalus).
[34] *Q*, II. 140a.

no quejas por lo que te falta.
(*Q*, II. 146a)

adonde no sobre habitación, ¿qué envidias y qué lamentas? (*Q*, II. 82a)

Verdad es que el pobre no tiene aduladores, empero tiene ocasión de serlo; no teme ladrones, empero témenle por ladrón. De todo esto se asegura el pobre que está contento de serlo. (Ibid. 146b)

¿Con qué agradecerás a la pobreza el hacerte exento de aduladores...? ...Tan seguro estarás de ladrones, que antes te temerán por testigo y huirán de ti por estorbo, que te acecharán por el provecho. (Ibid. 82b)

Nació el mendigo pobre...Enterráronle los ascos del olfato, los melindres de la vista, los horrores de la imaginación, si faltó caridad en los vecinos. (Ibid. 147a)

'Carecerás de sepultura.' Cuando lo ordene la inhumanidad, no lo consentirán la vista y el olfato de los vivos. (Ibid. 373a/b)

The delight Quevedo took in working out rhetorical variations upon Senecan *sententiae* is self-evident.

Although Seneca is not actually named in this *Fantasma*, other classical authors are cited in order to prove that on the question of poverty 'de tanto bien comunicó Dios algunas vislumbres a los gentiles', 'alcanzaron esta piadosísima verdad los gentiles', and 'en la gentilidad, hasta los poetas pusieron en el infierno al rico avariento'.[35] In the first case, however, having quoted Xenophon's view that those who need least goods are closest to God, Quevedo introduces Christ's injunction to the rich man to give all he had to the poor with the remark, 'Evangelicemos pues esta vislumbre'. Another example of 'evangelization' is his ingenious linking of Christ's temptation by the Devil with one of his favourite passages from Epicurus cited by Seneca.[36] After Christ, his chief exemplar of the right attitude to the goods of this world is Job, 'el ejemplo del buen pobre y del buen rico', who held the correct opinion of all things.[37] Thanks to his proto-Stoic wisdom, despite his misfortunes Job could not be robbed of his most precious possessions, 'de su paciencia, de su desengaño, de su constancia ni de su verdad.'[38]

The first half of the third *Fantasma*, 'Desprecio', is a *tour de force* of *conceptista* satire on hypocritical self-scorners, especially

---

[35] *Q*, II. 142b, 143a, 146b.
[36] See the passage ending 'Lo propio es dar a uno piedras, para que teniendo hambre se harte, que darle oro si desea ser rico, para que no sea pobre; siendo así que para enriquecer no es el remedio añadir dinero, sino quitar codicia' (*Q*, II. 140b). Cf. *Ep*. 21, 7.     [37] *Q*, II. 147b.     [38] *Q*, II. 148b.

flatterers. In the second half, however, Quevedo turns to 'verdadero y santo desprecio', and teaches that scorn is a question of
correct opinion: 'Por esto muchos desprecios son estimación, y
muchas estimaciones desprecios. Muda sus nombres el sentimiento
vulgar, que ni sabe lo que precia ni lo que desestima.'[39] While
he quotes several passages from Paul's Epistles, his examples of
both right and wrong attitudes are all classical. Commenting on
Claudian's despair at seeing the righteous scorned, he contends
that they have much to be thankful for.[40] Later he cites the 'grandes
y doctas palabras' and 'muy ponderada enseñanza' of Lucan's
praise of Amiclas and gives the example of Sulla's scorn for
Caesar, justified not when the latter was weak but when, having
gained supreme power, 'se precipitó en el más vil y sangriento
desprecio.'[41] His final example of the right attitude to worldly
honour, and the one he clearly admires most, is neither Christ
nor Job, but Scipio, an *exemplum* quoted from 'el grande Séneca'
and whose imitation he recommends: 'Scipión defendió su patria
peleando, y se defendió de su patria huyendo. A generosa y bien
sana imitación nos convida. Seamos despreciados, y viviremos
seguros. Despreciemos cuantas cosas nos quisieren hacer orgullo
nuestro desprecio; despreciemos a nosotros propios, no empero
despreciemos a alguno'.[42]

The *Fantasma* most directly influenced by Seneca is the last,
'Enfermedad'. Not only is the entire epistle a gloss on Seneca's
consolation for three hardships endured by the sick—fear of
death, pain, and the interruption of pleasures—but even its
dedication to a bishop whose constancy in illness had impressed
Quevedo is inspired by the Stoic's reflections on the fortitude
of the dying Aufidius Bassus.[43] Before proceeding to deal with the
hardships of illness enumerated by Seneca, however, the author of
the *Sueños* adds a further hardship—the unpleasantness and
expense of doctors and medicines—which he treats largely by

[39] *Q*, II. 153b. Earlier Quevedo had said: 'Afean el desprecio los malos
nombres con que le infaman los ambiciosos' (*Q*, II. 150a).

[40] See *Q*, II. 152a.

[41] *Q*, II. 153b.

[42] *Q*, II. 154a. Quevedo cites *Ep.* 86, 1, the source of his sonnets in praise of
Scipio (see *OP*, I. 431) and Osuna (p. 425).

[43] See *Q*, II. 154b–155a. Cf. *Ep.* 30. Quevedo's *Fantasma* is inspired by *Ep.*
78. A. Rothe, 'Quevedo und seine Quellen', *RF*, lxxvii (1965), 338–43, shows
that almost all the other classical authorities in 'Enfermedad' were lifted from
Stobaeus.

recourse to Senecan arguments. Doctors and medicines are of
no use to a life which is an illness from start to finish; health,
like wealth, cannot be enjoyed unless it is spent; doctors are super-
fluous if one follows the (Stoic) precept to 'seguir la naturaleza';
and they are powerless to hold up the process by which life leads
remorselessly to death.[44] The satirist of the *Sueños* can be heard
clearly in the comparison of doctors with executioners: 'Si los
ajusticiados hubieran podido dar la honra a sus ministros como
el interés, la brida del esparto no invidiara a la de las mulas.'[45]
As consolation for the 'hardship' of doctors and medicines, he
asserts, first, that fear of them promotes temperate living, noting
wittily that 'Sólo el hombre sabe lo que le hace mal, y sólo al
hombre le sabe bien lo que le hace mal', and, secondly, that lack
of faith in medicine encourages 'desengaño de nuestra fragilidad,
para prevención de nuestra conciencia'.[46] Later, when he paraphrases a passage from Seneca, he introduces both doctors and
medicines into the argument of 'el grande Español' that death is
the ultimate remedy for man's ills.[47]

When he turns to fear of death, the first hardship in illness
mentioned by Seneca, Quevedo predictably employs the Senecan
arguments that death is natural, inevitable, implicit in life, and
brought closer by gluttony, lechery, cupidity, revenge, and
gambling. As always, he displays a remarkable facility for imitating
the pointed *sententiae* he admired in the Stoic. Commenting on
Aristotle's definition of fear as the imagining of a future ill, he
argues, like Seneca, that death is neither an ill nor future, that it is
better to live well than long, and that death does not go by age.[48]
After citing the 'consuelo sagrado y verdadero' of Christian
authors, he turns his attention fully to Seneca. Quoting the
Stoic's lyrical description in Epistle 79 of the soul's return to
heaven, he takes it as evidence, not merely that Seneca was
unequivocal about immortality, but that 'en partes habla con
sentimiento casi católico'. What is more, he maintains that the
Stoic's words are so devout that they would constitute proof of

---

[44] See *Q*, II. 155a–156b. Quevedo's 'hardship', doctors and medicines, may
have been inspired by the reference to doctors in *Ep*. 78, 5.

[45] *Q*, II. 155b. Cf. *De los remedios*: '"Degollaránte." Lo mismo hace con
infinitos la medicina con sangrías en la cama, que el verdugo con algunos en
el cadahalso' (*Q*, II. 372a).

[46] *Q*, II. 157a.    [47] See *Q*, II. 158a. Cf. *Nat. Quaest*. VI. xxxii. 12.

[48] See *Q*, II. 157b–158a.

the authenticity of the correspondence between Seneca and Paul, were its style not so unlike that of its supposed authors. To confirm Seneca's belief in immortality he quotes from the letter cited at the end of the third *Fantasma* Seneca's conviction that Scipio's soul had returned to heaven, whence it had first come.[49] But the most unambiguous evidence that Quevedo's commitment to the Stoa was as strong as ever in the mid 1630s is to be seen in his outspoken defence of Seneca against Tertullian. Quoting the only reference to the Stoic in the latter's *De resurrectione carnis* — 'Ait et Seneca, omnia post mortem finiri, etiam ipsam'—he declares that the Father's reading of these words as a denial of immortality was mistaken and that, on the contrary, Seneca's words imply belief in the immortality of the soul:

No coligió bien Tertuliano contra nuestro Séneca, pues necesaria-mente de aquellas palabras se colige que Séneca afirmó la inmortalidad del alma y otra vida; pues si todo lo mortal se acaba con la muerte, y la misma muerte, forzoso es que se acabe con nueva vida y con nacer de nuevo a vida eterna. Lenguaje es sacrosanto matar la muerte, y ser muerte de la muerte. Cristo nuestro Señor la dió muerte con su vida, para que viviésemos sin temerla.[50]

Quevedo's interpretation is only 'necessary' if one assumes, as he does, that 'si . . . se acaba . . . la misma muerte, forzoso es que se acabe con nueva vida': whether Seneca ever made any such assumption he does not stop to consider, let alone argue. However, in what would seem to be an attempt to show that Seneca's views on the relationship between body and soul coincided with those of Christianity, he cites for the benefit of those who hate the Stoic for being a Spaniard or envy him for being so admirable his contention that death is identical with the state preceding birth, a view which in itself, of course, does not necessarily imply belief in immortality any more than the words cited by Tertullian.[51]

When he turns to Seneca's second hardship of illness, physical pain, Quevedo quotes virtually the whole of his model's treatment of the topic and makes a point of the fact that he is doing so: 'Hasta aquí son palabras de Séneca. Dígolo porque las he tradu-cido; que si no, fuera locura persuadirme que ellas no se daban

---

[49] See *Q*, II. 158b. Cf. *Ep*. 86, 1.
[50] *Q*, II. 159a. Cf. Migne, *Patrologia Latina*, II. 841B. The passage cited by Tertullian is *Troades*, v. 395.    [51] See *Q*, II. 159a.

a conocer entre mis borrones.'[52] His insistence on the fact that the
passage preceding these words is translated from Seneca—he had
introduced it with 'Séneca dice'—seems intended to draw attention to his ability as a translator of Seneca and to the similarity
between the Stoic's style and his own. Indeed, with the statement
'Atreveréme a decir algo, no añadiendo a Séneca, sino imitándole'
he recalls his sustained attempt at copying Senecan style in *De
los remedios de cualquier fortuna*. Much of his argumentation against
this hardship of illness and the last (interruption of pleasures) is
in fact paraphrased from the epistle upon which the entire
*Fantasma* is modelled:

No es posible no sentir los males,
mas es fácil sufrirlos y es gloria
vencerlos. Un nervezuelo en una
muela podrida triunfa del sufrimiento y de la paciencia y fortaleza
de un hombre, y le disfama la boca
con quejas, y los ojos con lágrimas,
y el rostro con visajes mujeriles.
(*Q*, II. 160a)

Toto contra ille pugnet animo;
vincetur, si cesserit, vincet, si se
contra dolorem suum intenderit.
(*Ep*. 78, 15)
'Dolorem gravem sentio.' Quid
ergo? Non sentis, si illum mulie-
briter tuleris? (Ibid. 78, 17)

¿Piensa el hombre que porque en
la cama no hace alguna cosa está
ocioso? Engáñase; que la cama
con la enfermedad es teatro para
ostentar las fuerzas del alma y las
del cuerpo. Sus batallas tiene el
lecho, y sus hazañas la dolencia.
Si el hombre luchando con los
dolores los vence, más es buen
soldado que mal enfermo; si
agradece al mal la intermisión de
los deleites, gloriosa victoria ad-
quiere su alma; gran valentía es
luchar bien con la calentura y
demás accidentes: si no te fuerzan,
si no te afligen, si no te derriban,
grande y provechoso ejemplo eres.
¡Oh si los enfermos tuvieran
auditorio y aplauso, cuán grande
ocasión de gloria fuera estar
enfermo! Voz es de Séneca: 'No
te vea alguno, nadie te atienda,
mírate tú a ti propio, tú te alaba.'
(Ibid. 160b–161a)

'Sed nihil', inquit, 'agere sinit
morbus, qui me omnibus abduxit
officiis.' Corpus tuum valetudo
tenet, non et animum. Itaque
cursoris moratur pedes, sutoris aut
fabri manus inpediet; si animus
tibi esse in usu solet, suadebis
docebis, audies disces, quaeres
recordaberis. Quid porro? Nihil
agere te credis, si temperans aeger
sis? Ostendes morbum posse
superari vel certe sustineri. Est,
mihi crede, virtuti etiam in lectu-
lo locus. Non tantum arma et acies
dant argumenta alacris animi in-
domitique terroribus; et in vesti-
mentis vir fortis apparet. Habes,
quod agas: bene luctare cum morbo.
Si nihil te coegerit, si nihil exo-
raverit, insigne prodis exemplum.
O quam magna erat gloriae materia, si spectaremur aegri! Ipse te
specta, ipse te lauda. (Ibid. 78,
20–1)

---

[52] *Q*, II. 160a. Cf. *Ep*. 78, 7–10.

Llámase desdichado el enfermo, y crece su mal con sus lamentos, porque en el verano, con los hielos entretenidos a pesar del calor, no bebe copiosamente en julio la condición del invierno; porque no bebe los vinos que con la peregrinación han adquirido mayor fuerza y precio; porque no ve en su mesa los ostiones y marisco que la gula fue a buscar entre las ondas, que la golosina descerraja de las clausuras de sus conchas; porque no puede ser pródigo de su vida a persuasión de la miseria de su lujuria. ¡Oh malaventurado enfermo, que lloras la falta de aquellas cosas mismas por quien sientes la falta de tu salud propia! (*Q*, II. 161a)

'O infelicem aegrum!' Quare? Quia non vino nivem diluit? Quia non rigorem potionis suae, quam capaci scypho miscuit, renovat fracta insuper glacie? Quia non ostrea illi Lucrina in ipsa mensa aperiuntur? . . . Hoc enim iam luxuria commenta est: ne quis intepescat cibus, ne quid palato iam calloso parum ferveat, cenam culina prosequitur. . . . Cenabis tamquam aeger, immo aliquando tamquam sanus. (*Ep.* 78, 23–4)

Towards the end of the *Fantasma* Quevedo puts forward Job's fortitude as the correct attitude towards illness and, here too, links him with the Stoa. Whereas in the *Doctrina estoica* and the preface to *La cuna y la sepultura* he had connected Job with Zeno and Epictetus, Quevedo now contends that Seneca, too, learned from the proto-Stoic: 'Job nos verifica lo que de Séneca hemos referido, y Séneca me persuado lo aprendió de Job.'[53] Job's constancy, illustrated by passages from Job 6: 24 and 16: 13–18, is presented as the source of Seneca's Epistle 78.

In the last chapter we saw how in *La cuna y la sepultura* Quevedo built up to a note of Stoicizing Christianity by means of Stoical and sceptical arguments. In his consolatory letter to Antonio de Mendoza, in order to depreciate life and thereby lessen the terrors of death, he likewise employed an amalgam of Stoic and Christian authorities and ideas.[54] The prayer for the liberation of the soul from the shackles of the body at the end of that letter is followed by a brief commentary in which he does not, as might be expected after the prayer, stress man's sinfulness but, yet again, the *miseria* of life's brevity. The *Virtud militante* ends on a similarly Stoical–Christian note, a gloss on Christ's words on the Cross in which the dying Christian is to address Christ in the following terms:

[53] *Q*, II. 161a/b.
[54] See *EQ*, pp. 253–60, and Blüher, *Seneca in Spanien*, pp. 343–7.

Y pues veo que mueres, siendo vida, ¿por qué temeré morir, siendo muerte? Si te veo desnudo y pobre, siendo señor de todo, ¿por qué temeré la pobreza, siendo nada? Si te veo despreciado, siendo Hijo de Dios, ¿por qué, yo, concebido en pecado, temeré el desprecio? Si te veo herido por muchas partes, y que desde la planta del pie hasta la cima de la cabeza no hay sanidad en tu cuerpo, y que no hay dolor como tu dolor, ¿por qué yo, gusano vilísimo, temeré el dolor de la enfermedad? Nada temeré sino mis pecados y tu justicia, mas de tal manera la temeré, que de ti, ofendido como juez, me ampare como hijo.[55]

If the Passion provides the most outstanding example of constancy in the face of adversity, the way to overcome incorrect opinion of the 'externals' treated in each of the *Fantasmas* is imitation of Christ. As before in *La cuna y la sepultura*, what in theory seemed to Quevedo to be a classical-Christian dilemma is resolved in practice into a Stoic–Christian synthesis.

[55] *Q*, II. 163b.

# VI

## LA CONSTANCIA DE JOB
## AND PROVIDENCIA DE DIOS

### 1. Job and the Senecan Tests of Fortune

TWO more posthumous works of Quevedo's, *Providencia de Dios* and *La constancia y paciencia del santo Job*, both written during his long imprisonment in León, show that our author's admiration for the Stoics and his belief in the utility of Stoical ideas and arguments in religious writing remained with him until the end of his life.[1] The two works have much in common. Indeed, the second was first published as a continuation of the first and it may have been intended by Quevedo as one of the 'vidas de los más ilustres y considerables' that he says at the end of the first work he was thinking of writing with a view to illustrating the workings of Providence.[2] *Providencia de Dios*, subtitled 'Doctrina estudiada en los gusanos y persecuciones de Job', uses Job as its chief example of the correct attitude to Providence; and *La constancia de Job*, subtitled 'Descansado discurso de los designios de la Divina Providencia', stresses Job's success in dealing first with prosperity and then with adversity. In both works Job is shown to have acted virtuously in all circumstances, thanks to his proto-Stoic knowledge of the real worth of 'internals' and 'externals', and in both Seneca is Quevedo's chief classical authority. As Rothe has pointed out, the titles of the two works recall Seneca's *De providentia* and *De constantia sapientis*.[3]

In *La constancia de Job* Quevedo sets out to expound God's reasons for his treatment of Job: to provide an example of the

---

[1] For the date of writing of *Providencia de Dios*, see Ettinghausen, 'Acerca de las fechas', pp. 170–3. That at least part of *La constancia de Job* was written between the composition of the two parts of *Providencia de Dios* may be inferred from the reference to 'hoy 20 de octubre de 41' (*Q*, II. 228b).

[2] See *Q*, II. 211a/b. It may be because *La constancia de Job* had already been written that Quevedo does not mention Job among the heroes of Antiquity whose Lives he proposed writing.

[3] See *Quevedo und Seneca*, p. 3.

kind of love that man owes him, and to prefigure the sufferings of Christ and the martyrs. His treatment of the first of the divine purposes takes the form of a commentary on Job 1 and 2, the chapters in which Job is seen at his most Stoical. Thanks to his virtue in prosperity and his patience in adversity, he is shown to have passed the Senecan tests of good and ill fortune with flying colours. If Job routed Satan it was because, unlike his adversary, he knew and practised the philosophy of the Stoics: 'El demonio cuenta por bienes solos los deste mundo, que no lo son; Dios las virtudes, que solamente son bienes.'[4] As if to stress that the doctrine that virtue is the only true good is a Stoic one, Quevedo states that Seneca and Epictetus were aware of it and that they were inspired by the example of the first Christians: 'Desta verdad mucha noticia tuvo Séneca; mayor Epicteto. Vivieron en el tiempo que los apóstoles vivían: estudiaron esta doctrina en las acciones de los primitivos cristianos; fueron sus ojos discípulos de sus persecuciones y cadenas; oyeron su sangre, que desde la de Abel hizo oficio de lengua y articuló voz derramada en los mártires.' Indeed, it is at this point that Quevedo defines the kind of love due to God and does so in terms of the Stoic concept of the correct opinion of things: 'Ya estamos en uno de los dos fines deste libro, que fue que Dios es amado por sí; y que los que son sus siervos tienen en precio sólo su temor y amor, no sólo no teniendo por bienes los de naturaleza y fortuna, sino despreciándolos por carga y embarazo.'[5] Although Epictetus is held up here as superior to Seneca, it is the latter who is quoted in support of the assertion that riches and prosperity are a greater peril to virtue than is adversity; and the passage which Quevedo cites from Seneca is coupled with one from Augustine in such a way as to suggest that the saint actually learned from the Stoic: 'Esto alcanzó Séneca, y lo dijo en la consolación a Helvia: *Neminem adversa fortuna comminuit, nisi quem secunda decepit. Después dijo lo mismo san Agustín: *Nulla infelicitas frangit, quem nulla felicitas corrumpit.*'[6]

The Stoic doctrine of 'internals' and 'externals' also underlies the treatment of that part of the Book of Job (1: 13–2: 13) on

---

[4] *Q*, II. 222b.

[5] Ibid. For the Senecan notion that 'externals' are a burden to the soul, see above, p. 74.

[6] *Q*, II. 222b. Cf. *Ad Helv.* V. 4, and Quevedo's sonnet, 'A quien la buena dicha no enfurece' (*OP*, I. 215).

which Quevedo had based his theory of the biblical origin of the Stoa in the *Doctrina estoica* and the preface to *La cuna y la sepultura*. Commenting on Job's losses, he declares that power and honours are 'engaños opulentos y mentiras magníficas' and that what counts is not 'externals', in themselves neither good nor bad, but the attitude adopted towards them: 'Los que Dios da, o son prueba del ánimo o ejercicio de la virtud; los que quita, alivio, rescate y premio.'[7] Again, he makes it clear that he is treating Job as a Stoical example. Quoting the speech in *De providentia* in which Demetrius the Cynic offers all his possessions and even his life to the gods, he asserts that this speech should be read as a commentary on Job's actions:

Estas palabras díjolas el filósofo con los labios, Job con las obras. Todo esto pronuncia la acción referida. Paciencia tan generosa, tan liberal resignación en Dios, sentimiento tan cortésmente santo, queja tan inflamada de amor, no es de casta de conocimiento gentil. Habló el idólatra el silencio del texto; viole como los estoicos, y dijo lo que coligió. Séales premio a Séneca y a él que suplen con sus plumas parte de comento a libro tan sagrado, y con cláusulas en que se conoce interior medula de su mente, dignas de que cada día las pronuncien afectos católicos.[8]

Quevedo's determination to prove that Job exemplifies the moral philosophy of the Stoics leads him to explain that when the proto-Stoic asked his wife, 'Shall we receive good at the hand of God, and shall we not receive evil?', he was using the term 'evil' in the popular sense but meant by it what the Stoics understood by 'externals': 'es de advertir que ninguna cosa que da Dios es mala, y que aquí llama males, no los que lo son sino los que los hombres disfaman con ese nombre.'[9] Turning the Stoic concept of *indifferentia* into the perfectly paradoxical notion that, when they are given by God, so-called evils are not merely not evils but are actually good, he observes: 'A Job le quitó todos aquellos bienes para darle pobreza, soledad, desprecio y enfermedades asquerosas. Que éstos son bienes, dándolos Dios, los sucesos cada día lo enseñan.'[10]

Before setting out to expound the second reason for God's

[7] *Q*, II. 224a.
[8] *Q*, II. 224b. Cf. *De prov.* V. 5–6. R. A. del Piero, 'Dos citas latinas de Quevedo', *RF*, lxix (1957), 69–70, comments on the way Quevedo adapts the passage from Seneca to make it more consonant with Job.
[9] *Q*, II. 227b–228a.          [10] *Q*, II. 228a.

treatment of Job, Quevedo abandons his verse-by-verse commentary at the point (Job 2: 14) where Job begins to exhibit
something less than Stoic constancy. At the beginning of the work
God's second purpose had been described as the exaltation of the
sufferings of Christ and the martyrs. Now it is referred to as
having to do with Providence. In order to contest the views of
Job's friends concerning God's treatment of him, Quevedo enlarges upon the Senecan idea propounded earlier that both brands
of fortune, good and bad, are divine tests of the virtuous. Like
the Seneca of *De providentia* he seeks not to prove the existence
of Providence but to reconcile its existence with the fact that the
righteous often suffer and the wicked often prosper. Job is his
textbook example because, apart from Christ and Paul, his
righteousness and the misfortunes he suffered are unparalleled
in the Scriptures. In answer to Eliphaz the Temanite's contention
that misfortune is divine retribution, he cites the examples of
Cain and Abel (an unpunished murderer and an innocent victim),
Lazarus and the miser, and Christ's Passion.[11] But his principal
text is Job's statement (9: 22) that God consumes both the innocent
and the impious, and he again stresses the Stoical point that what
matters is not the possession or lack of worldly goods but the use
to which they are put if possessed and the attitude adopted if they
are lacking: 'En el malo y despiadado se ve que las riquezas son
tierra; en el justo y piadoso, que pueden ser cielo. En éste la
miseria y trabajos muestran que son examen, prueba y mérito y
regalo; en aquél las desdichas, la pobreza y las afrentas, que son
castigo.'[12] The solution to the problem of evil which Quevedo
sees illustrated by Job is, then, a Stoical one, and Seneca and
Epictetus are chief among the pagans he cites as expressing 'Christian' views on the question of Providence. Just as earlier he linked
a passage from Seneca with one from Augustine, he couples
another with a verse from the Psalms: 'Llega el furor impío
de los hombres a juzgar a Dios. Séneca lo dijo: "Muchos hay
propicios a otros hombres; a Dios pocos." Más expresamente
David, en el salmo L: *Ut justificeris in sermonibus tuis, et vincas
cum judicaris.*'[13] And with the remark 'Aprenda el poco piadoso

---

[11] See *Q*, II. 232b–233a.
[12] *Q*, II. 234b. Cf., e.g., *De prov.* II. 1: '"Quare multa bonis viris adversa
eveniunt?" Nihil accidere bono viro mali potest; non miscentur contraria.'
[13] *Q*, II. 235a. The passage cited here is *Ep.* 93, 1.

cristiano del filósofo gentil', he quotes the injunction of the 'stoico Epicteto' to submit to the will of the gods and equates faith in Providence with 'buenas opiniones' of God.[14]

In his commentary on the Book of Job which Quevedo cites in *La constancia de Job*, the Jesuit Juan de Pineda had pointed out that Job's reactions to misfortune are for the most part quite unlike those recommended by the Stoics.[15] Shortly after *Providencia de Dios* and *La constancia de Job* Quevedo wrote a Life of St. Paul in which he contrasted Job's patience with the Apostle's Christian joy in adversity in the same terms as he uses elsewhere to contrast the fortitude of the Stoics with the joy of the martyrs.[16] In *La constancia de Job*, however, he studiously ignores those passages, which become more frequent as the Book proceeds, in which Job's words are charged with despair. Instead, he is throughout intent on treating Job's sufferings as the epitome of correct opinion in good and ill fortune and as a prefiguration of the Passion. As in the second part of the *Política de Dios*, whose chapter on Job (II. xx) he named the most important in the entire treatise, in *La constancia de Job* Quevedo concentrates on demonstrating Job's victory over adversity by means of a Christian patience which is indistinguishable from Stoic imperturbability.

Among the *exempla* adduced by Quevedo, one, which is neither classical nor biblical, is especially important: his own experiences at the time he wrote the work. Our author had made a literary example of himself as early as the first *Sueños* and provided two exemplary self-portraits in the *Virtud militante*. In the first *Fantasma*, developing the Senecan idea that man's desire for long life is tantamount to wishing for more death, he depicted himself as more dead than alive, 'sepultura de mi propia muerte ... entierro de mi misma vida'; and in the last, undated, *Fantasma* he declared that he had lived a long and healthy life without calling on the assistance of doctors or medicines.[17] In *La constancia de Job* he introduces a pathetic account of his arrest and imprisonment in León in 1639 with the words: 'Quiero hablar de mí mismo: deberé a mi pluma lo que quien leyere deberá a mi ejemplo.'[18]

[14] *Q*, II. 235a. Cf. *Manual*, XXXI. 1.

[15] See the commentary on Job 1: 20, 3: 2, in Pineda, *Commentariorum in Iob Libri tredecim* (Seville, 1598), pp. 113, 201. For Pineda's influence on *La constancia de Job*, see R. A. del Piero, 'Quevedo y Juan de Pineda', *MP*, lvi (1958), 82–91.

[16] See *Q*, II. 20a.      [17] See *Q*, II. 138b, 155b.      [18] *Q*, II. 228a.

Written after nearly two years of hardship suffered in the most depressing conditions, the account of his imprisonment in *La constancia de Job* follows closely the *Memorial* he had addressed to Olivares a fortnight before. In both he describes his illnesses and penury, his loneliness and his abandonment by his friends, all of which misfortunes correspond with the list of Job's afflictions that occurs shortly before the account in *La constancia de Job*: 'pobreza, soledad, desprecio y enfermedades asquerosas.'[19] His statement in the *Memorial*, 'no me falta para muerto sino la sepoltura', anticipates his description of Job: 'Aun no estaba como cuerpo muerto, sino como esqueleto ya roído de la hambre del sepulcro';[20] and his reference to having had to cauterize his own ulcers parallels his references to Job's having to scrape his boils with a potsherd. Whereas in the *Memorial* he gives an unrelievedly black picture of his ills, presumably in the hope of persuading Olivares to procure his release, in *La constancia de Job* his attitude towards his afflictions is one of Stoic resignation illuminated by the kind of joy in suffering that he praised in the martyrs. After describing his misfortunes he solemnly declares that the afflictions he has suffered constitute God's greatest blessings to him. These are the result of the loss of worldly goods which, he says, had previously clouded his mind with *engaño*. His account of these blessings is written in the pointed, paradoxical style which had attracted him in Seneca. It ends by ascribing to God the kind of powers that the Stoics attributed to their ideal sage:

Pues yo testifico en la presencia de Dios trino y uno a todos los que esta confesión mía leyeren, que en ninguna otra cosa en este mundo en mi favor se ha mostrado tan liberal su mano omnipotente. . . . Quiso (él sea bendito) cobrar mi penitencia en la moneda de los bienes de la tierra, que antes embaraza que enriquece. Mi remedio estuvo en que me quitó lo que yo debiera haber dejado, y me dio la medicina de que huía. Hízome discípulo de los trabajos. . . . Lo más y primero que me enseñaron fue a desaprender el mal que sabía. Diéronme a conocer los que me engañaban el conocimiento. Hicieron que me dejasen ingratos los que no me dejaban molestos. Hiciéronme fácil el amar a los enemigos, que no me quieren dejar, dándome a conocer los amigos que me han dejado. Librar con prisiones, descansar con tormentos, regalar con castigos, enriquecer con pérdidas, sanar con enfermedades, — sólo Dios lo hace. . . .[21]

19 *Q*, II. 228a. Cf. the *Memorial* (*EQ*, pp. 429–31).
20 *EQ*, p. 430; *Q*, II. 244a.    21 *Q*, II. 228b.

In the dungeon in the monastery of San Marcos where he wrote
these words four years before his death, Quevedo was still seeking
to become a *proficiens* in the philosophy of Christ by emulating the
patience of the biblical Stoic.

## 11. *Stoicism for Atheists*

*Providencia de Dios* is an energetic onslaught on disbelievers
in the immortality of the soul and divine Providence. The idea
of writing this twofold treatise may well have been suggested to
Quevedo by the Jesuit Leonardus Lessius' *De providentia numinis
et animi immortalitate* (Antwerp, 1613), from which he took his
list of classical deniers of God and Providence at the beginning
of the work.[22] In the first part, in which he attempts to prove
the immortality of the soul, apart from Job he cites hardly any
biblical examples or Christian authorities. In fact he states
repeatedly that he uses classical authors as independent witnes-
ses of Christian doctrine: 'No traigo autoridades de la Sagrada
Escritura y de los santos, porque los ateístas, negando que hay
Dios, Providencia y alma inmortal, consiguientemente desprecian
a todo lo que con Dios se autoriza.'[23] Knowing as we do his passion
for employing classical authority in his moral works, the regret
he voices here at having to stoop so low should almost certainly
not be taken at its face value. His discussion of immortality
opens with the assertion that the atheist must remember that
he rejects not only 'las resurrecciones sagradas' but also 'tantas
apariciones como refieren aun los autores profanos, griegos y
latinos'.[24] Although he ridicules the view of Plutarch and Tacitus
that animals are rational beings, and that man's soul need therefore
be no more immortal than theirs, he soon gives the impression of
being quite content to base his case on non-Christian writers:
'Si desprecias los santos, oye a todos los filósofos, historiadores,
poetas y oradores. Si tienes hastío de lo divino y de la Iglesia, oye
a los idólatras en esta parte: a los platónicos, peripatéticos, stoicos,
pitagóricos.'[25]

As might be expected, Quevedo is at no loss for arguments to
counter the atheist's possible objection that the universal and
natural fear of death is proof of the soul's mortality. Once again

---

[22] See *Q*, II. 167b–168b. Cf. Lessius, pp. 2–4.
[23] *Q*, II. 169b.  [24] Ibid.  [25] *Q*, II. 170b.

he has recourse to variations on the Senecan equation of life and death.[26] One of the first classical authors he cites is Lucan, 'docto poeta en la noche de la gentilidad', on whose remark about man's capacity to face death with equanimity he comments: 'No puedes negar que el tener las almas capaces de muerte en los gentiles, hizo inmortales y gloriosos y aclamación de todos los siglos y naciones a Scévola, a Lucrecia, a Catón, a Socrates y a Marco Bruto y a otros muchos'.[27] The names he mentions are those of Seneca's most cherished heroes, whose death by suicide—and, still more, that of 'infinitos gloriosos mártires'—he puts forward as evidence of the efficacy of belief in immortality. That he is thinking of Stoic heroes is made quite clear by his statement that 'aquellos capitanes y filósofos' were fortified by 'la igualdad del ánimo'.[28] Stoic suicide, condemned out of hand in the *Doctrina estoica*, is here employed as a useful argument for immortality. Towards the end of the first part of *Providencia de Dios* Quevedo again reminds the atheist that 'algunos (y no pocos) no temieron la muerte que les daban; otros la tomaron por descanso y medicina y libertad; muchos la desprecian por cualquier cosa cada día; y muchos más la han codiciado enamorados de ella en los innumerables mártires.'[29] Once again the classical example of Stoic suicides is coupled with the superior example of the Christian martyrs. If the former met death with equanimity, the latter, armed with faith, hope, and charity, died as though in love with death and outdid the feats which the Stoics claimed for their sage:

> Que esto sea así, recorre tu memoria por toda la jerarquía de innumerables mártires, y los verás dar música con himnos a los garfios que los arrancan las entrañas, abrazar cariñosos las cruces que los suspenden, salir a recibir con las gargantas el golpe de los cuchillos; bendecir las fieras que los despedazan, y ser apacible alimento a su hambre; guisarse en el fuego con alegría, que los sazona para Dios en la inmortalidad.[30]

As contemporary evidence of Christian love of death he cites the example of the Jesuit Marcelo Mastrilli, an account of whose life and martyrdom in Japan he had begun in 1640.[31]

---

[26] See *Q*, II. 188b.　　　　　　　　　　　　　　　　[27] *Q*, II. 175a.

[28] Ibid. For the Stoic concept of *aequanimitas* in Quevedo's letter to Antonio de Mendoza, see Blüher, *Seneca in Spanien*, p. 343.

[29] *Q*, II. 188b.　　　　　　　　　　　　　　　　　　[30] *Q*, II. 189a.

[31] See *Q*, II. 189a/b. Cf. *Q*, II. 71–4.

Apart from Lucan, the classical writers most enthusiastically praised in the first part of *Providencia de Dios* are Homer, 'aquel antepasado de toda la sabiduría de Grecia (de quien deciende la Academia y el Pórtico, peripatéticos y pirrónicos . . .)',[32] Juvenal, whose description of the difference between the souls of men and beasts Quevedo praises as 'elegancia casi devota',[33] and 'mi Séneca'. The Stoic is first quoted to support the contention that human justice punishes the sinner but leaves sin to be judged hereafter;[34] his reflections on the death of Aufidius Bassus, cited in the *Virtud militante*, are treated as revealing the same attitude towards death as Job 28;[35] and his advice to the poor and weak to examine the miseries endured by the rich and the powerful is borrowed once more.[36] Another of Quevedo's favourite passages in Seneca—his account of the return to heaven of Scipio's soul—was inserted by our author after the first redaction of the work to support a quotation from Ecclesiastes and as evidence that Seneca believed in the immortality of the soul.[37] Finally, the first part of the work originally ended with Seneca's glowing portrayal of the soul's struggle to free itself from the body and make its way to an after-life of eternal peace, a conclusion which Quevedo 'perfected' at a later date by adding a quotation from his Christian Seneca, Chrysologus.[38]

The current of Stoical ideas and arguments runs even more strongly through the second part of the work. Here Quevedo argues, as in *La constancia de Job*, that in order to comprehend the workings of Providence it is necessary to hold the correct opinion of wordly goods. The *vulgus*, with its false opinion of things, is unable to appreciate that 'externals' are in themselves 'indifferent' unless used virtuously:

. . . todo lo entienden al revés estos sacrílegos, que se usurpan judicatura sobre las disposiciones de Dios. ¿Cómo pues los bienes, honras y

---

[32] *Q*, II. 191a.     [33] *Q*, II. 178a.

[34] See *Q*, II. 179a. The passage cited, 'no cuelgan al robador porque hurtó; sino para que no hurte más, ni otro se atreva a hurtar', is perhaps *De ira*, I. xix. 7: 'nam, ut Plato ait, nemo prudens punit, quia peccatum est, sed ne peccetur; revocari enim praeterita non possunt, futura prohibentur'.

[35] See *Q*, II. 182b. Cf. *Ep.* 30.     [36] See *Q*, II. 185b. Cf. *Ep.* 115, 17.

[37] See *Q*, II. 187a and n. (a). The passage cited is *Ep.* 86, 1.

[38] See *Q*, II. 191b–192a. The passage cited is *Ad Marc.* XXIV. 5. In the autograph MS. of Part I of *Providencia de Dios* (Biblioteca Nacional, Madrid, MS. Vit. 7–7, fol. 68ᵛ) the quotation from Chrysologus, Sermon LXXIV, is in different ink from the rest of the page.

dignidades del mundo harán al malo bueno, si al bueno le hacen malo
y al perverso peor? ¿Quién pues los tendrá sin riesgo? Quien los rehusó,
quien los teme, quien los desprecia, quien los padece; quien los tiene,
sin que ellos le tengan.[39]

It is here, in one of his last works, that we find Quevedo actually
employing the Stoic term *indifferentia* for the first time. Thanks
to the seemingly indiscriminate distribution of good and ill
fortune among the righteous and the wicked, both prosperity and
adversity can be seen to be neither good nor bad in themselves:
'No de otra suerte se conociera que puestos, dignidades, honras y
riquezas, desprecio, abatimiento, persecuciones y pobreza, son de
sí cosas indiferentes, buenas o malas por la virtud o la iniquidad de
los que usan de unas y otras.'[40] Here and later Quevedo expresses
the notion of the equality of so-called good things and so-
called ills as much by the way he throws together what are
popularly regarded as opposites as by stating that the differences
between them are an illusion: 'No de otra manera los tesoros,
las felicidades, las honras, los grandes puestos, la pobreza, la
calamidad, el abatimiento son venenos en unos, y remedios y
antídotos en otros.'[41] Job is chosen as the 'catedrático que me
preside en estas conclusiones' because, by holding the correct
opinion of things, he maintained his faith in Providence.[42]
The apostles and the martyrs are proof that torture and death
can become 'corona, victoria y triunfo de los justos', and that
Providence can enable Christians to emulate the Stoic Paradoxes,
'abrasar en llamas al mártir, no sólo sin ofenderle sino ilustrándole,
y ser nueva vida y eterna los cuchillos y las sogas a la garganta . . .
hacer que los hombres subiendo bajen, y bajando suban; que
padeciendo gocen, que gozando padezcan; que muriendo vivan,
y viviendo mueran.'[43] As usual, Quevedo makes the most of the
stylistic possibilities afforded by Stoical ideas. The same is true
of his Senecan polemics against false opinion of wealth and power
which include the familiar arguments that nature wisely buried
precious stones and metals under mountains and that one is not
rich so long as one covets more wealth.[44] Once again, the Stoic
concept of false opinion is expressed by the idea of 'back-to-front'.
The avaricious are linked with the impious as men who practise

39  *Q*, II. 197a.                          40  *Q*, II. 197b.
41  *Q*, II. 198a.                          42  *Q*, II. 198b.
43  *Q*, II. 196b, 207a.       44  See *Q*, II. 197b, 199a.

'al revés' the correct use of 'externals' on which faith in Providence depends.[45]

The classical writers cited in the second part of *Providencia de Dios* include an even greater proportion of Silver Latin authors than in the first, and several of the quotations from them are identical with passages cited in *La constancia de Job*. Martial's Epigram (iv. 21) on Selius, who disbelieved because when he denied God he remained unpunished, is used here to illustrate a passage from Augustine.[46] Claudian's despair at seeing the wicked prosper is cited here as well as in the *Virtud militante* and *La constancia de Job*, where Quevedo adds the poet's statement that he believed that the wicked are raised up so that their downfall may be the greater, and comments: '¡ Grave discurso y verdadero! Rastreó Claudiano algún paso de la divina Providencia.'[47] Lucan and Juvenal are quoted in support of the Senecan thesis that prosperity is conducive to vice and adversity to virtue, and the satirist's words are warmly praised as worthy of having been pronounced by a Christian.[48] Once again we come across the stoic example of Anaxarchus; and the fable of Midas is linked with the story of Nebuchadnezzar's statue.[49]

Part II of *Providencia de Dios* is quite remarkable for the number of its quotations from Seneca, none of which, however, is from *De providentia*. A series of six passages from the Stoic follows on the quotation from Claudian. The first two affirm the existence of the Divinity, deducing it from the common belief of all peoples and from the benefits bestowed by the gods; and the last four describe the nature of God.[50] Commenting on the fact that in the last passage Seneca writes 'gods' when he says that men seek after them but uses the singular when he says that God comes to men, Quevedo exclaims: '¡ Grandes palabras, confines a los mayores misterios de nuestra fe!'[51] In the *Virtud militante* he declared that

---

[45] *Q*, II. 199b.
[46] See *Q*, II. 192b–193a. Cf. *Q*, II. 236a.
[47] *Q*, II. 235a. Cf. *Q*, II. 151b–152a, 194b. R. A. del Piero, 'Quevedo y la *Polyanthea*', *HispI*, ii (1958), 52, argues that the quotations from Claudian in *La constancia de Job* and *Providencia de Dios* were taken, like several more in both works, from a compendium of quotations.
[48] See *Q*, II. 200b, 207b, 208a.         [49] See *Q*, II. 210a, 200a/b.
[50] See *Q*, II. 194b–195a. The passages cited are *Ep.* 117, 6, *De benef.* IV. iv. 3, *Nat. Quaest.*, preface, 13–14, *De benef.* IV. vii. 2, *Nat. Quaest.* II. xlv. 1–3, and *Ep.* 73, 15–16.
[51] *Q*, II. 195a.

he would accept the Seneca–Paul correspondence as genuine, were it not for its style. Now, while reiterating this view, he affirms that he is none the less convinced by such passages in Seneca's works as those he has cited that the Stoic communicated with the apostle.[52] In the note to his translation of Seneca's Epistle 41 he protests that he is not trying to make Seneca into a Christian theologian.[53] This, however, is precisely what he now does, declaring that if in the last of the six passages cited Seneca speaks like a mystic, in *Naturales quaestiones* he speaks like a schoolman, treating of predestination and free will. Although the Stoic misunderstood the apostle when he used the pagan term 'fate' for 'predestination', he was a better Christian than Luther.[54] Finally, Quevedo declares that he has no better answer to offer atheists than Seneca, whom he eulogizes as fulsomely here as in any of his earlier works:

No he podido dar a los ateístas y herejes tapaboca más afrentoso que éste con la mano de Séneca, filósofo gentil, sin baptismo, y maestro de Nerón (primer perseguidor en Roma de los cristianos entre los emperadores), y el más feliz ingenio y la pluma de mejor sabor que se reconoce por todos en aquellas tinieblas; tan útilmente modesto en su doctrina, que san Jerónimo le colocó en el catálogo de los escritores eclesiásticos, y san Augustín frecuentemente le citó, y otros gravísimos escritores católicos.[55]

Later in the second part of *Providencia de Dios* Quevedo links with Psalm 52: 5 the passage from Epistle 93 which in *La constancia de Job* he had paralleled with a verse from the first Psalm. He also remarks on a passage in Epistle 31 that in half a line 'nuestro cordobés' explained the reason why Providence is denied

[52] See *Q*, II. 195a. Quevedo's view is similar to Lipsius'. The latter, too, rejects the extant correspondence as spurious, but believes that a genuine correspondence took place (see Seneca, *Opera quae extant omnia* (Antwerp, 1652), p. xxv).

[53] See *Q*, II. 385a.

[54] See *Q*, II. 195a. The passage cited is *Nat. Quaest.* II. xxxviii. 3. In one of his *Migajas sentenciosas* Quevedo states that St. Teresa was a 'maestra . . . de espíritu' and that Seneca 'lo fué de moralidad' (*BP*, p. 1005b); and in his undated *Homilía de la Santísima Trinidad* he declares: 'De Dios grandes cosas dijeron los filósofos, y más y mayores que todos, Séneca' (*Q*, II. 353b). From Quevedo's comments in *Providencia de Dios* it is not obvious that 'la diferencia entre Providencia y Fortuna, Fatalidad, Destino y la Causalidad, en Quevedo no tiene importancia. Estos temas estoicos han perdido vigencia en su pensamiento' (C. Láscaris Comneno, 'La mostración de Dios en el pensamiento de Quevedo', *Crisis* (Madrid/Murcia), ii (1955), 436).

[55] *Q*, II. 195a/b.

by the wicked, and paraphrases a favourite passage in Epistle 115 in support of Lucan's view that misfortune is deceptive.[56] At the end of the work he borrows from *De providentia* the notion that, while God alone is outside adversity, virtuous men can at least overcome it; and he takes over the example of the general (God) who assigns his bravest men (the virtuous) to the most testing exploits.[57]

Particularly in view of the roles allotted by Quevedo to the Stoic doctrine of the correct opinion of things and to Seneca as a philosopher who intuited as much of the truth revealed by Christianity as a pagan could, it is difficult to accept the view that in *Providencia de Dios* our author 'ha superado el senequismo para entregarse por completo a San Agustín'.[58] Certainly, despite his declaration at the beginning of the work that he would rely on the authority of the classics to combat atheism, Christian authors (including Augustine) are cited in both parts. However, his treatment of the problem of evil has only passing references to Original Sin as its cause and to Redemption as its cure. His solution to the problem, in both *Providencia de Dios* and *La constancia de Job*, is essentially that first put forward by the Stoics, for whom 'the so-called prosperity of the wicked is no prosperity, for it concerns only external goods—mere *adiaphora*; whereas the adversity of the righteous is no real adversity, inasmuch as it does not harm the soul'.[59] If, as O. H. Green suggests, one of the most basic differences between Stoic and Christian thought is 'the opposition of Stoic error and the Christian sense of guilt through sin',[60] it is one which Quevedo found perfectly surmountable. The relationship between Stoicism and Christianity in these two works of Quevedo's last years is fundamentally the same as we have observed in *La cuna y la sepultura* and the *Virtud militante*. What the Stoics achieved by means of natural reason assisted, in Quevedo's view, by the divine inspiration afforded by the examples of Job and the apostles and martyrs is used as

---

[56] See *Q*, II. 196a, 200b. Quevedo justifies by referring to Persius his transformation of Seneca's statement that no one knows God (*Ep.* 31, 10) into the statement that only very few know him.

[57] See *Q*, II. 210a. Cf. *De prov.* VI. 6, IV. 7–8.

[58] C. Láscaris Comneno, 'Senequismo y agustinismo en Quevedo', *RFi*, ix (1950), 476.

[59] Davidson, *The Stoic Creed*, p. 224.

[60] *Spain and the Western Tradition: The Castilian Mind in Literature from 'El Cid' to Calderón* (Madison, Wisc., 1963–6), iii. 314.

evidence of the rationality of Christian dogma. Their arguments against desire of apparent 'goods' and fear of apparent ills provide the means whereby bad Christians and atheists may be brought round to concern for 'internals'. A key to Quevedo's attitude towards the Stoa is provided by his remarks on Torquato Tasso early in *Providencia de Dios*. Commenting on Tasso's assertion that (as the Stoics taught) the soul is corporeal, and on his statement that, while believing like a Christian, he wished to be allowed the liberty to think like a philosopher, our author retorts tartly: 'Pudiera discurrir mejor como cristiano filósofo'.[61] For Quevedo, as we have had abundant occasion to note, the truth of philosophy and the truth of Christianity are by no means necessarily incompatible: it is the business of the Christian philosopher to reconcile with Christianity the achievements of the greatest philosophers of Antiquity.

[61] *Q*, II. 169a. In his preface to *De constantia* Lipsius had claimed: 'philosophum ego agam, sed Christianum' (cited in C. H. Hay, *Montaigne lecteur et imitateur de Sénèque* (Poitiers, 1938), p. 46).

# CONCLUSION

THE first serious attempt at tracing the development of Quevedo's Neostoicism has been made recently by K. A. Blüher in his history of Seneca's influence in Spain. Blüher's analysis of Quevedo's Stoical works is, however, marred by his uncritical acceptance of the theory put forward by C. Láscaris Comneno that *Providencia de Dios* marks a final and definitive transition from 'un neosenequismo de tipo interiorista' to 'un agustinismo con metodología suareciana'.[1] Because he maintains that after 1635 Quevedo entirely subordinated Stoicism to Christianity,[2] Blüher does less than justice to *Providencia de Dios* and barely mentions *La constancia y paciencia del santo Job* at all. However, Quevedo subordinated Stoicism to Christianity before as well as after 1635, as we have seen in every one of the works we have examined. Indeed, his attitudes towards the Stoics and his interest in their teachings remained remarkably consistent from first to last. Moreover, it is precisely in the year 1635 that he chose to publish, in the *Doctrina estoica*, his most unequivocal profession of faith in the Stoa; and in both *La constancia y paciencia del santo Job* and *Providencia de Dios* the Stoic who in the *Doctrina estoica* had been made the scapegoat for the Stoics' unchristian teaching concerning suicide is said to have spoken of God like a Christian. In *Providencia de Dios* Quevedo actually comes closer than in any of his earlier works to resuscitating the medieval belief that Seneca was a friend of Paul and a crypto-Christian, a belief which had been discredited for more than a century.[3] All of which, together with his spirited defences of the Stoic against the criticisms of Tertullian and Chrysologus in the *Virtud militante*, would seem to indicate his continued determination to reconcile the Stoa with Christianity and, if anything, a strengthening of his commitment to the Stoics. Whereas in *La cuna y la sepultura* Seneca and Epictetus are scarcely so much as mentioned

---

[1] 'Senequismo y agustinismo', p. 463. Cf. Blüher, *Seneca in Spanien*, pp. 326, 360, 365.
[2] See Blüher, p. 360.
[3] Ibid., pp. 195–6.

by name, in the *Virtud militante, La constancia y paciencia del santo Job*, and *Providencia de Dios* their anticipation of Christianity is argued quite explicitly.

Quevedo's brand of 'Christian Stoicism' is by no means a peculiarly Spanish phenomenon. Indeed it has no parallel in Spain in the extent to which it manifests features that characterize the Neostoic movement at large. Referring to the majority of the movement's adherents, L. Zanta remarks: 'Ne nous attendons pas à trouver parmi ces restaurateurs du stoïcisme de vrais philosophes, soucieux de faire revivre dans toute son intégrité la pensée antique, mais plutôt des littérateurs, des moralistes, des historiens, des humanistes.'[4] Quevedo's Neostoicism is in fact typical in its lack of interest in imitating the kind of attempt at objectively reconstructing the philosophy of the Stoa undertaken by Lipsius and Scioppius. Although undoubtedly inspired by his contact with the Fleming, and despite his extensive plagiarism of the *Manuductio ad stoicam philosophiam*, in his *Doctrina estoica* he is far closer in spirit to such Neostoics as Du Vair and Charron in France and Hall in England. Like them he is fascinated by the possibility of showing that the Stoics anticipated Christian teaching and by the ways in which their moral philosophy can be utilized to prepare the ground for the implantation or reinforcement of Christian faith. He might well have been surprised by the ease with which he could have subscribed to the sentiments of contemporaries beyond the Pyrenees: to Simon Goulard's declaration, 'Pour se resoudre contre les divers et fascheux evenemens de ceste vie, pour acquiescer à la providence divine, pour mespriser la mort et desirer l'immortalité bien-heureuse, pour reprimer l'insolence des passions ... je ne sçache entre les Payens historien, philosophe, orateur, ni auteur quelconque que je voulusse preferer à Seneque';[5] to Thomas Lodge's exclamation, 'Would God Christians would endeuour to practise his [Seneca's] good precepts, to reform their owne in seeing his errours; and perceiuing so great light of learning from a Pagans pen, ayme at the true light of deuotion and pietie, which becommeth Christians';[6] to Thomas James' assertion that 'no kinde of philosophie is more profitable and neerer approching unto Christianitie . . . then the philosophie of the

---

[4] *La Renaissance du stoïcisme*, p. 30.
[5] Quoted by Busson, *La Pensée religieuse française*, pp. 380–1.
[6] *The Workes of Lucius Annaeus Seneca* (London, 1614), fol. b4[v].

Stoicks';[7] to Bishop Hall's remark that after reading the Stoic philosophers he found 'a little envy and pity striving together within me';[8] or to Sir Thomas Browne's exhortations 'now to "live by old Ethicks, and the classical rules of Honesty", and now to "Look beyond Antoninus, and terminate not thy morals in Seneca or Epictetus. Be a moralist of the Mount, and Christianize thy Notions".'[9] His continual blurring of such distinctions between Stoicism and Christianity as the concepts of error and sin and of 'internals' and things of the soul makes him, like Charron and St. Francis of Sales, a Neostoic and an Augustinian at one and the same time.[10]

By virtue of his avowed personal attachment to the Stoa, his many connections with the Neostoic movement in Spain and abroad, and his capacity for adapting Stoical means to Christian ends, he is unquestionably Spain's most important contributor to the movement and one of its most persuasive spokesmen. It is largely thanks to him that by the middle of the seventeenth century a Spaniard writing for a Spanish audience could state that he left the defence of Seneca to 'algun Estoico de estos tiempos'.[11] But Quevedo is not a philosopher in any meaningful sense of the word. Although he certainly knew of Lipsius' *Physiologia stoicorum*, he shows no more interest in metaphysics, Stoic or otherwise, than the majority of Neostoics.[12] From Seneca and Epictetus he learned principally to take pathos and paradox to the extreme of equating such things as life and death, riches and poverty, health and illness, honour and scorn: to yoke together not merely disparate but opposite ideas. In *La cuna y la sepultura*, the *Virtud militante*, *La constancia y paciencia del santo Job*, and *Providencia de Dios* he is profoundly inspired by the ingenious manipulation of logically fallacious but emotively powerful arguments that he

[7] Du Vair, *The Moral Philosophie of the Stoicks . . . Englished by Thomas James . . .*, ed. R. Kirk, Rutgers Univ. Studies in English, no. 8 (New Brunswick, N.J., 1951), p. 3.

[8] *The Works of Joseph Hall*, vi (Oxford, 1837), 4.

[9] Quoted by B. Willey, *The Seventeenth-Century Background . . .* (Harmondsworth, 1962), pp. 44–5.

[10] See Levi, *French Moralists*, p. 2.

[11] Alonso Núñez de Castro, *Seneca impugnado de Seneca en questiones politicas y morales*, 2nd ed. (Madrid, 1661), fol. d2$^r$.

[12] See C. Láscaris Comneno, 'La epistemología en el pensamiento filosófico de Quevedo', *Bol*, xlv (1955), 911; Méndez Bejarano, *Historia de la filosofía*, pp. 327 ff.; and A. Castro, 'Escepticismo y contradicción en Quevedo', *HUM*, xviii (1928), 13.

imitated in *De los remedios de cualquier fortuna*. The same is true
of much of his serious verse, especially his poems on the futility
of honour and wealth and the brevity of life. In such sonnets as
'Vivir es caminar breve jornada' or 'Miré los muros de la patria
mía', life's fleetingness is made an almost physical sensation by the
masterly play of imagery, sound, and metre; and in the sonnet
entitled 'Signifícase la propria brevedad de la vida, sin pensar,
y con padecer, salteada de la muerte', assonance and alliteration
combine with rhyme and rhythm to make tangible the equation of
life with death.[13] Here, and in such potent denunciations of concern with riches as the sonnets 'Quitar codicia, no añadir dinero',
'Todo lo puede despreciar cualquiera', and '¿Qué otra cosa es
verdad sino pobreza . . .?',[14] his favourite Stoical themes are
expressed with an intensity that makes it hard to imagine that he
did not feel as well as think in Senecan terms.

A fundamentally Stoical attitude to life also runs through
Quevedo's satirical works. As R. M. Price has put it, 'the satirist
in one style is a moralist in another.'[15] His satire on stupidity in
word and deed in his early *Memoriales*, *Premáticas*, and *Genealogías*
reveals a scorn for the *vulgus* that harks back to the Stoics and the
Latin satirists; and his unwillingness to categorize or arrange in
order of demerit the varied butts of his attacks recalls the Stoics'
doctrine that all vices are equal. With the possible exception
of the first, all the *Sueños* contain Stoical ideas. The fourth in
particular, *El mundo por de dentro*, written in the same period as
his first known Stoical work, is inspired throughout by Stoical
attitudes. Lamenting the insatiability of human desires, Quevedo
states that concern with 'externals' arises out of 'la ignorancia
de las cosas', i.e. failure to arrive at the correct opinion of things.[16]
Casting himself in the role of the *vulgus*, he is sharply rebuked
by Desengaño for showing off his bookish erudition instead of
using his wits to distinguish appearance from reality.[17] And as
for Desengaño's sermon on the need to prepare for death, it is

---

[13] See *OP*, I. 150, 155–6, 184–5. Green, *Courtly Love*, p. 63, also suggests
that the pervasive awareness of death in Quevedo's love poetry 'might plausibly
be attributed to his Stoicism'.
[14] See *OP*, I. 151, 201–2, 219.
[15] 'A Note on Three Satirical Sonnets of Quevedo', *BHS*, xl (1963), 88.
[16] *Q*, I. 326a. For the Senecan ideas in the third *Sueño*, see Rothe, *Quevedo
und Seneca*, pp. 32–7.
[17] See *Q*, I. 328b.

Senecan through and through.[18] In two later satirical works, *Discurso de todos los diablos* and *La hora de todos y la Fortuna con seso*, he concentrates on making the point that Fortune's goods are 'indifferent'. In the former, Lucifer mocks Satan's efforts to tempt Job by persecuting him when he should have known that the greatest test of virtue is prosperity;[19] while in the latter Fortune blames men's false opinions for her evil repute. Some, she contends, fail to take the opportunities she holds out to them; others, under the illusion that they would be better off with the things they envy in their neighbours, snatch things from her that she never intended for them.[20] As in *La constancia y paciencia del santo Job* and *Providencia de Dios*, the implication throughout is that virtue and happiness depend upon correct opinion. Jupiter's conclusion that Fortune's alleged capriciousness is perfectly just coincides exactly with the Stoic doctrine that 'externals' are in themselves neither good nor bad.[21]

Stoical attitudes are also clearly discernible in Quevedo's best-known work, the picaresque novel *La vida del Buscón*, written at the same time as the first *Sueños*. Contrary to the view of the critic who referred to 'el viril estoicismo, que impulsa al héroe a una lucha constante contra un medio que le es siempre hostil',[22] Pablos is portrayed as the antithesis of the Stoic sage, an example of and a warning to the *vulgus*. From the outset he is motivated by the desire to better himself, at first, it seems, morally as well as socially.[23] But by the time he decides at Alcalá to follow the proverb 'Haz como vieres' he has surrendered whole-heartedly to the values of the *vulgus*, his total preoccupation with which he discloses, for example, when he tells how he spent a sleepless

---

[18] See *Q*, I. 326a/b. Cf., e.g., *Ad Polyb.* XI. 2, and *Ep.* 24, 23; 30, 18; 61, 1.

[19] See *Q*, I. 379a. Cf., e.g., *De prov.* IV. 9–10. For Quevedo's depiction of Seneca in the *Discurso* as the model *privado*, see Blüher, *Seneca in Spanien*, pp. 341–2, 375–6.

[20] See *Q*, I. 385a.

[21] 'La Fortuna encamine su rueda y su bola por las rodadas antiguas, y ocasione méritos en los cuerdos y castigo en los desatinados; a que asistirá nuestra providencia infalible y nuestra presciencia soberana. Todos reciban lo que les repartiere; que sus favores u desdenes por sí no son malos, pues sufriendo éstos y despreciando aquéllos, son tan útiles los unos como los otros. Y aquél que recibe y hace culpa para sí lo que para sí toma, se queje de sí propio, y no de la Fortuna, que lo da con indiferencia y sin malicia' (*Q*, I. 424b–425a).

[22] L. Santa María, ed., *Vida del Buscón* (Madrid, 1954), pp. xiii–xiv.

[23] 'Yo les dije que quería aprender virtud, resueltamente, y ir con mis buenos pensamientos adelante' (*Q*, I. 487a).

night thinking how best to spend the dowry he hoped to obtain by tricking a young noblewoman into marriage. Shortly after his plans are thwarted by his ex-master, the lady's cousin, his loss of all moral identity is remarked upon by his landlady: 'Te han visto aquí ya estudiante, ya pícaro, ya caballero, y todo por las compañías'.[24] A. A. Parker is the first to have pointed out the importance of 'the moral judgement that is implicit in Quevedo's treatment of his theme'.[25] As P. N. Dunn has noted, Pablos is at first quite capable of distinguishing reality from appearance, and his moral disintegration as the novel proceeds results from his ceasing to exercise this ability.[26] The end of the novel, with its final, Senecan *sententia*, 'nunca mejora su estado quien muda solamente de lugar, y no de vida y costumbres', is, as D. B. J. Randall suggests, 'more than a little pertinent to Quevedo's story'.[27] Having once abandoned any idea of virtue, Pablos' exclusive preoccupation with honour and wealth is made to lead him from one disaster to another. Misfortune pursues him from the moment he decides to 'mejorar su estado' not in a moral but in a purely material and social sense. The moral of the life of this obstinate sinner, as Quevedo makes Pablos brand himself in his parting words to the reader, is almost certainly to be taken as that expressed in one of our author's *Migajas sentenciosas*: 'No está en más nuestro acertar, que en no imitar al pueblo.'[28]

Quevedo's Stoical and satirical writings should be viewed as the two sides of one coin. Both arise out of the belief that moral corruption is the result of false opinion and, in particular, of attachment to power and wealth. This belief is most explicitly and interestingly revealed in *España defendida y los tiempos de ahora*, written in 1609. In chapter five Quevedo breaks off from defending Spain's reputation to contrast her past with her present. In his view her glory always consisted above all in her military exploits. So long as she was true to her tradition of vigorous belligerency the Lord of hosts enabled her to beat back the Moors

---

[24] *Q*, I. 521b.

[25] 'The Psychology of the *Pícaro* in *El Buscón*', *MLR*, xlii (1947), 58.

[26] See 'El individuo y la sociedad en *La vida del Buscón*', *BH*, lii (1950), 383–5.

[27] 'The Classical Ending of Quevedo's *Buscón*', *HR*, xxxii (1964), 107. See also Rothe, *Quevedo und Seneca*, pp. 30–2, for the view that Quevedo's source is *Ep.* 28, I, rather than Horace, *Ep.* I. xi. 27.

[28] *BP*, p. 1123b.

and conquer the New World. And because she attended to the
defence and expansion of her territory she was fonder of robust
virtue than of peace, rest, or comfort. The envy of her foes produced in her a 'miedo provechoso', a fear that had the inestimable
value of instilling caution and discipline into her inhabitants.[29]
As in his notes to Florus' *Epitome* of Roman history and in his
famous 'Epístola satírica y censoria' (the latter variously subtitled
'Contra las costumbres presentes de los castellanos' and 'En
recomendación de las costumbres antiguas de España'), in *España
defendida* he bids his fellow-countrymen recall the manly virtues
of their forebears:

> Pues si bajamos los ojos a las costumbres de los buenos hombres de
> Castilla, de quinientos y de cuatrocientos años a esta parte, ¡qué
> santidad, qué virtud y qué verdad veremos, que no imitamos ni here-
> damos, contentándonos con lo menos, que es el nombre! ¡Qué leyes
> tan lícitamente nacidas de las divinas, tan cuidadosamente veneradas de
> ellos! ¡Qué cosas no advirtieron con castigos en los *Fueros Juzgos*
> castellanos, donde se ven con rigurosas penas cosas que por nuestros
> pecados nos han persuadido los tiempos a que merecen premio![30]

The contrast between Spain's past and present is, in Quevedo's
view, due to what he considers a break with her warlike traditions,
which he evidently regards as dating from the Peace of Vervins
(1598) and the Peace of London (1604) and sees culminated in the
twelve-year truce with the Dutch signed less than six months
before he dedicated *España defendida* to Philip III.[31] For him, as
for Juvenal, the fatal effects of peace upon nations are amply
proved by the history of Rome:

> Mientras tuvo Roma a quien temer y enemigos, ¡qué diferentes
> costumbres tuvo! ¡Cómo se ejercitó en las armas! ¡Qué pechos tan
> valerosos ostentó al mundo! Mas luego que honraron sus deseos
> perezosos al ocio bestial con nombre de paz santa, ¡qué vicio no se
> apoderó de ella! ¡Y qué torpeza embarazó los ánimos que antes bastaron

---

[29] See *BP*, pp. 522a–524a. For *España defendida*, see R. Lida, 'La *España
defendida* y la síntesis pagano-cristiana', *Letras hispánicas*, pp. 142–8.

[30] *BP*, p. 523b. Cf. *OP*, I. 294–301. For Quevedo's notes to Florus, see H.
Ettinghausen, 'Quevedo Marginalia: His Copy of Florus's *Epitome*', *MLR*, lix
(1964), 391–8.

[31] This would seem to be the implication of his statement: 'a mi opinión
España nunca goza de paz: sólo descansa, como ahora, del peso de las armas,
para tornar a ellas con mayor fuerza y nuevo aliento' (*BP*, p. 522b). For the
considerable opposition in Spain to the truce of 1609, see Elliott, *Imperial
Spain*, p. 299.

a sujetar el mundo! Vióse entonces que la prudencia de los hombres sobra para vencer el mundo; mas no sabe vencerse a sí.[32]

Spain, 'viuda en parte del antiguo valor', is threatening to go the same way for the same reason. Her moral fibre is snapping because the martial spirit that inspired her to great things has been sapped by the powerful knight of Quevedo's famous *letrilla*, Don Dinero: 'Han empezado a contentarse los hombres de España con heredar de sus padres virtud, sin procurar tenerla para que la hereden sus hijos. Alcanzan a todas partes las fuerzas del dinero, o, por lo menos, se atreven, bien que el oro nació con tal imperio en la cudicia de los hombres; pobres, conquistamos riquezas ajenas; ricos, las mismas riquezas nos conquistan.'[33] The gold and silver of America have been lost to foreigners in payment not, in his view, for decades of exorbitant military expenditure but for new-fangled, effeminate fashions which have led to 'vicios desconocidos de naturaleza'. We find ourselves here in the very midst of the world of the *Sueños*. Spanish matrons, once renowned for their modesty, pride themselves on lewdness and adultery; and husbands have turned the state of matrimony into a trade.[34] As Lucifer points out in his closing speech in the *Discurso de todos los diablos*, only the Devil stands to gain by peace.

As for *España defendida*'s flattering tributes to Philip III's reforming zeal, they call to mind Quevedo's remark apropos of Seneca's *De clementia* that it was an 'estratagema muchas veces bien lograda, para reprehender a los monarcas, alabarlos de lo que no hacen ni tienen ni quieren'.[35] In particular, it is difficult to take at face value, only two years after the discovery of the scandalous embezzlement by Pedro Franqueza of one-fifth of the Crown's annual income, Quevedo's praise for Philip's wisdom in appointing virtuous, poor men to high office or his declaration that Spain's situation would be desperate but for the dedication of

---

[32] *BP*, p. 522a/b.

[33] Ibid., p. 524a. Although in his second letter to Lipsius Quevedo laments the loss of Spanish men and money in Flanders—'Ibi miles noster, opesque consumuntur' (Ramírez, *Epistolario*, p. 400)—it should be noted, first, that he is echoing Lipsius' complaint—'opes ac miles vester hic exhauriuntur aut consumuntur' (ibid., p. 391)—and, secondly, that he is at least as upset about the effects of *otium* in Spain: 'Vos belli praeda estis. Nos otij, et ignorantiae. . . . Hic nos consumimur: et desunt qui verba faciant, non qui dent' (p. 400).

[34] See *BP*, p. 524b.                                    [35] *Q*, II. 127a.

his ministers to the service of God, king, and country.[36] When, perhaps some sixteen years later, he wrote his 'Epístola satírica y censoria', relying on irony no longer, he was to call upon Olivares in no uncertain terms to replace Philip IV's favourite pastimes (the theatre, riding, and jousting with reed spears) with 'la militar valiente disciplina' and to emulate Pelayo, the first Spanish victor over the Moors, and thereby begin to restore the 'virtud desaliñada' and 'robusta virtud' of old.[37] When Seneca and Juvenal evoked a past golden age in contrast to the black present, they may well have thought back wistfully to the expansion and consolidation of the Empire, the defence of Roman traditions, and the attempts at curbing luxury and adultery of the age of Augustus. Quevedo could scarcely fail to recall and idealize the reign of Philip II that had kept Spain unflinchingly to her imperial mission and had backed it up with the militant ideology of the Counter-Reformation. His perfect monarch, as depicted in *Política de Dios*, is characterized by Philip II's proverbial self-reliance and distrust of ambitious favourites. At least one of Quevedo's references to him, dating possibly from the same period as the 'Epístola satírica y censoria', seems to support the view that our author regarded him as the last royal upholder of Spain's best traditions: 'era su semblante ejecutivo, y su silencio elocuente, y su *paz belicosa*.'[38] He certainly idolized his friend the Duke of Osuna, in whose aggressive policies in defence of Spanish hegemony in Italy he himself took an active part until the duke's disgrace in 1620.

Quevedo's despair at Spain's failure to fulfil her destiny underlies his satirical as well as his political writing. Despite his protestations that the target of the *Sueños* was vices and not classes, it is impossible to avoid the fact that the most constant object of his satire is the trades and professions and that he regards these twin branches of the nascent bourgeoisie as totally and unscrupulously dedicated to the pursuit of wealth. The *Sueños*, *Discurso de todos los diablos*, and *La hora de todos y la Fortuna con seso* continually expose the tricks of all kinds of trades, and the

---

[36] See *BP*, pp. 524b, 525a. For Pedro Franqueza see Elliott, pp. 297–8. J. O. Crosby, 'Quevedo and the Court of Philip III: Neglected Satirical Letters and New Biographical Data', *PMLA*, lxxi (1956), esp. 1122–3, comments on the letter of 1615 in which Quevedo, describing the eagerness with which courtiers allowed themselves to be bribed, does not conceal his contempt for them.

[37] See *OP*, I. 296, 300, 301.         [38] *Q*, II. 480a (my italics).

vices of other people who are satirized are frequently denounced in money terms.[39] Besides his repeated attacks on pastry-cooks, tavern-keepers, tailors, cobblers, jewellers, apothecaries, and so forth, his references to businessmen in general are especially symptomatic of his attitudes. In the first *Sueño*, for example, he says that what struck him most when he witnessed the Last Judgement was seeing 'dos o tres mercaderes que se habían vestido las almas del revés, y tenían todos los cinco sentidos en las uñas de la mano derecha.'[40] In the second, the possibility of carrying off to hell a large number of traders is given as the ultimate reason why judges are the devils' favourite prey: 'porque de cada juez que sembramos, cogemos seis procuradores, dos relatores, cuatro escribanos, cinco letrados y cinco mil negociantes, y esto cada día.'[41] In the third, the road to hell is said to be distinguishable above all by the crowds of 'mercaderes, joyeros y todos oficios'.[42] In the last, Money itself appears in person to claim that it carries out on its own all the functions of the three traditional enemies of the soul.[43] And in the *Discurso de todos los diablos* Lucifer upbraids a devil for wasting time by unnecessarily making sure that a merchant did not return his ill-gotten gains.[44] Although in *La hora de todos* Quevedo voices popular complaints against Spain's enemies abroad more clearly and insistently than before, the main force of his satire is still brought to bear upon the medical and legal professions and such obviously money-grubbing types as pawnbrokers, *arbitristas*, office-hunters, card-sharpers, and Genoese bankers. One passage in this work, the conversation between an alchemist and a coal-merchant, is especially revealing. On hearing the alchemist's account of the riches that are to be had for the asking, the coal-merchant becomes transformed into greed personified, just as Licenciado Cabra in the *Buscón* is miserliness incarnate: 'Oíale el mezquino con una atención canina y lacerada, y tan encendido en codicia con la turbamulta de millones, que le tecleaban los dedos en ademán de contar. Habíale crecido tanto el ojo, que no le cabía en la cara.'[45] But, as the alchemist points out, the coal-merchant is himself an expert at alchemy, for he makes gold and silver out of the basest

---

[39] e.g. Judas remarks on Luther and Muhammad in the first *Sueño*: 'bien conocéis vos que soy mucho mejor que éstos, porque si os vendí remedié al mundo, y éstos, vendiéndose a sí y a vos, lo han destruído todo' (*Q*, I. 301b).

[40] *Q*, I. 299a.          [41] *Q*, I. 306a.          [42] *Q*, I. 309a.

[43] See *Q*, I. 336a/b.       [44] See *Q*, I. 364b.       [45] *Q*, I. 401a.

things, including the stones he sells as charcoal, the earth and
filth he mixes with his coal, and the tricks he plays with his steel-
yard. And the coal-merchant readily admits that buying cheap
and selling dear is the real philosopher's stone and that trade can
make one doubloon give birth to another in the space of a month.[46]

The bitterness and frequency of Quevedo's onslaughts on the
trades and professions doubtless reflect in large measure the
resentment of the poorer nobility, particularly those like himself
on fixed or irregular incomes, at the ability of those classes to
protect themselves from galloping inflation by raising prices and
reducing the quality of their goods and services.[47] The plight of a
typical nobleman forced to spend conspicuously in order to keep
up his position at Court is graphically portrayed just after the
middle of the seventeenth century in Noydens's *Historia moral
del dios Momo*: '¿No sabéis que la primera cosa que preguntan los
señores antes de ponerse el ferreruelo y espada, es quién aguarda
allá fuera, para salir por puerta diferente y dexar burlados al
sastre, al platero, al bordador y a otros que esperan su salida
en la antesala?'[48] What little we know about Quevedo's dealings
with professional and trades people suggests that his own ex-
perience was not entirely a happy one. As a student at Valladolid
he quarrelled with a doctor over payment of a sixty-ducat bill.
On more than one occasion during their interminable lawsuits,
the inhabitants of the village of La Torre de Juan Abad sought
to deprive him of his *señorío* and created grave financial difficulties
for him. And it is largely thanks to the unscrupulous printers
who pirated his works or sought an easy profit by falsely attributing to him the writings of others that his name appeared on the
Index. On several occasions, and not only in his treatment of
Pablos in the *Buscón*, he reveals a strong dislike for the social

[46] See *Q*, I. 401b–402a.
[47] J. Lynch, *Spain under the Habsburgs*, ii (Oxford, 1969), refers to the 'vast
service sector' that supplied the Court at the beginning of the seventeenth
century (p. 139) and to 'the poor nobility who resented the pretensions of trades-
men, professional people and other urban groups' (p. 130).
After completing this study in 1969, I have discovered that my reading of
Quevedo's satirical works has been anticipated by R. Jammes (*Études sur l'œuvre
poétique de Don Luis de Góngora y Argote* (Bordeaux, 1967), esp. p. 55), and
N. Salomon (*Recherches sur le thème paysan dans la 'Comedia' au temps de Lope de
Vega* (Bordeaux, 1965), p. 259.
[48] Quoted by A. Domínguez Ortiz, *La sociedad española en el siglo XVII*, i
(Madrid, 1963), p. 252.

pretensions of the lower orders. To mention but two examples, in the fourth *Sueño* he cries out at the hypocrisy not only of a *caballero* aping a *señoría* and an *hidalgo* a *caballero*, but, most strongly, at that of a man who earns his living as a tailor dressing like an *hidalgo*;[49] and in the third *Sueño* he consigns a bookseller to hell for giving fools the same opportunities as educated men by selling cheap translations of the classics, so that 'hasta el lacayo latiniza, y hallarán a Horacio en castellano en la caballeriza.'[50] Contempt for the values of the *vulgo* is one thing Quevedo had in common with his literary foe, Góngora, who also saw the source of Spain's troubles in commerce[51] and, besides, prided himself on writing verse that left the uneducated baffled. Like Góngora and many more of their class, and like the 'English Seneca', Joseph Hall, he dreamed of putting the clock back to 'a dim imaginary past when men lived without the false trimmings of civilization.'[52] As far as he is concerned, eliminating the trimmings means eliminating those classes that make their living by supplying them. However, as he argues in *Providencia de Dios*, while money is certainly not good, it is not in itself an evil either. The uneven distribution of wealth is not merely justified, but wonderfully equitable, for ideally there should be only two types of people: the rich acting like fathers to the poor by supplementing Nature's bounty with charity; and the poor, content in the knowledge that what they lack is 'indifferent', accepting charity when it is offered— and thereby, incidentally, helping the rich achieve salvation.[53]

Parallels with these attitudes in Seneca and Juvenal are both striking and illuminating. Neither of the Romans, for all their

[49] See *Q*, I. 326b.
[50] *Q*, I. 311a. C. Aubrun says of Pablos: 'Chaque fois qu'il est sur le point de sortir de sa condition première, l'auteur l'enfonce dans la fange d'un grand coup de talon' ('La gueuserie aux XVIe et XVIIe siècles en Espagne et le roman picaresque', in *Littérature et société: problèmes de méthodologie en sociologie de la littérature* (Brussels, 1967), p. 144). A. Mas, *La Caricature de la femme, du mariage et de l'amour dans l'œuvre de Quevedo* (Paris, 1957), p. 329, notes that 'Quevedo n'est pas moins attaché, en effet, au maintien des hiérarchies sociales qu'au respect des distinctions naturelles'.
[51] See R. O. Jones, 'The Poetic Unity of the *Soledades* of Góngora', *BHS*, xxxi (1954), 196–200.
[52] A. Chew, 'Joseph Hall and Neo-Stoicism', *PMLA*, lxv (1950), 1139. Jones, ('Some Notes on More's *Utopia*', p. 482), suggests that for Quevedo and his generation *Utopia* was no longer a 'standing criticism of all Christendom' but 'offered simply a wistful glimpse of an unattainable past'.
[53] See *Q*, II. 199b.

tirades against the evils of money, made the slightest criticism of the structure of society. Seneca's thesis in *De vita beata* that the possession of wealth is compatible with commitment to the Stoa (which reads uncomfortably like an attempt at justifying his own very considerable fortune) rests ultimately upon the argument that inherited riches, since they are acquired without resorting to base dealing, are a gift of Fortune about accepting which the philosopher need have no moral qualms. What is more, for Seneca, too, the virtuous rich are entrusted with the social responsibility of seeing to it that the deserving poor do not go unrewarded. But, since indiscriminate giving is a shameful waste, the rich should, he says, make sure they have pockets from which much can appear but nothing can fall.[54] As for Juvenal, according to tradition the son of a wealthy freeman, he views the world bitterly from the position of one who has actually lost his place in the social hierarchy and has seen the ranks to which he had once aspired filled by low-born and even foreign climbers: 'He is sorry for middle-class men like himself who cannot get advancement. And he has a particular grievance about unworthy men who get ahead in the equestrian career. The man he hates most, next to the emperor Domitian, is the Egyptian Crispinus, who rose from being a fish-peddler to hold one of the two top posts open to knights, the command of the imperial guard.'[55] There is every reason to suppose that Seneca and Juvenal were Quevedo's favourite Latin authors not only because he admired their style and their philosophy, in a conventional sense, but also, and perhaps especially, because, in what R. H. Tawney described as 'a world heaving with the vastest economic crisis that Europe had experienced since the fall of Rome',[56] he shared their assumptions and pre-occupations about society.

Quite apart, then, from his personal need for the comfort of Stoic ethics at the most critical and conscience-stricken periods of his life, Quevedo's Neostoicism would appear to have its deepest roots in his awareness of what have been called 'the terrible paradoxes of the Castile of Philip III' and his successor, and in the conviction he shared with Osuna and Olivares that 'Spain could

[54] See *De vita beata*, XXIII.
[55] G. Highet, *Juvenal the Satirist* (Oxford, 1962), p. 37. See also P. Green, trans., *The Sixteen Satires* (Harmondsworth, 1967), pp. 23–35.
[56] *Religion and the Rise of Capitalism* (Harmondsworth, 1964), p. 76.

remain true to itself only if it remained true to its imperial tradition'.[57] At the practical level of living in this world, the example and teaching of the Stoics, 'útil y eficaz y verdaderamente varonil y robusta' as he calls it in the preface to *La cuna y la sepultura*, could provide support, by its 'devaluation' of 'externals', for the conservative wisdom of moral regeneration through indifference to circumstances. On the one hand Stoicism could counter the effects of 'vulgar' greed for money, honour, and power. On the other it could give consolation and a sense of moral superiority to those members of the nobility who, like Quevedo, had been made to realize that social and economic advantage no longer necessarily went hand in hand with noble birth.

[57] Elliott, *Imperial Spain*, pp. 294, 320.

# APPENDIX I

## QUEVEDO'S COPIES OF SENECA'S WORKS

WHEREAS Quevedo himself refers to the large number of different editions of Epictetus that he consulted for his translation of the *Manual* and even compares some of their readings,[1] he never identifies the editions of Seneca from which he took his quotations and made translations. Only one of them has been identified up to now: the Lyon 1555 edition, a copy of which, bearing his name on the title-page and with extensive annotations in his hand, is in the collection of the Count of Doña Marina (see below, Appendix II). However, the identity of two more editions used by him can be inferred from an examination of his translation of eleven of Seneca's Epistles and from his prefatory *Juicio* to his *De los remedios de cualquier fortuna*.

I

In his prologue to the first part of his *Vida de Marco Bruto*, the only work he published after his release from his last imprisonment in León, Quevedo states that among the papers which were confiscated on his arrest and never returned to him were '*Noventa epístolas de Séneca, traducidas y anotadas*'.[2] Only eleven such Epistles have come down to us, together with four imitations of Senecan Epistles, and appear in the same curious order in three eighteenth-century manuscripts.[3] However, particularly in view of the fact that only two of them are annotated, there is no way of knowing that these were among the ninety he referred to as lost.

When they are compared with the Latin editions from which they might have been made, it becomes clear that the eleven Epistles were translated from Lipsius' text and that Quevedo made fairly extensive use of his commentary. Thus, in Epistle 44 he translates Seneca's 'mehercules multis quattuordecim sunt clausi' as 'mas de verdad para muchos se cierran los catorce asientos', having, obviously, consulted Lipsius' note on 'quattuordecim': '*Gradus in theatris, proprij & sepositi equitibus.*'[4] Similarly, when he renders 'atrius plenum fumosis

---

[1] See *Q*, III. 385.      [2] *Q*, I. 132.
[3] Biblioteca Nacional, Madrid, MS. 4066; Real Academia Española, Madrid, MS. 29; and collection of Professor J. O. Crosby.
[4] Seneca, *Opera quae extant omnia* (Antwerp, 1652), p. 456. Cf. *Q*, II. 385b.

imaginibus' by 'el camarín cubierto con retratos ahumados de ilustres progenitores', his elaboration on Seneca's words relies on Lipsius' note: '*Romanus propiè mos collocandi in tabularijs per atria imagines majorum: atque ex ijs nobilitas aestimata.*'[5] Again, when Seneca remarks in Epistle 54 that he will refer to his chest ailment by its Greek name, and then does not, Quevedo adds both the alternatives suggested by Lipsius.[6] And the same thing happens when he translates 'singulis enim & genium & Junonem dederunt' in Epistle 110 by 'a cada hombre dieron un Genio, a cada mujer una Juno', a rendering inspired by the beginning of Lipsius' note: '*Hoc ita accipe, non ut singuli utrumque habuerint, sed ut alterum: & clarius esset, aut genium aut Junonem. Nam viris Genij attribuebantur, faeminis Iunones.*'[7]

In his note to Seneca's Epistle 41 Quevedo delivers the following panegyric of Lipsius in order to point a contrast with Muret:

Exclama el doctísimo Justo Lipsio en el argumento desta epístola: *O pulchram, altamque epistolam!* Leía sin pasión, juzgaba sin envidia, no se conocía en sus comentos su patria, lo francés no pasa del nacimiento a la pluma. ¡O mi Lipsio, grande honra de Francia! tanto como España debe a Córdoba porque le dió a Séneca, te debe España porque se le resucitas y se le defiendes.[8]

The fact that here he actually quotes the opening exclamation of the title given to the Epistle by Lipsius would appear to prove beyond any doubt that the Fleming's was the edition he used for his translation. But when, in the following paragraph, he accuses Muret of showing anti-Spanish feeling in his edition and actually quotes part of his commentary on the Epistle, it would seem that Quevedo must also have consulted his edition. And then, when he cites Hernán Núñez's note to part of Epistle 105, it would appear that he must have consulted his commentary as well.[9]

Quevedo did not, in fact, have to go to the trouble of consulting all these books. Evidence that he actually used none of them is contained in his remark, quoted above, that Lipsius' exclamation at the beginning of Epistle 41 occurred 'en el argumento desta epístola'. In Lipsius' edition of Seneca the titles of the Epistles are not headed 'Argumentum'; but they are in an edition based on Lipsius' text that was frequently reprinted in Paris between 1607 and 1628. In these editions the Fleming's

---

[5] Seneca, ed. cit., p. 457. Cf. *Q*, II. 385b.
[6] See Seneca, ed. cit., p. 474. Cf. *Q*, II. 386a.
[7] Seneca, ed. cit., p. 640. Cf. *Q*, II. 387a.
[8] *Q*, II. 384a.
[9] 'Pinciano lee: *poculum faciet*, menos a propósito, y contradiciendo al contexto' (*Q*, II. 386b). Cf. Hernán Núñez de Guzmán, *In omnia L. Annaei Senecae philosophi scripta* (Venice, 1536), fol. 79ᵛ.

titles to the Epistles are each headed 'Argumentum I. Lipsi'.[10] What is more, one of the very few divergences from Lipsius' text occurs at the beginning of Epistle 54, and it is followed by Quevedo.[11] Since these Paris editions reproduce not only Lipsius' commentary but also those of Muret, Hernán Núñez, and others, one of these multi-commentary editions was evidently the source also of Quevedo's quotations from these three commentators in his notes to Epistles 41 and 105.

## II

In the *Juicio* to *De los remedios de cualquier fortuna*, Quevedo paraphrased the note that Lipsius appended to *De remediis fortuitorum* in his edition of Seneca, and also followed his rather than Erasmus' reading of the text in at least two places in his translation.[12] Although Lipsius' note also appears in the multi-commentary editions published in Paris, one of which, as we have seen, Quevedo used for his translation of the Epistles, it appears that he went to a copy of Lipsius' Seneca when he wrote his *Juicio*, for in the Paris editions the note is headed: 'Ad excerpta notae. Nicol. Faber.' Had our author used one of these editions he would, therefore, almost certainly have wrongly attributed the note to Nicolas Lefèvre. From other evidence we know that he used a copy of the second (1615) or third (1632) edition of Lipsius' Seneca in the year 1635.[13] It seems likely that when he wrote the *Juicio*, presumably not long before *De los remedios de cualquier fortuna* was published in 1638, he used one of these two editions.

[10] There are copies of the 1607, 1613, 1619, 1627, and 1628 editions in the Biblioteca Nacional, Madrid.

[11] In Lipsius' edition (ed. cit., p. 474) this Epistle begins: 'Longum mihi commeatum dederat mala valetudo.' The Paris editions have 'desiderat' for 'dederat', and Quevedo translates: 'Larga prevención desea mi poca salud' (*Q*, II. 385b).

[12] See above, p. 62.

[13] See Ettinghausen, 'Neostoicism in Pictures', p. 96.

# APPENDIX II

## QUEVEDO'S ANNOTATIONS TO SENECA

QUEVEDO's annotations in his copy of the first volume of the Lyon 1555 edition of Seneca's works were first published by L. Astrana Marín in 1932.[1] His method of presenting them has, however, been criticized by P. U. González de la Calle, who points out that his bare page-references to this rare edition of Seneca make it almost impossible to relate Quevedo's notes to Seneca's text.[2] Without himself having seen Quevedo's or any other copy of the Lyon edition, González de la Calle has attempted to identify the passages to which Quevedo's notes to the Epistles refer. Not surprisingly, he is not always successful.[3] What is more, without having seen them in the original, but claiming none the less to be inspired by 'justos anhelos de seriedad y de exactitud científicas', he has even sought to rectify some of what he calls the 'lamentables y notorios yerros' in Astrana's transcription of the notes.[4] As it happens, an examination of Quevedo's copy of the Lyon edition reveals that Astrana did indeed make serious errors of transcription. As many as twenty-three of Quevedo's notes are entirely missing in his edition; the note he refers to as being on p. 286 of the book is not to be found there; and the note he transcribes from p. 302 is not by Quevedo but by one of the book's earlier owners.[5] The one who wrote this particular note was Jerónimo Antonio de Medinilla y Porres, the only one apart from Quevedo whose name appears on the title-page. His name, moreover, was written first, for Quevedo's signature and inscription were placed so as to fit the space left by his.

Quevedo's inscription, with its reference to 'otros compañeros',[6] suggests the possibility that the book was used by a group of friends. Quevedo undoubtedly knew Medinilla, for he wrote a preface for his

---

[1] See Quevedo, *Obras completas*, ed. L. Astrana Marín, 'Prosa' (Madrid, 1932), pp. 1315–17.

[2] See *Quevedo y los dos Sénecas*, p. 307.

[3] e.g. he gives the reference *Ep.* 79, 15–17 to the note on p. 338 of Quevedo's copy of Seneca when it is in fact a note to *Ep.* 66, 47 (see González de la Calle, p. 324).

[4] González de la Calle, p. 308.

[5] See Quevedo, *Obras completas*, ed. cit., p. 1316. Astrana identifies two other hands besides Quevedo's and Medinilla's, one sixteenth-, the other late seventeenth-century.

[6] See below, Quevedo's first note.

translation of More's *Utopia* and declared therein that it was he who had urged Medinilla to undertake it.[7] Furthermore, the two men were not only fellow knights of St. James who must have met frequently at Court, but, as Gobernador of Villanueva de los Infantes, Medinilla was practically Quevedo's neighbour when our author resided at La Torre de Juan Abad. Indeed, in his preface, written from La Torre in 1637, Quevedo refers to his 'gran providencia y desinterés, en el gobierno que tuvo destos partidos.'[8] After 1637 we know of only one reference to him by Quevedo: the curious wish expressed in his will that he be buried in the same tomb as Medinilla's widow in the monastery of Santo Domingo at Villanueva until his remains could be taken to Madrid.[9] To judge by the fact that Quevedo added to the original draft of his *Defensa de Epicuro* on a number of occasions before its publication in 1635, the loan or gift of Medinilla's copy of Seneca, on which much of the first draft is based, constitutes the earliest-known evidence of their friendship.[10]

Quevedo's marginalia tell us a good deal about the kinds of things that struck him as he read Seneca. In addition to almost all Seneca's references to Epicurus, he marked three passages in which Brutus is mentioned, and cited them at the beginning of his *Vida de Marco Bruto* (see below, Nos. 4, 91, and 92). He also made eight textual emendations (Nos. 2, 3, 43, 48, 51, 65, 88, and 89); and he expressed disagreement with Erasmus' objection to Seneca's insistence upon a thorough grounding in philosophy (No. 97). Some half-dozen passages appear to have been noted by him out of antiquarian interest in Roman customs (Nos. 55–8, 62, and 63). Two are marked for their references to the Stoics (Nos. 20 and 45); and several more caught his imagination by their mention of Stoical heroes: Marcellus (No. 93), the elder Cato (No. 60), and Scipio (No. 54). In addition he noted Seneca's views on the question whether Homer should be regarded as a philosopher (No. 61), and he compared the Stoical virtue of his contemporary, the judge Berenguer de Aoíz, to that of Menenius Agrippa (No. 96).[11] He was also attracted by some of Seneca's references to the courage and primitive virtues of the ancient Germans (Nos. 71, 75,

[7] See *Q*, II. 493, and F. López Estrada, 'La primera versión española de la *Utopia* de Moro, por Jerónimo Antonio de Medinilla (Córdoba, 1637)', in *Collected Studies in Honour of Américo Castro's Eightieth Year*, ed. M. P. Hornik (Oxford, 1965), pp. 291–309.

[8] *Q*, II. 493b. See López Estrada, p. 295.

[9] See *Q*, II. 678a, 679a. Medinilla died two years after Quevedo, on 13 July 1647 (see Archivo del Palacio Nacional, Madrid, *Caja* 663/13).

[10] Quevedo's earliest extant references to Medinilla are in a letter of January 1635 (see López Estrada, p. 296).

[11] For Aoíz and Quevedo's epitaph for him, see Crosby, *En torno a la poesía de Quevedo*, pp. 137–8.

and 76) and Spaniards (Nos. 87 and 90). The only Stoical idea he noted, apart from ingratitude (No. 8), was that of the need to prepare for death (Nos. 13, 41, 49, 50, 52, 53, and 73). Somewhat surprisingly, he marked only one of Seneca's discussions of the nature of God (No. 7); and he may have been struck by the parallel of the Roman Catholic attitude to images in Seneca's commendation of the worship of the images of ancestors (No. 46). What evidently excited him most was Seneca's style. He admiringly points out that one Epistle is devoted to problems of style (No. 69); and he translates or calls attention to some thirteen politico-moral *sententiae* (Nos. 9, 10, 12, 40, 59, 65–7, 72, 74, 77–8, and 94). Most of the facets of his interest in the Stoic that have been observed in his own Stoical writings are reflected in these notes, except that he left no annotations at all to the text of *De remediis fortuitorum*, despite the fact that he used this edition for his translation; and his marginalia give remarkably little indication of his passion for Christianizing Stoicism.

In the edition of the marginalia which follows, passages corresponding to Quevedo's annotations are reproduced only when they contain underlinings, and these are indicated. Where there is no underlining in the text, a precise reference to Seneca's works will enable the reader to locate the passage in question. Mere marks in the margins of the book, of which there are many, are not reproduced since, even if they are by Quevedo, they do not represent an articulate response to the passages to which they correspond. Line divisions in the notes are indicated; the notes themselves appear in italics; letters lost when the book's margins were cut are restored and appear in square brackets; spelling and punctuation are reproduced without any change; notes omitted by Astrana Marín are asterisked; and, where an annotated passage is cited in Quevedo's works, this is stated.

1. Title-page:
   *h*[?]*istrumento de los libros de Don Fran^{co}. / de Quevedo Villegas. con otros compañeros —*

*2. *De benef.* I. iii. 7 (p. 5):
   '. . . ut scias illas Vestales nõ esse uirgines. Inueniã aliũ poëtam, apud que praecingãtur, & spicis prodeãt. Ergo & Mercurius unà stat, non quia beneficia ratio cõmendat . . .' *Nota / dele, et le*[*ge*] */ egle*[?]*], et* [*Mer*]*/curius una / stant —*

*3. *De benef.* I. iii. 8 (p. 5):
   '. . . & uerbis non ultra, quàm ad intellectum satis est . . .' *lege verbis / vltra, et de*[*le*] */ non —*

4. *De benef.* II. xx. 1 (p. 30):
   + / *De Marco / Bruto*
   Cited in *Vida de Marco Bruto* (*Q*, I. 130).

5. *De benef.* IV. ii. 1 (p. 69):
'In hac parte nobis pugna est, cũ Epicureorum delicata & umbratica turba...' + | *De Epicu/ro. in uer*[?] | *et senecam* [*u*]/*bi concilieb*[?] | *et lege. Nobis p/ugna* [*es*]/*t cun epicur*[*eo*]/*run, in hac pa/rte delicat et vm/bratica turba* | [a line] | *Perperam* | *in hac quest*[*i*]/*one Seneca* | *contra Epic*[*u*]/*reos arguit* | *vt mihi vide/tur*
Cited in *Defensa de Epicuro* (*Q*, III. 421 and 430).

6. *De benef.* IV. iv. 1 (p. 70):
*nihil agit* | *Deus dixit Ep/icurus, non quia* | *aliquid non* | [*n*]*egat sed quia* | [*o*]*mni agit, si* | *uere passione, et perturbaçione. modo vvlgar es de/çir que el que haze vna cosa sin trabajo i sin que le cueste* | *nada, que no haze nada en hazello.*
Cited in *Defensa de Epicuro* (*Q*, III. 430).

7. *De benef.* IV. viii. 3 (p. 73):
+ | *todos los* | *Dioses afir/ma que son* | *vn Dios, i po*[*r*]/*que en Dios to/do es Dios lla/man con no/mbre de un* | *Dios la Cleme/ncia, i de otro* | *la Justiçia* | *i de otro la Fer/tilidad.*

*8. *De benef.* V. xvi. 1 (p. 112):
+ | *ingratvs*

9. *De benef.* VI. xxxi. 11 (p. 143):
'... quantum ab exercitu turba distaret.' *ai mucha dif*[*e*]/*rençia de Ex*[*e*]/*rcito, a Multi/tud.* —

10. *De benef.* VI. xxxiii. 1 (p. 144):
'... dic illis non quod uolunt audire, sed quod audisse semper uolent.' *Di no lo q̃; vno* | *quiere oir sino* | *lo que siempre* | *querra aber oi/do*

11. *Ep.* 2, 5 (p. 179):
'Hodiernum, hoc est, quod apud Epicurũ nactus sum.' *Epicuro*

12. *Ep.* 3, 4 (p. 181):
'Vtrumq; enim uitium est, & omnibus credere, & nulli...' *Ω / viçio es creer* | *a todos, i a ni/nguno, aquel* | *mas honesto,* | *este mas seguro*

13. *Ep.* 4, 9 (p. 183):
'Haec & huiusmodi uersanda in animo sunt, si uolumus illam ultimam horã placidi expectare, cuius metus oẽs alias inquietas facit.' + | *Padecer vna* | *humanida/d afrentosa*

*14. *Ep.* 6, 6 (p. 186):
'Metrodorum, & Erymachum, & Poliaenum, magnos uiros non schola Epicuri, sed contuberniũ fecit.' ∩ | *Epicuro*
Cited in *Defensa de Epicuro* (*Q*, III. 423).

15. *Ep.* 7, 11 (p. 188):
'Egregie hoc tertium. Epicurus cum uni ex consortibus studiorum suorum scriberet...' *Epicuro*

16. *Ep.* 8, 8 (p. 190):
'Potest fieri, ut me interroges, quare ab Epicuro tã multa bene dicta
referã potius quàm nostrorũ? quid est tamẽ, quare tu istas Epicuri
uoces putes esse non publicas?' *Epicuro | ePicuro*
Cited in *Defensa de Epicuro* (*Q*, III. 423).

17. *Ep.* 9, 1 (p. 190):
*Epicuro*

18. *Ep.* 9, 20 (p. 194):
'Epicurus, similem illi uocem emisit, quam tu boni consule, etiã
hunc diẽ iam expuxi. Si cui, inquit, sua non uidentur, amplissima,
licet totius mundi dominus sit, tamen miser est.' *Epicuro.* | [a line]
Cited in *Defensa de Epicuro* (*Q*, III. 423).

19. *Ep.* 12, 11 (p. 200):
'Epicurus, inquis, dixit, quid tibi cum alieno? Quod uerum est,
meũ est. Perseuerabo Epicurum tibi ingerere, ut isti qui in uerba
iurant, nec quid dicatur aestimant, sed à quo, sciant, quae optima
sunt esse comunia.' *Epicur/o* —
Cited in *Defensa de Epicuro* (*Q*, III. 423).

20. *Ep.* 13, 4 (p. 202):
'. . . & saepius opinione quàm re laboramus. Non loquor tecum
Stoica lingua, sed hac submissione.' *nota | + | stoica*
Cited in *Defensa de Epicuro* (*Q*, III. 426).

21. *Ep.* 13, 17 (p. 204):
'Quid est autem turpius qum senex uiuere incipiens. Non adijcerem
autorẽ huic uoci, nisi esset secretior . . .' *Epicuri | vox.*
Cited in *Defensa de Epicuro* (*Q*, III. 423).

22. *Ep.* 13, 17 (p. 205):
'. . . nec inter uulgata Epicuri dicta, quae mihi & laudare, &
adoptare permisi.' *Epi/curo*

23. *Ep.* 18, 9 (p. 217):
'Certos habebat dies ille magister uoluptatis Epicurus, quibus
maligne famem extingueret, uisurus an aliquid deesset ex plena et
cõsummata uoluptate, uel quantũ deesset, et an dignũ, quod quis
magno labore pensaret . . .' *Epicuro*
Cited in *Defensa de Epicuro* (*Q*, III. 423).

24. *Ep.* 19, 10 (p. 220):
'Vt se res habet ab Epicuro uersura facienda est. Ante, inquit,
circunspiciendum est, cum quibus edas & bibas, quàm quid edas
& bibas.' *Epicur.*
Cited in *Defensa de Epicuro* (*Q*, III. 423).

25. *Ep.* 20, 9 (p. 223):
'Inuieas licet, etiã nunc libenter pro me dependet Epicurus.
Magnificẽtior (mihi crede) sermo tuus in grabato uidebitur & in
panno . . .' ∩ / *Epicuro*

26. *Ep.* 20, 11 (p. 224):
'Nec scio ego Epicuri angelus, si pauper iste contempturus sit
diuitias . . . nisi apparuit aliquem illa non necessitate pati sed malle.'
*Epicuro*

*27. *Ep.* 21, 3 (p. 225):
'Si gloria, inquit, tangeris, notiorẽ te epistolae meae facient, quàm
omnia ista quae colis, & propter quae coleris.' *Epicuro*
Cited in *Defensa de Epicuro* (*Q*, III. 423).

*28. *Ep.* 21, 5 (p. 225):
'Quod Epicurus amico suo potuit promittere, hoc tibi promitto
Lucili.' *Epicuro*

29. *Ep.* 21, 7 (p. 226):
'Ad hunc Epicurus illã nobilẽ sententiã scripsit, qua hortatur, ut
Pythoclea locupletẽ non lublica, nec ancipiti uia faciat. Si uis,
inquit, Pythoclea diuitem facere, non pecuniae adijciendum, sed
cupiditatibus detrahendum est.' *Epicuri*
Cited in *Defensa de Epicuro* (*Q*, III. 423).

30. *Ep.* 21, 9 (p. 226):
*Epicuri*
Cited in *Defensa de Epicuro* (*Q*, III. 424).

31. *Ep.* 22, 5–6 (p. 228):
'Epicuri epistolam ad hanc rem pertinentem legi, Idomeneo quae
scribitur, quem rogat, ut quantum potest fugiat & properet, antequam aliqua uis maior interueniat, & auferat libertatem recedendi.
Idem tamen subijcit, nihil esse tentandum, nisi cum apte poterit,
tempestiueq́; tentari.' ∩ / *Epicu/ro*

32. *Ep.* 23, 9 (p. 232):
'Possum enim uocem tibi Epicuri tui reddere, & hanc epistolam
liberare. Molestũ est semper uitam inchoare, aut si hoc modo magis
sensus potest exprimi, male uiuunt, qui semper uiuere incipiunt.'
*Epicuri*
Cited in *Defensa de Epicuro* (*Q*, III. 424).

33. *Ep.* 24, 18 (p. 236):
'. . . nec ullius uiscera, & renasci posse quotidie, & carpi.' *Epicuro*

\*34. *Ep.* 24, 22–3 (pp. 236–7):
'Obiurgat Epicurus non minus eos, qui mortĕ concupiscunt, quàm eos qui timent . . . cum uitam tibi inquietam feceris motu mortis?'
*Epicuro*
Cited in *Defensa de Epicuro* (*Q*, III. 424).

35. *Ep.* 25, 4–5 (p. 238):
'Panem & aquã natura desiderat, nemo ad haec pauper est, intra quae quisquis desiderium suum clausit . . . ut ait Epicurus. . . . Sic fac, inquit, omnia tanquã spectet aliquis.' *Epicu*
Cited in *Defensa de Epicuro* (*Q*, III. 424).

36. *Ep.* 25, 6 (p. 238):
'. . . quod idem suadet Epicurus, Tunc praecipue in te ipse secede, cũ esse cogeris in turba.' *Epicu*
Cited in *Defensa de Epicuro* (*Q*, III. 424).

37. *Ep.* 26, 8 (p. 240):
'. . . interim cõmodabit Epicurus, qui ait, Meditare utrũ cõmodius sit, uel mortem transire ad nos, uel nos ad eam.' ⌒ / *Epicur.*

38. *Ep.* 27, 9 (p. 242):
'Hoc saepe dicit Epicurus aliter atq; aliter. Sed nunquam nimis dicitur, quod nunquam satis discitur, Quibusdã remedia monstranda, quibusdam inculcanda sunt.' *Epicuro*

\*39. *Ep.* 46, 1 (p. 276):
'. . . leuis mihi uisus est, cum esset, nec mei, nec tui temporis, sed qui primo aspectu, aut Titi Liuij, aut Epicuri posset uideri . . .'
*brebis* / *dele esset* ['cum esset' is deleted in text and *esse* written in above 'mei'] / *Alauanza* / *de Epicuro* —
Cited in *Defensa de Epicuro* (*Q*, III. 424).

\*40. *Ep.* 47, 20 (p. 280):
'Nec hoc ignorant, sed occasionem nocendi captant, quaerendo acceperunt iniuriam, ut facerent.' *de los Reyes* / *i de su ira Jus/ta i Politica re/prehension*

41. *Ep.* 50 = Loeb *Ep.* 49, 11 (p. 285):
'Non ubiq; se mors tam prope ostendit, ubiq; tam propè est.' + / *no en todas par/tes se muestra* [*la*] / *muerte igual[me]/nte çercana a* [*no*]/*sotros mas en* [*to*]/*das partes esta* [*ta*]/*n çerca de nos[o]/tros.* —

\*42. *Ep.* 53 = Loeb *Ep.* 52, 3 (p. 291):
'Quosdã ait Epicurus ad ueritatẽ contendere sine ullius adiutorio . . .'
*Epicu[r]/us* —
Cited in *Defensa de Epicuro* (*Q*, III. 424).

\*43. *Ep.* 62 = Loeb *Ep.* 61, 1 (p. 318):
'Desinamus quod uolumus uelle.' *lege voluimus* / [a line]

44. *Ep.* 62 = Loeb *Ep.* 61, 4 (p. 319):
*Lucretius. | vitę satur co[n]/viua recede*

45. *Ep.* 65 = Loeb *Ep.* 64, 2 (p. 322):
*stoici*

46. *Ep.* 65 = Loeb *Ep.* 64, 9 (p. 323):
'Quid ni ego magnorū uirorū & imagines habeā, incitamenta animi,
& natales celebrem?' *Para la ad[o]/racion de la[s] | imagenes.*

47. *Ep.* 67 = Loeb *Ep.* 66, 47 (p. 338):
*epicu/ri laus | [a line]*
Cited in *Defensa de Epicuro* (*Q*, III. 424–5).

48. *Ep.* 71 = Loeb *Ep.* 70, 10 (p. 347):
'. . . adolescentis tam solidi, quàm nobilis, maiora sperantis, quàm
illo seculo quisquam sperare poterat, aut ipse ullo.' *non solidi lege,*
*sed stolidi, litera | adita stolidi est, maiora sperare, quam illo | seculo*
*quisquam sperare poterat, aut ipse vllo*

49. *Ep.* 71 = Loeb *Ep.* 70, 12 (p. 348):
'Exeat quà impetum cepit, siue ferrum appetit, siue laqueum . . .'
*[a]d Plinium. | [s]e occidere his | causis, ait pli/[n]ius esse per sapi/[e]ntiam*
*mori*

50. *Ep.* 71 = Loeb *Ep.* 70, 20 (p. 349):
'Quid est stultius quàm fastidiose mori?' *ergo per sapientiam mori*
*est | mori sine fastidio.*

*51. *Ep.* 78 = Loeb *Ep.* 77, 17 (p. 385):
'Tanti enim illā putas, ut tardius coenes, solemq́; si posses,
extingueres?' *ojo | solem[q] | si posses ex[t]/ingueres | [words deleted] |*
*vt tardius | cęnes —*

52. *Ep.* 78 = Loeb *Ep.* 77, 19 (p. 385):
'Inuitus relinquo officia uitae, quibus fideliter, & cum industria
fungor. Quid? tu nescis unum esse ex uitae officijs & mori?' *ojo |*
*siento dexa[r] | los ofiçios de [l]/a vida que h[ui]/o. porque ig[no]/ras*
*que es vno [de] | los oficios de la v[i]/da, morir —*

*53. *Ep.* 79 = Loeb *Ep.* 78, 6 (p. 387):
'Morieris non quia aegrotas, sed quia uiuis.' *ad Galion[e]/m —*

*54. *Ep.* 87 = Loeb *Ep.* 86, 1 (p. 428):
*ojo*

55. *Ep.* 87 = Loeb *Ep.* 86, 7 (p. 429):
'. . . quantū statuarum, quātum columnarum est nihil sustinentium,
sed in ornamentum positarum impensae causa?' *Columne | Mar-*
*moree | Ornamenti | causa*

**56. *Ep.* 87 = Loeb *Ep.* 86, 8 (p. 429):
'. . . ut sine iniuria munimēti, lumen admitteret.' *sin abertu[ra]* / [a line]

57. *Ep.* 87 = Loeb *Ep.* 86, 12 (p. 430):
'Nam, ut aiunt qui priscos mores urbis tradiderũt, brachia & crura quotidie abluebant, quae scilicet sordes opere collegerãt: caeterùm toti nundinis lauebantur.' *los brazos, i las* / *Piernas se la/baban cada di/[a] el Cuerpo ca/[d]a Mes.*

**58. *Ep.* 88 = Loeb. *Ep.* 87, 7 (p. 433):
*liber calen/darii.* —

59. *Ep.* 88 = Loeb *Ep.* 87, 8 (p. 433):
'Ista nec dominum meliorẽ possunt facere, nec mulã.' *El coche d[e]* / *Oro, no pued[e]* / *hazer mexor al dueño, ni [a]* / *las vestias que le tiran.*

60. *Ep.* 88 = Loeb *Ep.* 87, 10 (p. 434):
'. . . Catonem, uno caballo esse contentũ . . .' *Caton ocupa/ba vn solo Caba/[l]lo, i no todo* / *porque parte* / *[o]cupaba con* / *las alforxas,* / *[o] Maleta*

61. *Ep.* 89 = Loeb *Ep.* 88, 5 (p. 441):
'Nisi forte tibi Homerum Philosophum fuisse, persuadent. . . Demus illis Homerum philosophum fuisse, Nempe sapiens factus est, antequam carmina ulla cognosceret: ergo illa discamus, quae Homerum fecere sapientem.' *de Hom[e]/ri philos[o]/phia*

62. *Ep.* 91 = Loeb *Ep.* 90, 25 (p. 461):
'Quid uerborum notas, quibus quãuis citata excipitur oratio, & celeritate linguae manus sequitur?' *hablar de* / *mano.*

63. *Ep.* 91 = Loeb *Ep.* 90, 33 (p. 463):
'. . . quemadmodũ decoctus calculus in smaragdũ conuerteretur . . .' *cont[ra]/ha[ci]/an las esm[e]/raldas* —

**64. *Ep.* 91 = Loeb *Ep.* 90, 39 (p. 464):
'. . . uicinum uel pretio pellat aeris . . . uel iniuria . . .' *[e]l un mal, quot* / *iniuria venales* / *[f]eçerit agros.*

**65. *Ep.* 91 = Loeb *Ep.* 90, 39 (p. 464):
'Cum omnia fecerimus, multum habebimus, uniuersum habebamus.'
+ / *egle sed nihil* / *faciendo v. h.* / *[e]t sententię sub/[t]ilis acumen* / *[r]estitues.*

**66. *Ep.* 93 = Loeb *Ep.* 92, 2 (p. 471):
'Nam qui aliquo auxilio sustinetur, potest cadere. Si aliter est, incipient in nobis multum ualere non nostra . . .' *ojo.* / [note by Medinilla] / *debemonos repara[r]* / *con fuerças propias no [a]/jenas*

*67. *Ep.* 93 = Loeb. *Ep.* 92, 5 (p. 473):
'Vides autem quale sit, <u>sole te non</u> esse <u>contentum, nisi</u> aliquis igniculus alluxerit?' *ojo*

68. *Ep.* 93 = Loeb *Ep.* 92, 25 (p. 476):
+ / *Epicuri la-/us, et Beati-/[t]udo*
Cited in *Defensa de Epicuro* (*Q*, III. 425).

69. *Ep.* 115 = Loeb *Ep.* 114, 3 (p. 579):
+ / *del estilo / en escribir / es toda esta c[a]/rta llena de / verdadera / i docta ens[e]/ñanza —*

70. *De paupertate*, beginning (p. 650):
*Epicuro.*
Cited in *Defensa de Epicuro* (*Q*, III. 425).

71. *De ira* I. xi. 3 (p. 669):
*Germa[no]/rum Rob[ur] / et mores*

72. *De ira* I. xii. 5 (p. 670):
'Irasci pro suis nõ est pij animi, sed infirmi.' *[E]nojarse por los / [s]uios, no es de a/[n]imo impio si/[n]o enfermo.*

*73. *De ira* I. xii. 6 (p. 670):
'Nã & febres quaedã genera ualetudinis leuãt, nec ideò nõ ex toto illis caruisse melius est.' *Per sapientiam mori Plinius.*

74. *De ira* I. xvi = Loeb I. xix. 7 (p. 677):
'Nam, ut Plato ait, Nemo <u>prudens</u> punit, quia peccatum est sed ne peccetur.' *nadie castig[a] / porque se pe[co] / sino para qu[e] / no se peque.*
Paraphrased in *Providencia de Dios* (*Q*, II. 179a).

*75. *De ira* II. xv. 1 (p. 690):
*Libertas Ger/manorum, et / [s]citarum. obi/[?]am.*

76. *De ira* II. xvi = Loeb II. xv. 5 (p. 691):
'In frigora septẽtrioneq; uergentibus immansueta ingenia sunt . . .'
*Naciones septentri[o]/nales, imm/ansueta / habent ing[e]/nia ideo l[i]/bera.*

77. *De clem.* I. xii. 1 (p. 754):
*el Tirano se / diferencia del / Rey en los he/chos no en el / nombre*

78. *De clem.* I. xii. 1 (p. 754):
'Et L. Syllã appellari tyrannum quid prohibet, <u>cui occidendi finem fecit inopia hostium?</u>' *sylla dejo de matar gente porque le falto / gente que matar.*

79. *De vita beata* XII. 4 (p. 785):
'Ita nõ <u>ab</u> Epicuro impulsi luxuriãtur. . . . Nec aestimatur uoluptas illa Epicuri . . .' *Epicuro.*
Cited in *Defensa de Epicuro* (*Q*, III. 421-2).

80. *De vita beata* XIII. 1 (p. 785):
 *Epicuro*
 Cited in *Defensa de Epicuro* (*Q*, III. 422).

81. *De vita beata* XIII. 2 (p. 786):
 *Epicuro*
 Cited in *Defensa de Epicuro* (*Q*, III. 422).

82. *De vita beata* XIX. 1 (p. 790):
 'Diodorũ Epicureũ philosophum, qui intra paucos dies, finẽ uitae
 suae manu sua imposuit, negant ex decreto Epicuri fecisse, quod sibi
 gulã praecidit.' *Epicuro*

83. *De vita beata* XXVII. 5 (p. 800):
 '. . . Democrito quod neglexerit, Epicuro, quod consumpserit . . .'
 *Epicuro*

84. *De vita beata* XXVIII = Loeb *De otio* I. 4 (p. 801):
 'Quid nobis Epicuri praecepta in ipsis Zenonis principijs loqueris?'
 *Epicuro*

85. *De vita beata* XXX = Loeb *De otio* III. 2 (p. 802):
 *Epicuro*
 Cited in *Defensa de Epicuro* (*Q*, III. 423).

86. *De vita beata* XXXII = Loeb *De otio* VII. 3 (p. 806):
 *Epicurus*

*87. *Ad Albinam* VI = Loeb *Ad Helv.* VII. 2 (p. 936):
 'Tyrij Africam incolũt, in Hispania Poeni . . .' + / [*t*]*emporibus*
 *se*/[*d*]*es e Hispania* / *Pẹni incole*/[*r*]*ant*

88. *Ad Albinam* VIII = Loeb *Ad Helv.* VII. 8 (p. 937):
 'Vrum coeli grauitas . . .' *vtrum* / [a line]

89. *Ad Albinam* VIII = Loeb *Ad Helv.* VII. 8 (p. 937):
 '. . . an natura importuosi maris.' *importuosi* / [a line] / *maris.*
 *lege* / *si mauis, imp*[*e*]/*tuosi, magi*[*s*] / *Latinum est* / *quam impo*[*r*]/*tuosi*

90. *Ad Albinam* VIII = Loeb *Ad Helv.* VII. 9 (p. 937):
 '. . . & Hispani, quod ex similitudine ritus apparet. Eadem enim
 tegumenta capitum, idemq; genus calceamenti, quod Cantabris
 est, et uerba quaedam.' *Hispani, et Cantabri.*

91. *Ad Albinam* VIII = Loeb *Ad Helv.* VIII. 1 (p. 938):
 'M. Brutus satis hoc putat, quod licet in exiliũ euntibus uirtutes suas
 ferre secum.' *Brutus*
 Cited in *Vida de Marco Bruto* (*Q*, I. 130).

92. *Ad Albinam* IX = Loeb *Ad Helv.* IX. 4–5 (p. 940):
 'Brutus in eo libro quem de uirtute composuit, ait se uidisse
 Marcellum Mitylenis exultantem, & quantũ modo natura hominis

pateretur, beatissime uiuentem, neq; unqua bonarum artium
cupidiorem quàm illo tēpore. Itaq; adijcit, uisum sibi se magis in
exilium ire, qui sine illo rediturus esset, quā illū in exilio relinqui.
O fortunatiorē Marcellum, eo tempore quo exilium suum Bruto
approbauit, quàm quo R.P. cōsulatum. Quantus uir ille fuit, qui
effecit ut aliquis exul sibi uideretur, quod ab exule recedebat.'
+ / Magnani/ma Bruti / verba
Cited in Vida de Marco Bruto (Q, I. 130).

93. Ad Albinam IX = Loeb Ad Helv. IX. 6 (p. 940):
Magnus vir / [e]t gloriosus / [i]n exilio suo / Marcellus.

*94. Ad Albinam IX = Loeb Ad Helv. X. 2–4 (p. 940):
'Dij istos deaeq́; perdant, quorum luxuria tam inuidiosi imperij
fines transcendit . . . nec piget à Parthis, à quibus nondū poenas
repetimus, aues petere. . . . Quod dissolutus delicijs stomachus uix
admittat, ab ultimo portatur Oceano. Vomunt ut edant, edunt ut
uomant, epulas, quas toto orbe conquirunt nec concoquere dignātur.
. . . C. Caesar, quē mihi uidetur rerū natura edidisse, ut ostenderet
quid summa uitia in summa fortuna possent, centies sestertio
coenauit uno die, & in hoc omnium adiutus ingenio, uix tamen
inueuit quomodo prouinciarū tributum una coena fieret.' mir[a] /
dicta / in inglu/viem

95. Ad Albinam X = Loeb Ad Helv. X. 7 (p. 942):
'Maiores nostri, quorū uirtus etiā nunc uitia nostra sustētat, infelices
erant?' nota / [a line]

96. Ad Albinam XII = Loeb Ad Helv. XII. 5 (p. 945):
d. Beren/gel de Aois

97. Ad Albinam XVI = Loeb Ad Helv. XVII. 4 (p. 951):
'. . . uoluisset te sapiētum praeceptis erudiri potius quam imbui . . .'
+ / [two lines] / esto sin ra[z]/on reprehe[n]/de Erasm[o]

# APPENDIX III

## QUEVEDO'S QUOTATIONS FROM SENECA AND EPICTETUS

THE following is a list of the passages quoted by Quevedo from the works of Seneca and Epictetus. It does not include mere references or unacknowledged borrowings, nor does it contain quotations in his *Migajas sentenciosas*. Quotations from passages annotated by Quevedo in his extant copy of Seneca (see above, Appendix II) are asterisked.

### 1. *Seneca*

#### *Ad Helviam de consolatione*

| V. 4 | *La constancia de Job* | *Q*, II. 222b |
| *VIII. 1 | *Marco Bruto* | *Q*, I. 130 |
| *IX. 4–5 | ibid. | *Q*, I. 130 |

#### *Ad Marciam de consolatione*

| IV. 4 | *Carta de Plinio* | *Q*, II. 394b |
| IV. 4 | *Letter 212* | *EQ*, 429 |
| XXIV. 5 | *Providencia de Dios* | *Q*, II. 191b–192a |

#### *De beneficiis*

| *II. xx. 1–3 | *Marco Bruto* | *Q*, I. 130 |
| *IV. ii. 1 | *Defensa de Epicuro* | *Q*, III. 421 |
| *IV. ii. 1 | ibid. | *Q*, III. 430 |
| *IV. ii. 2 | ibid. | *Q*, III. 430 |
| *IV. ii. 3–4 | ibid. | *Q*, III. 430 |
| *IV. iv. 1 | ibid. | *Q*, III. 430 |
| IV. iv. 3 | *Providencia de Dios* | *Q*, II. 194b |
| IV. vii. 1 | *Prevención* | *Q*, III. 387 |
| IV. vii. 2 | *Providencia de Dios* | *Q*, II. 195a |
| IV. viii. 1 | *Prevención* | *Q*, III. 388 |
| IV. viii. 3 | ibid. | *Q*, III. 388 |
| IV. xxxv. 1 | *Su espada por Santiago* | *Q*, II. 432b |
| IV. xxxv. 2 | ibid. | *Q*, II. 432a |
| IV. xxxv. 3 | ibid. | *Q*, II. 432a |
| VI. xxiii. 2–3 | ibid. | *Q*, II. 431b |

*De ira*

| I. xviii. 1 | Política de Dios | Q, I. 56b |
| I. xix. 7 (?) | Providencia de Dios | Q, II. 179a |
| II. v. 5 | Alevoso manifiesto | Q, I. 280a |
| II. xxi. 7 | Virtud militante | Q, II. 127a |
| III. iii. 1 | ibid. | Q, II. 127a |
| III. xv. 4 | Doctrina estoica | Q, III. 417 |

*De otio*

| *III. 2 | Defensa de Epicuro | Q, III. 423 |

*De providentia*

| V. 5–6 | La constancia de Job | Q, II. 224a |

*De vita beata*

| *XII. 4 | Defensa de Epicuro | Q, III. 421–2 |
| *XIII. 1 | ibid. | Q, III. 422 |
| *XIII. 2 | ibid. | Q, III. 422 |

*Epistulae ad Lucilium*

| 1, 2–3 | Letter 134 | EQ, 258 |
| *6, 6 | Defensa de Epicuro | Q, III. 423 |
| *8, 8 | ibid. | Q, III. 423 |
| *9, 20 | ibid. | Q, III. 423 |
| 10, 4 | Epístolas de Séneca | Q, II. 385a |
| *12, 11 | Defensa de Epicuro | Q, III. 423 |
| *13, 4 | ibid. | Q, III. 426 |
| *13, 17 | ibid. | Q, III. 423 |
| *18, 9 | ibid. | Q, III. 423 |
| *19, 10 | ibid. | Q, III. 423 |
| *21, 2–4 | ibid. | Q, III. 423 |
| *21, 7 | ibid. | Q, III. 423 |
| *21, 8–9 | ibid. | Q, III. 423 |
| *23, 9 | ibid. | Q, III. 424 |
| *24, 23 | ibid. | Q, III. 424 |
| 25, 2 | Su espada por Santiago | Q, II. 458a |
| *25, 4–5 | Defensa de Epicuro | Q, III. 424 |
| *25, 6 | ibid. | Q, III. 424 |
| 31, 10 | Providencia de Dios | Q, II. 196a |
| 32, 3 | Letter 134 | EQ, 258 |
| 41, 1 | Epístolas de Séneca | Q, II. 384b |
| 41, 5 | ibid. | Q, II. 385a |
| *46, 1 | Defensa de Epicuro | Q, III. 424 |
| 47, 1 | De los remedios | Q, II. 370 |
| 47, 17 | ibid. | Q, II. 370 |
| *52, 3 | Defensa de Epicuro | Q, III. 424 |
| *66, 47 | ibid. | Q, III. 424–5 |
| 69, 6 | Doctrina estoica | Q, III. 416 |

| 73, 1 | Política de Dios | Q, I. 42a |
| 73, 1–2 | Doctrina estoica | Q, III. 413–14 |
| 73, 15–16 | Providencia de Dios | Q, II. 195a |
| 78, 6 | Virtud militante | Q, II. 155a |
| 78, 7–10 | ibid. | Q, II. 160a |
| 78, 21 | ibid. | Q, II. 161a |
| 79, 12–13 | ibid. | Q, II. 158b |
| 86, 1 | ibid. | Q, II. 154a |
| 86, 1 | ibid. | Q, II. 158b |
| 86, 1 | Providencia de Dios | Q, II. 187a |
| *92, 25 | Defensa de Epicuro | Q, III. 425 |
| 93, 1 | La constancia de Job | Q, II. 235a |
| 93, 1 | Providencia de Dios | Q, II. 196a |
| 101, 1 | Virtud militante | Q, II. 138b |
| 101, 1 | Letter 134 | EQ, 255 |
| 115, 14–16 | Juicios, prólogos | Q, II. 492a |
| 115, 14–16 | Virtud militante | Q, II. 130b |
| 115, 17 | Providencia de Dios | Q, II. 185b |
| 115, 17 | ibid. | Q, II. 200b |
| 117, 6 | ibid. | Q, II. 194b |

*Naturales Quaestiones*

| Pref. 13–14 | Providencia de Dios | Q, II. 194b–195a |
| II. xxxviii. 3 | ibid. | Q, II. 195a |
| II. xlv. 1–3 | ibid. | Q, II. 195a |
| VI. xxxii. 12 | Virtud militante | Q, II. 158a |

*Troades*

| vv. 407–8 | Virtud militante | Q, II. 159a |

*De paupertate*

| *Beginning | Defensa de Epicuro | Q, III. 425 |

Unidentified

| | Juicios, prólogos | Q, II. 484a |
| | Política de Dios | Q, I. 14b |
| | ibid. | Q, I. 57a |
| | Virtud militante | Q, II. 158a |
| | Letter 231 | EQ, 453 |

II. *Epictetus*

*Discourses*

| I. ix. 16–17 | Doctrina estoica | Q, III. 417 |
| I. xi. 39 | Juicios, prólogos | Q, II. 487a |

*Manual*

# BIBLIOGRAPHY

Foreign and Latin names of places of printing have been anglicized.

Achutegui, P. S. de, *La universalidad del conocimiento de Dios en los paganos según los primeros teólogos de la Compañía de Jesús (1534–1648)* (Rome, 1951).

Adam, A., *Sur le problème religieux dans la première moitié du XVII<sup>e</sup> siècle* (Oxford, 1959).

Alatorre, A., 'Quevedo, Erasmo, y el doctor Constantino', *Nueva Revista de Filología Hispánica*, vii (1953), 673–85.

Alonso, D., *De los siglos oscuros al de oro*, 2nd ed. (Madrid, 1964).

Alonso Cortés, N., 'Un nuevo dato para la biografía de Quevedo', *Revista Contemporánea*, xxviii (1902), 147–50.

Arnold, E. V., *Roman Stoicism: Being Lectures on the History of the Stoic Philosophy with Special Reference to its Development within the Roman Empire* (Cambridge, 1911).

Astrana Marín, L., *La vida turbulenta de Quevedo* (Madrid, 1945).

Atkinson, W. C., 'Seneca, Virués, Lope de Vega', *Homenatge a Antoni Rubió i Lluch. Miscel·lània d'estudis literaris històrics i lingüístics* (Barcelona, 1936), i. 111–31.

Aubertin, C., *Étude critique sur les rapports supposés entre Sénèque et saint Paul* (Paris, 1857).

Aubrun, C., 'La gueuserie aux XVI<sup>e</sup> et XVII<sup>e</sup> siècles en Espagne et le roman picaresque', in *Littérature et société: problèmes de méthodologie en sociologie de la littérature* (Brussels, 1967), pp. 137–45.

Ayala, F., 'Hacia una semblanza de Quevedo', *La Torre*, xv (1967), 89–116.

Barlow, C. W., *Epistolae Senecae ad Paulum et Pauli ad Senecam (quae vocantur)* (Rome, 1938).

—— 'Seneca in the Middle Ages', *Classical Weekly*, xxxv (1941–2), 257.

Barth, P., *Los estoicos*, trans. L. Recasens Siches (Madrid, 1930).

Bataillon, M., *Erasmo y España. Estudios sobre la historia espiritual del siglo XVI*, trans. A. Alatorre, 2nd ed. (Mexico/Buenos Aires, 1966).

Batllori, M., 'La agudeza de Gracián y la retórica jesuítica', *Actas del Primer Congreso Internacional de Hispanistas*, ed. C. A. Jones and F. Pierce (Oxford, 1964), pp. 57–69.

Baum, D. L., *Traditionalism in the Works of Don Francisco de Quevedo y Villegas*, University of North Carolina Studies in the Romance Languages and Literatures, No. 91 (Chapel Hill, 1970).

Bell, A. F. G., *Francisco Sánchez El Brocense* (Oxford, 1925).

—— *Luis de León. A Study of the Spanish Renaissance* (Oxford, 1925).

Belmonte, F., 'Estudio sobre el estoicismo en España', *Revista de España*, xxxi (1873), 313–40.

Bénichou-Roubaud, S., 'Quevedo helenista (el *Anacreón castellano*)', *Nueva Revista de Filología Hispánica*, xiv (1960), 51–72.

Bevan, E. R., *Stoics and Sceptics: Four Lectures delivered in Oxford during Hilary Term 1913* (Oxford, 1913).

Blüher, K. A., *Seneca in Spanien: Untersuchungen zur Geschichte der Seneca-Rezeption in Spanien vom 13. bis 17. Jahrhundert* (Munich, 1969).

Boissier, G., *La Religion romaine d'Auguste aux Antonins*, 2 vols. (Paris, 1874).

Bonilla y San Martín, A., *Fernando de Córdoba ¿1425–86? y los orígenes del renacimiento filosófico en España. Episodio de la historia de la lógica* (Madrid, 1911).

Borges, J. L., 'Quevedo', in *Otras inquisiciones* (Buenos Aires, 1960), pp. 55–64.

Bouillier, V., *La Fortune de Montaigne en Italie et en Espagne* (Paris, 1922).

Bourgery, A., *Sénèque prosateur* (Paris, 1922).

Bréhier, E., *Historia de la filosofía*, trans. D. Náñez, 2 vols. (Buenos Aires, 1944).

—— 'Introduction au stoïcisme', in *Les Stoïciens*, ed. P.-M. Schuhl (Tours, 1962).

Brun, J., *Le Stoïcisme*, 2nd ed. (Paris, 1961).

Bryant, J. H., *The Mutual Influence of Christianity and the Stoic School* (London/Cambridge, 1866).

Burnier, C., *La Morale de Sénèque et le néo-stoïcisme . . .* (Lausanne, 1908).

Busson, H., *La Pensée religieuse française de Charron à Pascal* (Paris, 1933).

Cardenal Iracheta, M., 'Algunos rasgos estéticos y morales de Quevedo', *Revista de Ideas Estéticas*, v (1947), 31–51.

Carrillo y Sotomayor, L., *Obras* (Madrid, 1611).

Castanien, D. G., 'Quevedo's *Anacreón castellano*', *Studies in Philology*, lv (1958), 568–75.

—— 'Quevedo's Translation of the Pseudo-Phocylides', *The Philological Quarterly*, xl (1961), 44–52.

—— 'Quevedo's Version of Epictetus' *Encheiridion*', *Symposium*, xviii (1964), 68–78.

Castellanos, D., 'Quevedo y su *Epicteto en español*', *Boletín de la Academia Nacional de Letras* (Montevideo), i (1947), 179–213.

Castro, A., 'Escepticismo y contradicción en Quevedo', *Humanidades*, xviii (1928), 11–17.

Chacón y Calvo, J. M., 'Quevedo y la tradición senequista', *Realidad*, iii (1948), 318–42.

Charlton, H. B., *The Senecan Tradition in Renaissance Tragedy* (Manchester, 1946).

Charron, P., *De la sagesse livres trois* (Bordeaux, 1601).

—— *Les trois veritez contre les Athees, Idolatres, Juifs, Mahumetans, Heretiques & Schismatiques* (Bordeaux, 1593).

Chew, A., 'Joseph Hall and Neo-Stoicism', *Publications of the Modern Language Association of America*, lxv (1950), 1130–45.

Correas, G., *El Enkiridion de Epikteto, i la Tabla de Kebes, filosofos estoikos* (Salamanca, 1630).

Cougny, E., *Guillaume du Vair: étude d'histoire littéraire* (Paris, 1857).

Counson, A., 'L'influence de Sénèque le Philosophe', *Le Musée belge*, vii (1903), 132–67.

Crosby, J. O., *En torno a la poesía de Quevedo* (Madrid, 1967).

—— 'Quevedo and the Court of Philip III: Neglected Satirical Letters and New Biographical Data', *Publications of the Modern Language Association of America*, lxxi (1956), 1117–26.

Davidson, W. L., *The Stoic Creed* (Edinburgh, 1907).

Davies, G. A., 'The Influence of Justus Lipsius on Juan de Vera y Figueroa's *Embaxador* (1620)', *Bulletin of Hispanic Studies*, xlii (1965), 160–73.

Davis, C. H., *Greek and Roman Stoicism and Some of its Disciples: Epictetus, Seneca and Marcus Aurelius* (London, 1903).

Delacroix, P., 'Quevedo et Sénèque', *Bulletin hispanique*, lvi (1954), 305–7.

Del Piero, R. A., 'Dos citas latinas de Quevedo', *Romanische Forschungen*, lxix (1957), 67–71.

—— 'Quevedo y Juan de Pineda', *Modern Philology*, lvi (1958), 82–91.

—— 'Quevedo y la *Polyanthea*', *Hispanófila*, ii (1958), 49–55.

—— 'Two Notes on Quevedo's *Job*', *Romanic Review*, l (1959), 9–24.

Domínguez Ortiz, A., *La sociedad española en el siglo XVII*, i (Madrid, 1963).

Dunn, P. N., 'El individuo y la sociedad en *La vida del Buscón*', *Bulletin hispanique*, lii (1950), 375–96.

Du Vair, G., *Les Œuvres* (Paris, 1618).

—— *The Moral Philosophie of the Stoicks . . . Englished by Thomas James . . .*, ed. R. Kirk, Rutgers University Studies in English, no. 8 (New Brunswick, N.J., 1951).

Edelstein, L., *The Meaning of Stoicism*, Martin Classical Lectures, vol. xxi (Cambridge, Mass., 1966).

Elliott, J. H., *Imperial Spain. 1469–1716* (London, 1963).

Epictetus, *The Discourses . . ., the Manual, and Fragments*, ed. W. A. Oldfather, 2 vols. (London/Cambridge, Mass., 1959). (See also Correas, G., and Sánchez, F.)

Erasmo, D., *El enchiridion o manual del caballero cristiano*, ed. D. Alonso, *Revista de Filología Española*, Anejo XVI (Madrid, 1932).

Espina, A., *Quevedo* (Madrid, 1945).

Ettinghausen, H., 'Acerca de las fechas de redacción de cuatro obras neoestoicas de Quevedo', *Boletín de la Real Academia Española*, li (1971), 161–73.

—— 'Neostoicism in Pictures: Lipsius and the Engraved Title-page and Portrait in Quevedo's *Epicteto y Phocilides*', *Modern Language Review*, lxvi (1971), 94–100.

Farrell, A. P., *The Jesuit Code of Liberal Education: Development and Scope of the 'Ratio Studiorum'* (Milwaukee, 1938).

Farrington, B., *The Faith of Epicurus* (London, 1967).

Fernández de Heredia, J. F., *Seneca y Neron*, 2nd ed. (Madrid, 1680).

Fernández Navarrete, P., *Los libros de beneficiis de Luçio Aeneo Seneca . . . traducidos por . . .* (Madrid, 1629).

—— *Siete libros de L. Æ. Seneca Traducidos por . . .* (Madrid, 1627).

Fleury, A., *Saint Paul et Sénèque . . .*, 2 vols. (Paris, 1853).

García-Borrón Moral, J. C., *Séneca y los estoicos. (Una contribución al estudio del senequismo.)* (Barcelona, 1956).

Gelder, H. A. E. van, *The Two Reformations in the Sixteenth Century* (The Hague, 1961).

Giacoman, H. F., 'El hombre visto como ser-para-la-muerte en Job, Séneca, San Agustín y Francisco de Quevedo', *Papeles de Son Armadans*, no. CLVIII (1969), 123–42.

Glaesener, H., 'Juste Lipse et Guillaume du Vair', *Revue belge de philologie et d'histoire*, xvii (1938), 27–42.

Glendinning, N., *Vida y obra de Cadalso* (Madrid, 1962).

Gonnet, P., 'Un manuel de perfection chez les anciens. Épictète et saint François de Sales', *L'Université catholique*, N.S., lii (1906), 563–92.

González de la Calle, P. U., *Quevedo y los dos Sénecas* (Mexico, 1965).

González de Salas, J. A., *Nueva idea de la tragedia antigua, o ilustracion ultima al libro singular de Poetica de Aristoteles Stagirita* (Madrid, 1633).

González Haba, M. J., 'Séneca en la espiritualidad española de los siglos XVI y XVII', *Revista de Filosofía*, xi (1962), 287–302.

González Palencia, A., 'Pleitos de Quevedo con la villa de la Torre de Juan Abad', *Boletín de la Real Academia Española*, xiv (1927), 600–19.

—— 'Quevedo y Tirso ante la Junta de Reformación', *Boletín de la Real Academia Española*, xxv (1946), 43–84.

Goyoaga y Escario, J. L. de, *Don Francisco de Quevedo y su significación en la literatura española* (n.p., n.d.).

Granada, L. de, *Collectanea moralis philosophiae, in tres tomos distributa: quorum primus selectissimas sententias ex omnibus Senecae operibus* . . . (Lisbon, 1571).

—— *Libro de la oración y consideración*, in Biblioteca de Autores Españoles, viii (Madrid, 1848), 1–202.

Green, O. H., *Courtly Love in Quevedo* (Boulder, Col., 1952).

—— *Spain and the Western Tradition: The Castilian Mind in Literature from 'El Cid' to Calderón*, 4 vols. (Madison, Wisc., 1963–6).

—— *Vida y obra de Lupercio Leonardo de Argensola* (Saragossa, 1945).

Green, V. H. H., *Renaissance and Reformation* (London, 1958).

Gregores, E., 'El humanismo de Quevedo', *Anales de Filología Clásica*, vi (1953–4), 91–105.

Grismer, R. L., 'Introduction to the Classical Influence on the Literatures of Spain and Spanish America (a Bibliographical Study)', in *Estudios de filología e historia literaria. Homenaje al R. P. Félix Restrepo S.I.* (Bogotá, 1950), pp. 433–46.

Gutiérrez, M., *Fr. Luis de León y la filosofía española del siglo XVI* (Madrid, 1885).

Hall, Joseph, *The Works*, 12 vols. (Oxford, 1837–9).

Hay, C. H., *Montaigne, lecteur et imitateur de Sénèque* (Poitiers, 1938).

Haydn, H. C., *The Counter-Renaissance* (New York, 1950).

Heller, J. L., and Grismer, R. L., 'Seneca in the Celestinesque Novel', *Hispanic Review*, xii (1944), 29–48.

Hermenegildo, A., *Los trágicos españoles del siglo XVI* (Madrid, 1961).

Herreras, D., *Séneca y la proyección europea de su obra*, Estudios de literatura comparada, 2 (Malaga, 1968).

Highet, G., *The Classical Tradition* (Oxford, 1951).

—— *Juvenal the Satirist* (Oxford, 1962).

Holland, F., *Seneca* (London, 1920).

Horozco y Covarruvias, J. de, *Emblemas morales* (Segovia, 1589).

—— *Paradoxas christianas contra las falsas opiniones del mundo* (Segovia, 1592).

*Index generalis in omnes libros Instituti Societatis Jesu* (Antwerp, 1635).

Isar, E. E., 'La cuestión del llamado "senequismo" español', *Hispanófila*, ii (1958), 11–30.

Iventosch, H., 'Quevedo and the Defense of the Slandered: the Meaning of the *Sueño de la muerte*, the *Entremés de los refranes del viejo celoso*, the *Defensa de Epicuro*, etc.', *Hispanic Review*, xxx (1962), 94–115, 173–93.

Jagu, A., *Épictète et Platon* (Paris, 1946).

Jammes, R., *Études sur l'œuvre poétique de Don Luis de Góngora y Argote* (Bordeaux, 1967).

Jáuregui, J. de, *El Retraído* (Valencia, 1635).

Jones, R. O., 'Some Notes on More's *Utopia* in Spain', *Modern Language Review*, xlv (1950), 478–82.

—— 'The Poetic Unity of the *Soledades* of Góngora', *Bulletin of Hispanic Studies*, xxxi (1954), 189–204.

Juderías, J., *Don Francisco de Quevedo y Villegas. La época, el hombre, las doctrinas* (Madrid, 1922).

Juvenal, *The Sixteen Satires*, trans. Peter Green (Harmondsworth, 1967).

Kelly, J. N. D., *Early Christian Doctrines* (London, 1958).

Klaniczay, T., 'Stoïcisme et maniérisme. Le déclin de la Renaissance en Hongrie', *Revue de littérature comparée*, xli (1967), 515–31.

Knowles, D., *The Evolution of Medieval Thought* (London, 1962).

Krailsheimer, A. J., *Studies in Self-interest from Descartes to La Bruyère* (Oxford, 1962).

Kristeller, P. O., *The Classics and Renaissance Thought*, Martin Classical Lectures, vol. xv (Cambridge, Mass., 1955).

Lanza Estéban, J., 'Quevedo y la tradición literaria de la muerte', *Revista de las Indias* (Bogotá), iv (1953), 367–80.

Láscaris Comneno, C., 'La epistemología en el pensamiento filosófico de Quevedo', *Bolívar* (Caracas), xlv (1955), 911–25.

—— 'La mostración de Dios en el pensamiento de Quevedo', *Crisis* (Madrid/Murcia), ii (1955), 427–40.

—— 'Senequismo y agustinismo en Quevedo', *Revista de Filosofía*, ix (1950), 461–85.

Leonardo de Argensola, L. and B., *Obras sueltas*, 2 vols. (Madrid, 1889).

Lessius, L., *De providentia numinis et animi immortalitate aduersus Atheos & Politicos* (Antwerp, 1613).

Levi, A., *French Moralists. The Theory of the Passions, 1585 to 1649* (Oxford, 1964).

Leyden, W. von, *Seventeenth-Century Metaphysics: an Examination of Some Main Concepts and Theories* (London, 1968).

Lida, R., *Letras hispánicas: estudios, esquemas* (Mexico/Buenos Aires, 1958).

—— 'Quevedo y su España antigua', *Romance Philology*, xvii (1963), 253–71.

Lida de Malkiel, M. R., 'La tradición clásica en España', *Nueva Revista de Filología Hispánica*, v (1951), 183–223.

Lipsius, J., *Libro de la constancia* . . . (Seville, 1616).

—— *Los seys libros de las Politicas o Doctrina Ciuil* . . . (Madrid, 1604).

—— *Manuductionis ad stoicam philosophiam libri tres* (Antwerp, 1604).

—— *Physiologia stoicorum* (Antwerp, 1604).

Lira Urquieta, P., 'El senequismo de Quevedo', in *Sobre Quevedo y nuestros clásicos* (Madrid, 1958), pp. 44–53.

López Estrada, F., *Introducción a la literatura medieval española*, 2nd ed. (Madrid, 1962).

—— 'La primera versión española de la *Utopia* de Moro, por Jerónimo Antonio de Medinilla (Córdoba, 1637)', in *Collected Studies in Honour of Américo Castro's Eightieth Year*, ed. M. P. Hornik (Oxford, 1965), pp. 291–309.

Lucas Marracín, I., *Séneca en tres ensayistas del barroco español: Quevedo, Saavedra Fajardo y Baltasar Gracián* (Madrid, 1970).

Lynch, J., *Spain under the Habsburgs*, 2 vols. (Oxford, 1964–9).

Marcilly, C., 'L'angoisse du temps et de la mort chez Quevedo', *Revue de la Méditerranée*, xix (1959), 365–83.

Marichal, J., 'Montaigne en España', *Nueva Revista de Filología Hispánica*, vii (1953), 259–78.

Martha, C., *Les Moralistes sous l'Empire romain: philosophes et poètes* (Paris, 1865).

Mártir Rizo, J. P., *Historia de la vida de Lucio Anneio Seneca español* (Madrid, 1625).

Mas, A., *La Caricature de la femme, du mariage et de l'amour dans l'œuvre de Quevedo* (Paris, 1957).

Massaloux, M., 'Quevedo traducteur des deux Sénèque'. Thèse en vue de l'obtention du Doctorat de Troisième Cycle. Presented in Paris, 1970.

May, T. E., 'Good and Evil in the *Buscón*: A Survey', *Modern Language Review*, xlv (1950), 319–35.

Mayo, T. F., *Epicurus in England (1650–1725)* (n.p., 1934).

Mazzeo, J. A., *Renaissance and Revolution: the Remaking of European Thought* (London, 1965).

Melio de Sande, J., *Dotrina moral de las epistolas que Luzio Aeneo Seneca escriuio a Luzilo* . . . (Madrid, 1612).

Méndez Bejarano, M., *Historia de la filosofía en España hasta el siglo XX* (Madrid, n.d.).

Menéndez Pelayo, M., *Bibliografía hispano-latina clásica*, ed. E. Sánchez Reyes, in *Obras completas*, xliv–liii (Santander, 1950–3).

—— *Historia de los heterodoxos españoles*, in *Obras completas*, xxxv–xlii (Santander, 1946–8).

—— *La filosofía española*, ed. C. Láscaris Comneno (Madrid, 1955).

Mérimée, E., *Essai sur la vie et les œuvres de Francisco de Quevedo (1580–1645)* (Paris, 1886).

Merlan, P., 'The Stoa', Part I, ch. 7 of *The Cambridge History of Later Greek and Early Medieval Philosophy* (Cambridge, 1967).

Moir, D., 'The Classical Tradition in Spanish Dramatic Theory and Practice in the Seventeenth Century', in *Classical Drama and its Influence. Essays Presented to H. D. F. Kitto*, ed. M. J. Anderson (London, 1965), pp. 193–228.

Montaigne, M. de, *Essais*, ed. A. Thibaudet (Bruges, 1958).

Montoliu, M. de, 'El alma estoica', ch. 4 of *El alma de España y sus reflejos en la literatura del siglo de oro* (Barcelona, n.d.).

Morel-Fatio, A., 'D. Bernardino de Mendoza', *Bulletin hispanique*, viii (1906), 20–70, 129–47.

Morreale, M., 'Luciano y Quevedo: la humanidad condenada', *Revista de Literatura*, viii (1955), 213–27.

Murray, G. G. A., *The Stoic Philosophy* . . . (London, 1915).

Nothdurft, K.-D., *Studien zum Einfluß Senecas auf die Philosophie und Theologie des zwölften Jahrhunderts* (Leyden/Cologne, 1963).

*Novissimus librorum prohibitorum et expurgandorum Index* . . . (Madrid, 1640).

*Novus Index librorum prohibitorum et expurgatorum* . . . (Seville, 1632).

Núñez de Guzmán, F., *In omnia L. Annaei Senecae philosophi scripta . . . castigationes utilissimae* (Venice, 1536).

Oates, W. J., *The Stoic and Epicurean Philosophers* (New York, 1940).

Oldfather, W. A., *Contribution toward a Bibliography of Epictetus* (Urbana, Ill., 1927).

Palmer, R. G., *Seneca's 'De remediis fortuitorum' and the Elizabethans*, Institute of Elizabethan Studies Publication, no. 1 (Chicago, 1953).

Papell, A., *Quevedo: su tiempo, su vida, su obra* (Barcelona, 1947).

Parker, A. A., 'The Psychology of the *Pícaro* in *El Buscón*', *Modern Language Review*, xlii (1947), 58–69. (Revised version in *Literature and the Delinquent* (Edinburgh, 1967).)

Patch, H. R., *The Goddess Fortune in Medieval Literature* (Cambridge, 1927).

Paz y Meliá, A., *Opúsculos literarios de los siglos XIV a XVI* (Madrid, 1892).

Pellicer y Saforcada, J. A., *Ensayo de una biblioteca de traductores españoles* . . . (Madrid, 1778).

Penney, C. L., *Printed Books 1468–1700 in the Hispanic Society of America* (New York, 1965).

Penzol, P., *El estilo de Don Francisco de Quevedo* (Madrid, 1931).

Pérez Clotet, P., *La 'Política de Dios' de Quevedo: su contenido éticojurídico* (Madrid, 1928).

Pérez de Montalván, J., *Para todos* (Huesca, 1633).

Piña, J. de, *Varias fortunas* (Madrid, 1627).

Pineda, J. de, *Commentariorum in Iob libri tredecim*, 2 vols. (Seville, 1598–1602).

Pire, G., 'De l'influence de Sénèque sur les *Essais* de Montaigne', *Les Études classiques*, xxii (1954), 270–86.

Plutarch, *Moralia*, 8 vols. (Oxford, 1795–1830).

Pohlenz, M., *Die Stoa*, 2nd ed. (Göttingen, 1959).

Popkin, R. H., *The History of Scepticism from Erasmus to Descartes* (Assen, 1960).

Prat, J., 'Francisco de Quevedo y el estoicismo español', *Revista de América*, iii (1945), 385–91.

Quasten, J., *Patrology*, 2 vols. (Utrecht, 1950–3).

Quevedo, F. de, *Epistolario completo* . . ., ed. L. Astrana Marín (Madrid, 1946).

—— *La cuna y la sepultura para el conocimiento propio y desengaño de las cosas agenas*, ed. L. López Grigera, *Boletín de la Real Academia Española*, Anejo XX (Madrid, 1969).

—— *Lágrimas de Hieremías castellanas*, ed. E. M. Wilson and J. M. Blecua, *Revista de Filología Española*, Anejo LV (Madrid, 1953).

—— *La vida del Buscón llamado Don Pablos*, ed. F. Lázaro Carreter (Salamanca, 1965).

—— *Obras*, ed. A. Fernández-Guerra y Orbe and F. Janer, Biblioteca de Autores Españoles, xxiii, xlviii, and lxix (Madrid, 1946–53).

—— *Obras completas*, ed. F. Buendía, i, 'Obras en prosa' (Madrid, 1961).

—— *Obra poética*, ed. J. M. Blecua, 4 vols. (Madrid, 1969– ).

—— *Política de Dios, govierno de Christo*, ed. J. O. Crosby (Madrid, 1966).

Ramírez, A., *Epistolario de Justo Lipsio y los españoles (1577–1606)* (Madrid, 1966).

Randall, D. B. J., 'The Classical Ending of Quevedo's *Buscón*', *Hispanic Review*, xxxii (1964), 101–8.

*Ratio atque institutio studiorum Societatis Jesu* (Rome, 1606).

Revenga y Proaño, A. de, *Los dos libros de clemencia; escritos por Lucio Anneo Seneca, Filosofo Español* . . . (Madrid, 1626).

Rice, E. F., Jr., *The Renaissance Idea of Wisdom* (Cambridge, Mass., 1958).

Riley, E. C., 'The Dramatic Theories of Don Jusepe Antonio González de Salas', *Hispanic Review*, xix (1951), 183–203.

Rist, J. M., *Stoic Philosophy* (Cambridge, 1969).

Rodríguez Marín, F., *Pedro Espinosa: estudio biográfico, bibliográfico y crítico* (Madrid, 1907).

Roersch, A., *Juste Lipse* (Brussels, 1925).

Røstvig, M.-S., *The Happy Man: Studies in the Metamorphoses of a Classical Ideal, 1600–1700* (Oslo/Oxford, 1954).

Rothe, A., 'Quevedo und seine Quellen', *Romanische Forschungen*, lxxvii (1965), 332–50.

—— *Quevedo und Seneca: Untersuchungen zu den Frühschriften Quevedos*, Kölner romanistische Arbeiten, N. F., Heft 31 (Geneva/Paris, 1965).

Round, N. G., 'Pero Díaz de Toledo: a Study of a 15th-Century *Converso* Translator in his Background'. D.Phil. thesis presented in the University of Oxford, 1966.

—— 'Renaissance Culture and its Opponents in Fifteenth-Century Castile', *Modern Language Review*, lvii (1962), 204–15.

Ruiz Montiano, G., *Espeio de bienhechores y agradecidos: que contiene los siete libros de Beneficios de Lucio Anęo Seneca, insigne Filosofo moral* . . . (Barcelona, 1606).

Sabrié, J.-B., *De l'humanisme au rationalisme: Pierre Charron (1541–1603). L'homme, l'œuvre, l'influence* (Paris, 1913).

Saint-Affrique, B. de, *Sénèque a-t-il été chrétien?* . . . (Montauban, 1884).

Salomon, N., *Recherches sur le thème paysan dans la 'Comedia' au temps de Lope de Vega* (Bordeaux, 1965).

Sams, H. W., 'Anti-Stoicism in 17th- and Early 18th-Century England', *Studies in Philology*, xli (1944), 65–78.

Sánchez, F., *Dotrina del estoico Filosofo Epicteto, que se llama comunmente Enchiridion* . . . (Madrid, 1612).

Sánchez Alonso, B., 'Los satíricos latinos y la sátira de Quevedo', *Revista de Filología Española*, xi (1924), 33–62, 113–53.

Sandys, J., *A History of Classical Scholarship*, 3 vols. (Cambridge, 1921).

San José, B. de, 'El senequismo y S. Juan de la Cruz', *El Monte Carmelo*, xliii (1942), 381–424.

Sanmartí Boncompte, F., *Tácito en España* (Barcelona, 1951).

Saunders, J. L., *Justus Lipsius. The Philosophy of Renaissance Stoicism* (New York, 1955).

Schiff, M., *La Bibliothèque du marquis de Santillane* (Paris, 1905).

Schulte, H., *El Desengaño: Wort und Thema in der spanischen Literatur des Goldenen Zeitalters* (Munich, 1969).

Scioppius, C., *Elementa philosophiae stoicae moralis* (Mainz, 1606).

Selig, K.-L., *The Library of Vicencio Juan de Lastanosa, Patron of Gracián* (Geneva, 1960).

Seneca, *Ad Lucilium epistulae morales*, ed. R. M. Gummere, 3 vols. (London/Cambridge, Mass., 1961–2).

—— *Moral Essays*, ed. J. W. Basore, 3 vols. (London/Cambridge, Mass., 1958).

—— *Opera, quae extant omnia* . . ., 2 vols. (Lyon 1555).

—— *Opera quae extant omnia* . . . (Antwerp, 1652).

—— *Questions naturelles*, 2 vols. (Paris, 1929). (See also Fernández Navarrete, P., Melio de Sande, J., Revenga y Proaño, A., and Ruiz Montiano, G.)

Serrano Poncela, S., 'Séneca entre españoles', in *Collected Studies in Honour of Américo Castro's Eightieth Year*, ed. M. P. Hornik (Oxford, 1965), 383–96.

Sierra Corella, A., *La censura de libros y papeles en España y los índices y catálogos españoles de los prohibidos y expurgados* (Madrid, 1947).

Simón Díaz, J., 'El helenismo de Quevedo y varias cuestiones más', *Revista de Bibliografía Nacional*, vi (1945), 87–118.

Solana, M., *Historia de la filosofía española*, 3 vols. (Madrid, 1941).

Spanneut, M., *Le Stoïcisme des Pères de l'Église, de Clément de Rome à Clément d'Alexandrie* (Paris, 1957).

Spearing, E. M., *The Elizabethan Translations of Seneca's Tragedies* (Cambridge, 1912).

Stelzenberger, J., *Die Beziehung der frühchristlichen Sittenlehre zur Etik der Stoa* (Munich, 1933).

Tamayo de Vargas, T., *Novedades antiguas de España* (Madrid, 1624).

Tarsia, P. A. de, 'Vida de Don Francisco de Quevedo Villegas', in *Obras de Don Francisco de Quevedo Villegas*, x (Madrid, 1794).

Vilanova, A., 'El tema del gran teatro del mundo', *Boletín de la Real Academia de Buenas Letras* (Barcelona), xxiii (1950), 153–88.

Villey, P., *Les Sources et l'Évolution des 'Essais' de Montaigne*, 2nd ed., 2 vols. (Paris, 1933).

Vives, J. L., *Introducción a la sabiduría*, Biblioteca de Autores Españoles, lxv (Madrid, 1873), 239–60.

—— *Del socorro de los pobres, o de las necesidades humanas*, Biblioteca de Autores Españoles, lxv (Madrid, 1873), 261–91.

Wagner de Reyna, A., 'Die Philosophie der Enttäuschung des Francisco Quevedo', *Deutsche Vierteljahrsschrift für Literaturwissenschaft und Geistesgeschichte*, xxx (1956), 511–25.

Wenley, R. M., *Stoicism and its Influence* (Norwood, Mass., n.d.).

Wight Duff, J., *A Literary History of Rome in the Silver Age* (London, 1927).

Willey, B., *The English Moralists* (London, 1964).

—— *The Seventeenth-Century Background: Studies in the Thought of the Age in Relation to Poetry and Religion* (Harmondsworth, 1962).

Williamson, G., *The Senecan Amble* (London, 1951).

Zanta, L., *La Renaissance du stoïcisme au 16ᵉ siècle* (Paris, 1914).

Zeller, E., *The Stoics, Epicureans and Sceptics*, trans. O. W. Reichel (London, 1880).

# INDEX